D0765758

To March for Others

POLITICS AND CULTURE IN MODERN AMERICA

Series Editors: Margot Canaday, Glenda Gilmore,
Michael Kazin, and Thomas J. Sugrue

Volumes in the series narrate and analyze political and social change in the broadest dimensions from 1865 to the present, including ideas about the ways people have sought and wielded power in the public sphere and the language and institutions of politics at all levels—local, national, and transnational. The series is motivated by a desire to reverse the fragmentation of modern U.S. history and to encourage synthetic perspectives on social movements and the state, on gender, race, and labor, and on intellectual history and popular culture.

To March for Others

The Black Freedom Struggle and the United Farm Workers

LAUREN ARAIZA

PENN

UNIVERSITY OF PENNSYLVANIA PRESS

PHILADELPHIA

Published by
University of Pennsylvania Press
Philadelphia, Pennsylvania 19104-4112
www.upenn.edu/pennpress

Printed in the United States of America on acid-free paper
10 9 8 7 6 5 4 3 2 1

Library of Congress Cataloging-in-Publication Data
Araiza, Lauren.
   To march for others : the black freedom struggle and the United Farm
Workers / Lauren Araiza — 1st ed.
      p.   cm. (Politics and culture in modern America)
   Includes bibliographical references and index
   ISBN 978-0-8122-4557-8 (hardcover : alk. paper)
      1. Untied Farm Workers of America—History—20th century. 2. African
Americans—Civil rights—History—20th century. 3. Mexican American
agricultural laborers.—Civil rights—History—20th century. 4. African
Americans—Relations with Mexican Americans—History—20th century.
5. Civil rights movements—United States—History—20th century.
6. United States—Race relations—History—20th century. 7. United
States—Ethnic relations—History—20th century. I. Title. II. Series: Politics
and culture in modern America.
E185.61.A66   2014
323.1196'0730904   2013020887

for Charlie

CONTENTS

ABBREVIATIONS

AFL	American Federation of Labor
AFL-CIO	American Federation of Labor and Congress of Industrial Organizations
AWOC	Agricultural Workers Organizing Committee, AFL-CIO
BPP	Black Panther Party
CIO	Congress of Industrial Organizations
CMM	California Migrant Ministry
COFO	Council of Federated Organizations
CORE	Congress of Racial Equality
CSO	Community Service Organization
DRUM	Dodge Revolutionary Union Movement
EEOC	Equal Employment Opportunity Commission
FEPC	Fair Employment Practices Commission
FLOC	Farm Labor Organizing Committee
FRUM	Ford Revolutionary Union Movement
IAF	Industrial Areas Foundation
ICWU	International Chemical Workers Union
ILWU	International Longshore and Warehouse Union, AFL-CIO
LCFO	Lowndes County Freedom Organization
LULAC	League of United Latin American Citizens
MALDEF	Mexican American Legal Defense and Education Fund
MFDP	Mississippi Freedom Democratic Party
MFLU	Mississippi Freedom Labor Union
NAACP	National Association for the Advancement of Colored People
NCNP	National Conference for New Politics
NDOC	New Democratic Organizing Committee

NFWA	National Farm Workers Association
NLRA	National Labor Relations Act
NLRB	National Labor Relations Board
NUL	National Urban League
OLAS	Organization of Latin-American Solidarity
PFP	Peace and Freedom Party
SCLC	Southern Christian Leadership Conference
SIU	Seafarers International Union, AFL-CIO
SNCC	Student Nonviolent Coordinating Committee
SSOC	Southern Students Organizing Committee
UAW	United Auto Workers, AFL-CIO
UE	United Electrical Workers
UFW	United Farm Workers, AFL-CIO
UFWOC	United Farm Workers Organizing Committee, AFL-CIO
UPWA	United Packinghouse Workers of America, AFL-CIO
USW	United Steelworkers, AFL-CIO

Introduction

ON March 17, 1966 a group of around sixty Mexican American farm laborers representing the National Farm Workers Association (NFWA) began marching nearly 250 miles from the farming town of Delano through California's Central Valley to the state capitol in Sacramento. Led by Cesar Chavez, who had founded the union in 1962 and would go on to become one of the foremost labor leaders in the United States, the farmworkers undertook this arduous, twenty-five-day pilgrimage to draw attention to their strikes and boycotts of grape growers in Delano. The *Sun-Reporter*, a progressive African American newspaper in San Francisco, reported on the march two days into it. In the midst of explaining the particulars of the union's crusade, reporter Eleanor Ohman abruptly admonished her readers: "Those who march for Negro freedom have to also march for freedom of other men, for economic freedom and justice." Ohman was echoing criticisms of the black freedom struggle that had arisen by 1966—that the movement needed to more directly confront economic inequality and, particularly in the multicultural West, should include other minorities in the pursuit of racial equality. According to Ohman, supporting the NFWA was both fitting and necessary for the movement's evolution.[1]

Although admirable, the potential for cooperation between the civil rights movement and the farmworkers' struggle—the latter commonly referred to as *la causa* (the cause)—faced many challenges. While both groups shared similarities, especially experiences of discrimination, their histories and cultures were distinct. For African Americans and Mexican Americans to come together in solidarity meant overcoming racial and ethnic differences, and in some instances those of language and religion. Geography could also divide them. In the South and Northeast, African Americans were generally unfamiliar with Mexican Americans, whose population in these areas was miniscule in the 1960s. In the West, most African Americans lived in urban areas far removed from the rural agricultural areas where the NFWA operated. Finally, and perhaps most significantly, for differing groups to come together in solidarity and cooperation, common interests must contend with self-interests. Forming alliances with others may not be a priority when one is still struggling to achieve unity within one's own group.[2]

Despite these challenges, significant cooperation between the civil rights movement and *la causa* did occur. Moreover, the alliances that developed between the United Farm Workers (UFW, as the NFWA later became known) and the organizations at the center of the black freedom struggle occurred in the context of widespread coalition building between the movements of the 1960s and 1970s. Although technically a labor union, the leaders and members of the UFW envisioned themselves and their struggle as part of "The Movement," the umbrella term for the various equality and justice struggles that unfolded in the United States from the 1950s to the 1970s. Yet existing histories of this period have tended to treat these movements independently. While providing in-depth knowledge of each movement, these works have created the false impression that each one operated in isolation. On the contrary, the social movements of the 1960s–1970s were marked by a pattern of continuous interaction and dynamic exchange. Sometimes the strategies, philosophies, and accomplishments of one movement merely influenced others. But in other instances, movements physically intersected. Participants overlapped, resources were shared, and efforts were merged to more effectively combat a shared enemy.[3]

While much historical scholarship argues that African American and Latino relations during the civil rights era were marked by conflict rather than cooperation, widespread coalition building occurred between the Chicano movement and the black freedom struggle. For example, the Brown Berets, a Chicano organization based in Los Angeles, joined with the Black Panther Party (BPP) to demand the release of Party leader Huey Newton from prison. Numerous Chicano activists, including members of the Crusade for Justice and the Alianza Federal de Pueblos Libres, participated in the Poor People's Campaign organized by the Southern Christian Leadership Conference (SCLC). African American and Chicano students, together with American Indian students, formed the Third World Liberation Front and organized protests that led to the creation of the Ethnic Studies program at San Francisco State University, the first in the nation. It was in just this sort of dynamic give-and-take that the UFW interacted with the black free-dom struggle.[4]

To explore more deeply the relationship between African American and Latino activism and how the black freedom struggle approached mul-tiracial coalition building, this book examines the interaction between the UFW and the five major organizations of the black freedom struggle: the Student Nonviolent Coordinating Committee (SNCC), National Association for the Advancement of Colored People (NAACP), National Urban League (NUL), SCLC, and BPP. These five organizations demonstrate the wide range of ideology and activism within the black freedom struggle. The NAACP, founded in 1909, was the largest and most established civil rights organiza-tion and pursued integration and equality in employment, education, and public accommodations primarily through the legal system. Founded a year later, the Urban League sought to improve the lives of African Americans in urban areas through employment and social services. In doing so, the League eschewed agitation and protest in favor of cultivating the support of white business leaders. The push for civil rights in the 1950s and 1960s led to the creation of organizations that employed new and varied methods. SCLC, led by Martin Luther King, Jr., sought to end discrimination by appealing to the morality of white Americans through Christianity and nonviolent protests. SNCC, founded by college students during the wave of sit-ins that swept the South in 1960, initially shared SCLC's commitment to Christian nonviolence, but soon diverged from the clergy-led organization as it embraced direct ac-tion protests, voter registration, and participatory democracy in the most vi-olent areas of the Deep South. The movement in the South generally did not address the experience of African Americans in the urban North and West. The BPP was founded in Oakland, California in 1966 to confront police bru-tality in that city. In contrast to SCLC and SNCC, the BPP pursued social justice and economic and political power through a daring combination of community service and armed self-defense. The prominence and effective-ness of all five of these organizations demonstrates the diversity of activists, ideologies, and protest strategies within the black freedom struggle.[5]

These five organizations were not only instrumental in shaping the di-rection of and providing leadership for the black freedom struggle, they all also actively supported the UFW. Comparing and contrasting these orga-nizations' relationships to the UFW thus conveys the range of attitudes and approaches toward multiracial coalition building within the movement. Some scholars argue that organizations do not truly represent group interests and that "some of the most dynamic struggles take place outside—indeed, sometimes in spite of—established organizations and institutions." While I acknowledge the importance of this sort of "infrapolitics," I maintain that organizations are useful tools in the study of coalition building. As scholar Laura Pulido has argued, "Organizations and groups are the essential building blocks of movements, as they provide the space where like-minded individuals coalesce and can accomplish a great deal more collectively than alone." Once individuals come together in an organization, they can then form coalitions with others.[6]

The UFW is an ideal vehicle for examining the black freedom struggle's positions on multiracial coalitions. Cultivating non-farmworker allies was a key component of UFW strategy because union leaders realized that farmworkers were not powerful enough on their own to be victorious against the forces of agribusiness. Distinct from family farms, agribusiness refers to massive, industrialized farms run by corporations. Chavez explained that in the case of agribusiness, "The power of the growers was backed by the power of the police, the courts, state and federal laws, and the financial power of the big corporations, the banks, and the utilities." In the face of this web of power, farmworkers confronted nearly insurmountable odds in their struggle; previous attempts to unionize farmworkers had been crushed—often violently— by the forces of agribusiness. Outside supporters were thus necessary to aid the economically and politically powerless farmworkers.[7]

Allies were particularly useful during boycotts, which the UFW employed to put economic pressure on growers. Chavez explained, "Alone, the farm workers have no economic power; but with the help of the public they can develop the economic power to counter that of the growers." In order for the boycotts to have negative economic consequences for the growers, as many people as possible needed to participate. The UFW appealed to a wide spectrum of potential supporters, including other labor unions, religious orders, students, activists of the New Left, housewives, politicians, and celebrities. Pursuing such a wide array of supporters both set the union apart from Chicano movement organizations and drew criticism from its more nationalistic elements. Corky Gonzales, founder of the Denver-based organization Crusade for Justice and an early leader of the Chicano movement, said of Chavez, "In order to have autonomy he had to have financial support. We work differently. We feel that no matter how long it takes, we have to develop our own leadership. We don't want those alliances." The UFW's reliance on coalitions with other groups to execute its political goals, and the eagerness with which its leaders pursued these alliances, makes the organization a fitting lens through which to study multiracial coalition building.[8]

Analyzing the relationships between the UFW and the black freedom struggle organizations allows for the examination of multiracial coalition building in both regional and national contexts. The UFW's base in California provides a window into the dynamics of interracial activism in the West, which was remarkable in its level of racial and ethnic diversity. Recent scholarship has revealed that activists in the West frequently engaged in multiracial coalition building as a practical strategy in the pursuit of social change. In contrast, when scholars of the movements in the South and Northeast address cross-racial cooperation, they focus on the relationships between black and white activists. However, some of the union's boycotts, particularly against California grapes in the late 1960s, were national. The spread of UFW boycotts nationwide, particularly to areas with small or nonexistent Mexican American populations, facilitates the analysis of multiracial coalition building on a larger scale and provides a counterpoint to the uniqueness of the West.[9]

Finally, the UFW is an apt lens through which to view the black freedom struggle's approaches to multiracial coalitions because the union enjoyed the support of such widely divergent organizations. While each of the five organizations examined here had the ultimate goal of African American equality, they differed widely in their ideologies, priorities, strategies, leadership, and constituencies. Nevertheless, each supported the UFW. Although Chicano and African American activists frequently cooperated during the 1960s and 1970s, the UFW was distinctive among Mexican American organizations in its sustained relationships with a wide variety of civil rights organizations. For example, the Brown Berets had cooperative relationships with similarly radical organizations such as the BPP, but not with more mainstream groups like the NAACP and the NUL. Likewise, the alliances between the militant Alianza Federal de Pueblos Libres and the likeminded Nation of Islam, US, and the BPP outlasted its relationship with SCLC, which dissolved after the Poor People's Campaign in 1968.[10]

This analysis of the relationship between the black freedom struggle and the UFW is a study of social movement politics, in that it focuses on how and why coalitions formed and the reasons they did or did not work. Coalition building is a complicated undertaking and involves several factors, the interplay of which determines the viability of an alliance. The coalitions formed between the black freedom struggle and the UFW were shaped by key facets

of personal and group identity: race, class, and region. Aspects of an organization—particularly ideology, praxis, historical context, and leadership—
were also instrumental in the development and outcome of coalitions.

Race was of primary importance in these interrelationships. To successfully overcome racial divides, individuals had to overlook such differences
in favor of interracial solidarity. The strongest coalitions considered here
rested on a shared sentiment among the participants that African Americans and Mexican Americans were commonly oppressed peoples of color.
In many ways, the discrimination against Mexican Americans in the West
took the same forms as that directed against African Americans in the Jim
Crow South. Both groups were segregated in schools, housing, and public accommodations. "White" and "Colored" signs in the South were replaced in the West by signs proclaiming, "No Mexicans or Dogs Allowed."
Both African Americans and Mexican Americans also experienced racial
discrimination in the workplace; African American factory workers and
Mexican American farmworkers were each prevented from becoming a
foreman or manager, positions reserved for whites. The recognition of this
shared experience was a key step in building a coalition by establishing mutual understanding.

Racial solidarity between African Americans and Mexican Americans
was facilitated by the evolution of Mexican Americans' racial identity. From
the 1930s until the 1960s, many middle class Mexican American activist organizations, such as the League of United Latin American Citizens (LULAC)
and the American GI Forum, invested in crafting a white identity, viewing
whiteness as essential for access to opportunity in the United States. Although not necessarily a rejection of African Americans, many black activists took it that way, especially when LULAC used the claim to whiteness
as a legal strategy in court cases challenging discrimination against Mexican
Americans. The strategy was largely ineffective, as defendants could argue
that since Mexican Americans were white, they were not being discriminated
against, and defendants were thus not compelled to end discriminatory practices. The ineffectiveness of the whiteness strategy, coupled with the domestic and international movements of the 1960s, led some Mexican Americans
to develop a Chicano identity that rejected whiteness in favor of a "brown"
identity. *Chicanismo* included racial pride, cultural expression, active resistance to discrimination, and unity with peoples of color around the world,
including African Americans. This transition was likely easiest for working-
class Mexican Americans who, due to their experiences with discrimination

and segregation, generally did not consider themselves white and therefore found commonality with African Americans.[11]

Especially in the West, the participation of whites and Asians in these political struggles was frequent and complicates the role of race in the relationship between the UFW and the black freedom struggle. Whites not only boycotted grapes and sent financial contributions to civil rights organizations, they also were important staff members within the UFW and SNCC. In some cases, they even played vital roles in the development of coalitions between movements. The UFW allied with the Agricultural Workers Organizing Committee (AWOC), many of whose members were Filipino, in their first strike against Delano grape growers in 1965. The role of whites and Filipinos thus moves this story beyond one of black/brown relations and proves that the coalitions between *la causa* and the black freedom struggle were truly multiracial.

Perhaps due to its prominence in our society, race has overshadowed other important factors in the study of dynamics between different racial groups. For example, much of the recent scholarship on African American and Mexican American relations focuses on racial similarities or differences. Although race figured prominently in multiracial alliances, it was by no means the only factor at work.[12]

Class identity also played a decisive role in the coalitions considered here. The formation of one's class identity included one's relationship to the economic system: one's occupation (or relationship to the means of production) and financial standard of living. However, class identity is also based on lived experience within the home and one's community. In these settings, an awareness of economic inequality and power, shaped before entering the workforce, created a firm sense of class position. For both African Americans and Mexican Americans, their class was intertwined with their race. Racial discrimination in the workplace relegated the majority of both groups to the working classes and justified their continued economic exploitation. While a common class identity does not guarantee solidarity, class provided another point of cooperation between the black freedom struggle and the UFW. Civil rights activists who had experience with agricultural labor and rural poverty were especially apt to feel class solidarity with the farmworkers. However, middle-class civil rights activists had to cross both the divides of class and race to connect with the Mexican American farmworkers.[13]

The importance of class takes on additional force here because both the black freedom struggle and *la causa* were fights for economic justice as well as racial equality. Both movements conceptualized the fight for equitable hiring practices, fair wages, and safe working conditions as integral to the pursuit of racial equality. Wendy Goepel Brooks, a white UFW organizer, succinctly explained, farm labor "has been a civil rights issue since the first Negro was brought to America to work in the fields as a slave." However, the emphasis on economic justice in both movements created the opportunity for coalition building around class while sidestepping the racial divide. Indeed, some civil rights activists were motivated to support the farmworkers because of a commitment to fighting economic inequality rather than a concern for racial discrimination against Mexican Americans.[14]

Region played an important role in narrowing racial and class divides. The UFW was based in California, a state renowned for its racial and ethnic diversity. The state's diversity made race relations more complex than in other regions and rigid Jim Crow segregation became impossible. Even when confined to segregated neighborhoods, African Americans lived and worked alongside other minority groups, including Mexican Americans. Sharing social spaces caused the two groups to participate in cultural exchanges, learning and enjoying each other's customs, foodways, music, and languages. They also became intimately familiar with each other's experiences of discrimination. This close knowledge often led to collaboration in the pursuit of social change. Multiracial coalition building was also a practical strategy for the civil rights organizations in the West because the African American population was small in relation to the entire region, making strategic alliances essential to achieving their goals. Furthermore, in reflection of the West's demographics, the fight for civil rights took on a decidedly multiracial form by demanding social justice on behalf of Latinos, Asian Americans, and American Indians, as well as African Americans. In contrast, race relations in the South operated around a black/white binary and thus the civil rights movement revolved around equality for African Americans. The lack of significant numbers of other minority groups (the Latino population in the South was less than 1 percent in both 1960 and 1970) also meant that multiracial coalition building was neither a priority nor a necessity. Although the Northeast—the urban areas in particular—were more diverse, there were few Mexican Americans in the region. Civil rights activists in the South and Northeast thus had little if any firsthand knowledge of Mexican Americans and their issues. It was therefore more challenging for civil rights organizations in these regions to find common cause with the UFW.[15]

Regional differences in the United States were not the only ways that geography affected coalition building. The rural Central Valley in which the UFW organized was the agricultural epicenter of the West, if not the entire country. The UFW's organizing program therefore revolved around the challenges faced by rural agricultural workers and addressed itself to the economic and social structures of rural areas. Of the five civil rights organizations considered here, only SNCC prioritized rural organizing. Members of SCLC and the BPP, however, had been raised in rural areas and had personal experience with farm work. Familiarity with the character of agricultural labor and rural poverty facilitated connections between the black freedom struggle and the UFW.

Race, class, and region all created a sense of common cause among individual activists, but these factors alone were not enough to sustain coalitions between large organizations. It was important that they had compatible ideologies and praxis. Although organizations did not have to have identical interests, philosophies, strategies, and tactics in order to form an alliance, likeminded organizations were better able to work together. Historical context was also an important factor in determining whether an organization would and could enter into a coalition. Although the UFW conceived of itself as part of the civil rights movement, it also embodied the labor movement. Whether an organization of the black freedom struggle supported the UFW thus depended on its historic relationships with both Mexican Americans and organized labor. Many activists were reluctant to support the UFW because of organized labor's history of discrimination against African Americans and its complicated relationship with the civil rights movement.[16]

Leadership also played a decisive role in coalition building in the black freedom struggle. No matter how similar or compatible organizations may have been, coalitions did not occur spontaneously. The formation of coalitions depended on the work of bridge leaders who, by crossing the divides that separated movements or organizations, created the impetus for alliances to develop. Although some scholars define bridge leaders as individuals, particularly women, who connect formal movement leaders to their constituencies, I argue that bridge leadership can operate between movements as well as within. These leaders were willing to overlook differences in favor of similarities and had to convince their colleagues and constituencies to do the same. Accordingly, individuals could also explain why alliances between analogous and likeminded organizations did not occur.[17]

As all of these factors indicate, the coalitions that formed between the UFW and the organizations of the black freedom struggle were complex and contextual, shaped by the dynamics of race and class, but also reflective of the organizations' histories, ideologies, praxis, circumstances, and geographic locations. Though SNCC, the NAACP, the Urban League, SCLC, and the BPP—five organizations that represented a wide spectrum of black activism—all supported the UFW, the extent of their support for the union varied. This book seeks to uncover the factors that explain the organizations' differing approaches to the UFW and, more broadly, to multiracial coalition building writ large.

Although the extent and duration of the alliances between the black freedom struggle and the UFW varied, they were all significant. As a historian of interracial activism has argued, "Whether coalitions were rare or common is not the important question here, but rather their significance and long-term import. Interracial cooperation influenced civil rights outcomes and trajectories disproportionate to the number of people involved." The support of the black freedom struggle, in addition to that of the farmworkers' other allies, helped the UFW to achieve the first union contracts for agricultural workers in the United States. Beyond material gains, these civil rights activists and the UFW members and organizers learned from each other. Working together informed their ideology and praxis, which contributed to their individual and organizational development and further strengthened their bonds. Furthermore, whether for one boycott or several, the coalitions between the UFW and these civil rights organizations mattered for revealing that the black freedom struggle was committed to "freedom for other men."[18]

CHAPTER 1

This Is How a Movement Begins

ELIZABETH Sutherland Martínez had chosen her dress just for the occasion—it was red and black to match the flag of the National Farm Workers Association. As one of two Mexican Americans on the staff of the Student Nonviolent Coordinating Committee nationwide, Martínez had traveled from New York City to California's Central Valley in March 1966 to show support for the union. Led by Cesar Chavez, the farmworkers were marching 250 miles from Delano to Sacramento to draw attention to their struggles against Schenley Industries, one of the largest grape growers in Delano. That evening, as the marchers rested, ate, and visited in a community center in a small, dusty town along the route, Martínez was asked to give a speech on behalf of SNCC. She hurried to the ladies' room, where she scribbled a short address on a steno pad, changed into her specially selected dress, and ran back to the hall. In Spanish, Martínez spoke for SNCC when she proclaimed, "We are with you and we are proud of your march and your victory because it is a victory for all the poor of the world."[1]

Along the highway leading through the heart of California's breadbasket, Martínez was far from SNCC's organizational base in the Deep South. However, SNCC's participation in and endorsement of the Delano to Sacramento march marked the high point of the alliance that had formed between the civil rights organization and the farmworkers union. Beginning in early 1965, SNCC and the NFWA came together in a productive relationship that demonstrated both organizations' profound understanding—based on hard-won experience—of the connection between racial discrimination and economic oppression. The NFWA recognized that California's largely Mexican

American farm laborers were both discriminated against as racial minorities and economically exploited by the state's agribusiness corporations. Therefore the NFWA confronted both forms of oppression in its endeavors. In its pursuit of racial equality on behalf of African Americans in the Deep South, SNCC also challenged America's economic caste system, which it saw as antithetical to a democratic society. SNCC's intent to confront not only American racial mores and the political system, but also the nation's economic and class structure, set it apart from other civil rights organizations. Therefore, the support that SNCC demonstrated for the farmworkers was characteristic of the organization and its ideals about race and class.[2]

This shared understanding of the connection between racial discrimination and economic oppression formed the basis of the alliance between SNCC and the NFWA because it enabled them to recognize that African Americans and Mexican Americans were victims of the same oppressive forces and led them to see the benefits of a multiracial coalition. On top of this ideological foundation, common organizational praxis of the two groups further facilitated their alliance. However, these factors only led to a coalition between SNCC and the NFWA because of the leadership of individuals who recognized the potential in such a relationship. The resulting alliance enabled each organization to expand its mission and activism by applying its principles across racial lines. As Martínez told the marchers, "It is necessary that blacks and Mexicans see that there is only one cause—justice."[3]

*   *   *

SNCC's founding reveals the degree to which the organization incorporated economic power in its fight for racial equality. In April 1960, black and white students gathered at Shaw University in Raleigh, North Carolina, at the invitation of Ella Baker and SCLC, who wanted to harness the energy of the student-led sit-ins of lunch counters and restaurants that had swept the South since the sit-ins in Greensboro, North Carolina, in February of that year. These sit-ins were conducted with the knowledge that African Americans possessed economic power as consumers that could be used as a weapon against racial discrimination. Franklin McCain, who as a student at North Carolina A&T College participated in the sit-in at Woolworth's in Greensboro, explained that they targeted that store because they were allowed—and encouraged—to purchase goods, but were not permitted to eat at the lunch counter: "They tell you to come in: 'Yes, buy the toothpaste; yes, come in and buy the notebook paper . . . .No, we don't separate your money in this cash register, but no, please don't step down to the hot dog stand...' The whole system, of course, was unjust, but that just seemed like insult added to injury." By recognizing their power as consumers, the students began to dismantle the system of racial segregation in southern public accommodations. Baker was concerned that the energy and power that the students had demonstrated would dissipate once they achieved their goal of access and integration. Founding SNCC member Julian Bond recalled that Baker thought that the student sit-in movement "had narrow vision and thought the whole world was nothing but lunch counters." The founding of SNCC at the meeting at Shaw University was thus an attempt to institutionalize the students' use of economic power to combat racial discrimination.[4]

As SNCC grew and evolved, it fought for racial equality through direct action tactics (such as sit-ins and marches) and through voter registration among African Americans, primarily in the Deep South. Through their efforts in their fight against racial discrimination, SNCC workers were exposed to the economic inequality and exploitation of African Americans. By living and working in small towns in the rural Deep South, SNCC "field secretaries" (the term given to those who organized for SNCC full time) witnessed firsthand the crippling poverty experienced by most African Americans in the region. Furthermore, some SNCC organizers had grown up in rural southern towns and brought their intertwined experiences of poverty and racism to their activism. For example, SNCC field secretary and Mississippi native Lawrence Guyot explained that when African Americans in Greenwood, Mississippi attempted to register to vote, "the county decided that what it would do was it would cut off all welfare supplies. So it did just that. All food was cut off." Ivanhoe Donaldson, who organized for SNCC in the Mississippi Delta town of Clarksdale, elaborated that when plantation workers tried to register to vote or organize others to do so, "plantation owners were not only being hostile in terms of pushing people off the plantation, but were economically isolating people from credit at stores or from banks." SNCC workers therefore drew a direct connection between gaining the vote, racial equality, and economic justice.[5]

The treatment of black sharecroppers was remarkably similar to that of Mexican American farmworkers in California. Like African Americans in the South, racial discrimination against Mexican Americans directly affected their

opportunities for employment and economic advancement. In the West's agricultural areas, such as the fertile Central Valley, many worked as migrant
farm laborers. The high numbers of Mexican Americans in agriculture resulted from labor policies influenced by racism. Many growers encouraged
the government recruitment of Mexicans, whom they stereotyped as docile
and obedient, which they argued made them ideally suited for farm labor.
Some believed that Mexicans were also uniquely physically adapted to agricultural work. Echoing earlier justifications of the enslavement of Africans,
a prominent landowner in California asserted in the *Saturday Evening Post*
in 1928, "Mexican casual labor fills the requirement of the California farm
as no other labor has done in the past. The Mexican withstands the high
temperatures of the Imperial and San Joaquin valleys." Paradoxically, employers also claimed that Mexicans were lazy and irresponsible and that they
should therefore be paid less than other workers. Similarly, southern planters
argued that African Americans were lazy and "shiftless," which justified both
low wages and strict white control and supervision. Furthermore, Mexicans
were desirable as workers because—due to racial biases against them and the
proximity of the border—they were easily deported when their labor was no
longer needed, as was the case during the Great Depression. The growers
also opened themselves up to the charge of discrimination against Mexican Americans by their indifference toward the unhealthy and dangerous
working conditions to which farmworkers were exposed, including extreme
temperatures, lack of fresh water and restrooms in the fields, and the use of
hazardous pesticides.[6]

California farmworkers had made several attempts to organize and improve their conditions. For example, in 1928 the Confederación de Unio-
nes Obreras (Federation of Labor Unions) was founded in Los Angeles and
promptly organized a strike of cantaloupe workers in the Imperial Valley
in Southern California. In the thirteen years following that strike, Mexican
American workers organized themselves into unions and conducted strikes
in the lettuce, pea, berry, beet, cotton, citrus, celery, and bean fields throughout California in pursuit of higher wages and improved working conditions.
However, growers had successfully crushed these efforts through race riots
and murders and by firing, evicting, and deporting workers who attempted
to organize or strike. Similarly, sharecroppers' attempts to organize in Arkansas and Alabama in the 1930s were met with evictions, arrests, race riots, and lynchings. Mike Miller—a white SNCC field secretary from San
Francisco's largely Latino Mission District neighborhood who ran that city's

SNCC office—recognized that African Americans and Mexican American agricultural workers experienced identical forms of overlapping racial discrimination and economic oppression. Miller therefore saw it as only fitting that SNCC reach out to California's exploited farmworkers.[7]

Miller orchestrated SNCC's involvement with the farmworkers during a time of transition for the organization. The Mississippi Freedom Summer Project of 1964, during which SNCC recruited white northern student volunteers to conduct voter registration among African Americans, heightened—and in some cases introduced—tensions regarding SNCC's structure, direction, and identity. In the wake of beatings, murders, voter intimidation, and the inability of the Mississippi Freedom Democratic Party (MFDP) to gain representation at the Democratic National Convention in Atlantic City, SNCC experienced a period of collective introspection. After the tumultuous summer, SNCC's national headquarters in Atlanta called for members to present position papers at a staff meeting in Waveland, Mississippi in November 1964. Miller saw the meeting at Waveland as an opportunity to expand the mission of SNCC to include the plight of workers. In response to a questionnaire distributed to SNCC offices nationwide that accompanied the call for papers, Miller wrote,

> That the question "what should be SNCC's position on African affairs?" is raised and the question, for example, "what is SNCC's position on the labor movement?" is not raised seems to me to ignore what we have to do here and now. . . . The day-to-day world in which we live is such that UAW affairs are probably more relevant to MFDP, COFO [Council of Federated Organizations], and SNCC than African affairs.

Many SNCC members were inspired by recent African liberation struggles and were thus motivated to form connections with countries freed from colonial rule. In fact, a SNCC delegation toured the continent and met with some of the leaders of the newly independent countries in September 1964. But Miller questioned the immediate relevance of Africa's anticolonial struggles and instead wanted to see SNCC aligned with the farm labor movement.[8]

Miller's interest in the plight of workers long predated his involvement in SNCC. He recalled, "When I was little, I was on my father's shoulders on picket lines." Miller's father, James Miller, wrote for the newspaper of the International Fishermen and Allied Workers of America, which was expelled from the Congress of Industrial Organizations (CIO) in 1950 for being "communist dominated." As an undergraduate at the University of California, Berkeley, Miller focused his attention on agricultural workers when he became acquainted with veteran labor organizer Anne Draper, who worked with the National Farm Labor Advisory Committee and organized support activities on the Berkeley campus for striking workers. Under Draper's influence, Miller organized rallies and food and clothing drives on behalf of the United Packinghouse Workers (UPWA) when it struck against cantaloupe growers in the Imperial Valley of California. In 1960, Miller organized the Student Committee for Agricultural Labor, which conducted grassroots organizing among farmworkers. [9]

Following his graduation from UC Berkeley, Miller attended graduate school in sociology at Columbia University. His passion for fighting on behalf of the oppressed followed him to New York City, where he organized public housing tenants on the Lower East Side. After six months, Miller was fired for being "too militant." He then returned to the Bay Area to resume his graduate studies at the Berkeley. There Miller became re-involved with SLATE, a campus political organization he had helped found as an undergraduate. [10]

Miller's experience could have led directly to a career on behalf of agricultural workers. However, SNCC was in need of his considerable organizing skills. In 1962 SLATE held a conference on "The Negro in America," in which SNCC chairman Charles McDew participated. At the request of McDew, Miller became the SNCC representative in the Bay Area. Miller joined the SNCC staff full time the following winter, while still a graduate student. Soon after, Sam Block, a SNCC field secretary working on voter registration in Greenwood, Mississippi, went to Berkeley and asked Miller to work in Mississippi, which he did in July 1963. [11]

After being severely injured when his car was run off the road by hostile whites in Mississippi, Miller returned to expand SNCC activities in the Bay Area by setting up a Friends of SNCC office in San Francisco, part of a network of volunteers who worked to support the organization's activities in the South. In addition, Miller and fellow activist Terence "Terry" Cannon established Freedom House, which organized against the redevelopment of the Fillmore District, a historically African American neighborhood in San Francisco. According to Cannon, the redevelopment project "was tearing the heart out of the black community there." Miller and Cannon's work against urban renewal was supported by the national SNCC office. Miller explained,

"SNCC support work went well in the Bay Area, so national headquarters waived the usual rule that 'field secretaries' in the north were only to work on southern support. I was able to divide my time between support work for the South and participation in several losing San Francisco battles against urban renewal." The San Francisco Friends of SNCC soon became a bona fide SNCC chapter, one of nine "northern offices" outside the Deep South and the only one in northern California. Miller asked Cannon to edit the office's newsletter, which quickly evolved into *The Movement*, the national publication of SNCC.[12]

Miller and his colleagues in San Francisco SNCC firmly believed that SNCC's organizing techniques could—and should—be applied to farmworkers in California. In their pursuit of civil rights, SNCC field secretaries practiced participatory democracy, which SNCC organizer Cleveland Sellers defined as "local people working to develop the power to control the significant events that affected their lives." Operating under that philosophy, SNCC field secretaries did not impose leadership, but rather worked to identify indigenous leaders in the community and cultivate their leadership skills. Furthermore, SNCC organizers did not dictate to people what they should be fighting for and how they should go about it. Instead, they conducted what historian Charles Payne refers to as "slow and respectful work" in order to discern people's interests and concerns before attempting to persuade them to register to vote. Miller described the ideal organizer who followed this model in an editorial in *The Movement*: "An organizer doesn't like to do all the talking. He talks; he listens; he asks questions. He operates on the principle that the people in the streets, in the neighborhoods, in the fields, in the plants, on the unemployed lines, on the welfare rolls know better than he what they want and need—but they don't know how to get it." Thus, a good organizer, according to SNCC, helped empower people to make meaningful and lasting changes in their communities.[13]

SNCC's organizing philosophy and tactics strongly resembled Chavez's mission to empower farmworkers. Like SNCC, Chavez knew that effective organizing was slow work because it relied on making personal connections. He explained,

> There are also some very simple things that have to be done in organizing, certain key things that nobody could get away without doing, like talking to people. If you talk to people, you're going to organize them. But people aren't going to come to you. You have

to go to them. It takes a lot of work. When you pick grapes, you
pick a bunch at a time. Eventually you pick the whole vineyard.
Organizing is no different.

Chavez began his career as an organizer through the Community Service
Organization (CSO), a Mexican American civil rights organization based in
Southern California. Founded in 1947 in the wake of Edward Roybal's first
campaign for Los Angeles city council, the CSO began as a mutual aid so-
ciety that encouraged political participation and integration of Mexican
Americans. Fred Ross, the white West Coast regional director of Saul
Alinsky's Industrial Areas Foundation (IAF), became CSO executive director.
Ross recruited and trained Chavez to be an organizer for the CSO in 1952.[14]

One of Ross's most important organizing tactics that he taught Chavez
was the house meeting. This method was completely dependent on personal
connections; once the organizer identified an interested person, she/he would
ask that person to hold a small meeting in their home and to invite a few
of their friends. The intimacy of the small house meeting would then allow
people to speak freely about their concerns. Chavez recalled, "When I talked
to people at their homes, it was unbelievable how their attitude changed, how
different it was from when I talked to them in the fields." After conducting
house meetings for several weeks, a mass meeting would be held to organize
a CSO chapter. Similarly, after SNCC organizers had been canvassing in African American communities for some time, they held mass meetings to bring
people together, create a sense of solidarity, and mobilize people to action.
As historian Charles Payne argued in his study of civil rights organizing in
Mississippi,

> Maybe canvassing is the prototypical organizing act. It is the initial
> reaching out to the community, the first step toward building
> relationships outside the circle of those favorably predisposed to
> the movement. Mass meetings were another step in that process.
> If canvassers could awaken an initial curiosity in people, mass
> meetings could weld curiosity into commitment.

The same argument could be made about the role of organizers and mass
meetings in the CSO, which demonstrates that many of the activities of the
early CSO resembled those of SNCC.[15]

The CSO and SNCC both sought political power for their communities through voter registration. However, since many CSO members were not U.S. citizens, Ross implemented citizenship classes that eventually become key components of every CSO chapter. The classes were open to all ages and included literacy instruction. Chavez recalled of the classes, "Where the kids sat during the day, the parents would sit at night, and we not only taught them the Constitution and basic English but we also taught them to fill out all the citizenship forms." In both format and content, CSO citizenship classes paralleled SNCC voter registration efforts. In the South, African Americans were prevented from registering to vote in many ways, including through the use of literacy tests. In some areas, African Americans who wished to register were asked to interpret a section of the Constitution. SNCC therefore devised education programs that taught literacy and government and instructed adults in the process of voter registration.[16]

After serving as the director of the CSO, Chavez resigned to work on behalf of farmworkers and founded the NFWA in 1962. However, he took Ross's lessons in organizing and applied them to the recruitment of farmworkers. The similarities between Chavez's and SNCC's approaches to organizing facilitated the eventual alliance between the two organizations. The work of Chavez and SNCC became even more closely aligned when SNCC began organizing migrant farmworkers on Maryland's eastern shore in 1964. It was this project that convinced Mike Miller that SNCC's techniques could be applied to Mexican American farmworkers in California. Even though the migrant farmworkers on the East Coast were primarily African American, Miller persuaded SNCC to explore the idea of voter registration among California's Mexican American farmworkers, whom he saw as suffering from the same racial discrimination and economic exploitation. In December 1964 Miller wrote a letter to the national SNCC staff outlining a proposal to organize farmworkers in California. Miller explained, "Some of you have heard me talk about the California Valley. It is our Delta. It is a land of immense richness and the deepest of poverty." Miller was especially interested in working with the NFWA, which he had learned of through Ross, whom he had met through his activities at UC Berkeley.[17]

Immediately after SNCC approved his program, Miller contacted the union in January 1965 through his friend Coleman Blease, a Sacramento lawyer who had worked with NFWA co-founder Dolores Huerta, to discuss voter registration. Blease wrote to Huerta in January of 1965, requesting a meeting between Chavez, Huerta, Miller, and Bob Moses, director of SNCC organizing in Mississippi. Blease opined, "I believe that any cooperative ven-

ture between SNCC and the Farm Workers Association would be most fruitful." Although Chavez did not attend the meeting, which occurred in late
January 1965, it established the first formal connection between SNCC and
the NFWA.[18]

Miller's actions demonstrate the importance of individual leadership in
coalition building. Although significant, parallel ideologies and praxis did
not necessarily lead to the formation of alliances between organizations. For
example, scholars have pointed out that although the NAACP had much in
common with LULAC, they did not work together, even when both organizations were fighting school segregation in the courts. Individuals were
necessary to recognize the potential of working with others and lead their
organizations to form a coalition. Miller's background in both labor and civil
rights organizing enabled him to serve as a bridge between the NFWA and
SNCC and guide the formation of their alliance.[19]

*   *   *

True to Blease's prediction, the newly formed alliance between SNCC and
the NFWA proved invaluable for the farmworkers just a few months after
the initial meeting between the two organizations. In July 1965, the NFWA
and the California Migrant Ministry (CMM)—an offshoot of the National
Council of Churches that both ministered to farmworkers and assisted
them in their fight for justice—organized a rent strike against the Tulare
County Housing Authority. The Housing Authority had doubled the rent at
the Woodville and Linnell labor camps, despite no increase in pay for the
farmworker residents and no improvement of the unsanitary, Depression-
era tin huts, which the County Health Department had condemned.
Finding themselves ill-prepared for a rent strike, the CMM's Reverend
Jim Drake and Gilbert Padilla, who had worked with Chavez in the CSO,
called on the San Francisco SNCC office to send organizers to assist. The
SNCC volunteers who heeded the call were especially helpful when 350
farmworkers and supporters marched six miles from the Linnell camp to
the Housing Authority offices. The influence of SNCC's use of nonviolent
direct action was clear in the rules given to the marchers, which began,
"All participants in this action project are asked to maintain discipline
and conduct themselves in a nonviolent manner. Nonviolence has been

Figure 1. Child in front of a dilapidated house in a farm labor camp. Courtesy of Walter P. Reuther Library, Wayne State University.

shown to be a powerful force when used by a dedicated group trained in understanding and discipline." The rules' emphasis on nonviolence reflected SNCC's founding statement, which proclaimed, "By appealing to conscience and standing on the moral nature of human existence, nonviolence nurtures the atmosphere in which reconciliation and justice become actual possibilities."[20]

Along with contributing strategy, SNCC also supported the rent strike by diligently reporting on it in *The Movement*. According to Cannon, the newspaper's staff "saw early just simply the need to publicize what was going on." Although San Francisco SNCC published the newspaper, it was disseminated to SNCC and Friends of SNCC offices nationwide. Through *The Movement*, many in SNCC first learned of racial and social problems outside the South. For example, to illustrate the similarities between farmworkers on the East and West Coasts, the front page of the August 1965 issue of *The Movement* placed an article on the Tulare County strike next to an article on the Tennessee Freedom Labor Union, an organization of black farmworkers and sharecroppers. Subsequent issues of *The Movement* included additional pieces on farmworkers and reprinted articles from *El Malcriado*, the NFWA newspaper. Along with Miller, the staff of *The Movement* operated as bridge leaders by highlighting the commonalities, rather than the differences, between the NFWA and the civil rights movement.[21]

The Movement took such a great interest in the rent strike because the newspaper's staff included members who shared a background in the labor movement and an interest in the struggles of agricultural workers. Editor Terry Cannon was a Midwestern Quaker whose mother had reported on sharecroppers during the Great Depression. One of *The Movement*'s most prolific photographers and writers was George Ballis. Following a short stint as a factory worker in Chicago, Ballis moved to Fresno, California, in January 1953 to edit the *Valley Labor Citizen*, a weekly pro-union newspaper. He soon became interested in farmworkers and began photographing them. Ballis became acquainted with SNCC and several of its staff members, including Mississippi field secretary Lawrence Guyot, in 1963 when he drove to the South with donations for the organization from the students of California State University, Fresno. In 1964, Ballis volunteered for SNCC as a photographer. When Mike Miller set up the SNCC office in San Francisco, Guyot suggested that Ballis be added to the staff. Ballis's interest in agricultural workers provided *The Movement* with a significant degree of knowledge and sophistication about the plight of the farmworkers.[22]

The Movement's staff also brought with them a profound understanding of economic inequality. Hardy Frye, another early staff member, grew up in Tuskegee, Alabama where he experienced the strict class divisions within the black community. As a young man in Tuskegee, he was not allowed to date the daughters of the black elite because he was "from the other side of the tracks." He later reflected that his early experiences shaped his activism: "I probably brought an ideology to my Movement work . . . and it was class based." His disgust with the city's black elite led Frye to join the Army in order to escape Tuskegee. Stationed in Texas, Frye met Latinos for the first time and began to recognize the similarities between their experiences with discrimination and those of African Americans. After being discharged, he moved to Los Angeles, where he was active in the Congress of Racial Equality (CORE). Through his activism, Frye met Mike Miller and helped establish the Sacramento Friends of SNCC while a student at Sacramento City College. He then went to Mississippi in 1964 as a volunteer for Freedom Summer, after which he returned to Sacramento and the Friends of SNCC chapter there. In this capacity, Frye worked closely with

Father Keith Kenney, parish priest of Our Lady of Guadalupe Church in Sacramento, who ministered to farmworkers in the area and strongly supported the NFWA.[23]

SNCC's support was enormously beneficial to the Tulare County rent strike. SNCC's organizing techniques, as well as the publicity in *The Movement*, helped the farmworkers put constant pressure on the county Housing Authority. In the face of legal challenges, a district judge upheld the legality of the rent strike and declared the rent increases illegal. After over three years of delay, 100 new residences were built at the Woodville and Linnell Labor Camps in 1968. The rent strike was also successful in educating farmworkers about the NFWA. Chavez noted, "Short of getting into an agricultural strike, the rent strike . . . was one of the best ways of educating farm workers that there was a Union concerned with their economic interests." Furthermore, the NFWA, CMM, and farmworkers greatly appreciated the SNCC members who helped with the rent strike and march and valued their experience. Padilla recalled, "Those young men, or these young people I should say, were guys who had been in Mississippi and stuff. So they were already trained in marches and how to deal. They came with the perspective."[24]

*   *   *

The alliance that had blossomed between SNCC and the NFWA was based on shared ideas and values: commitment to justice and equality, acknowledgement of the importance of personal connections in organizing, and a profound understanding of the relationship between racial discrimination and economic oppression. Furthermore, SNCC shared common organizing techniques and strategies with the CSO, in which the NFWA leaders had been trained as organizers. These qualities continued to sustain the relationship between the two organizations as the NFWA embarked on the most pivotal moment of its history. On September 16, 1965, Mexican Independence Day, the NFWA voted to join AWOC, a union of Filipino farmworkers, in their strike of grape growers in the Delano area. In the spring of 1965 AWOC staged a series of successful strikes in Coachella Valley, California to demand higher wages. When growers in Delano refused to meet the same demand for equal wages, the Filipino grape pickers went on strike at nine vineyards. Knowing that a farmworker strike could not succeed in Delano without the support of Mexican American farmworkers, AWOC leader Larry Itliong turned to Chavez. Chavez was initially caught off guard when Itliong approached him because the NFWA was still a growing organization and did not have the monetary reserves to support a strike by thousands of workers. Nevertheless, Chavez realized that only a united workforce could effectively pressure the growers into signing contracts. The coalition between AWOC and the NFWA echoed the CSO's earlier cross-racial alliances with Asian American groups in Los Angeles to achieve political progress. Moreover, the alliance with the Filipino AWOC demonstrated that although the membership of the NFWA was overwhelmingly Mexican American, its fight for economic justice and equality for farmworkers was truly multiracial.[25]

As soon as the NFWA joined the strike, the growers, police, and townspeople became increasingly hostile and violent toward the farmworkers. Chavez recalled, "Growers pushed people around on the picket lines, ran tractors between pickets and the field to cover them with dust and dirt, drove cars and pickups with guns and dogs dangerously close to pickets at high speeds." Chavez had studied Gandhi and was determined that the strike be nonviolent, which was becoming increasingly difficult as violence toward the strikers continued and tensions in the town of Delano escalated due to the arrival of press covering the strike. Furthermore, NFWA organizer Wendy Goepel Brooks acknowledged that "the farm workers were not necessarily at all nonviolent by nature, to put it mildly." Recalling the influence of SNCC's strategy of nonviolent direct action during the Tulare County rent strike, Chavez personally asked the San Francisco SNCC office to send organizers to Delano to teach courses on nonviolent resistance to the farmworkers. In doing so, he placed great importance on the experience the SNCC activists had gained in the southern civil rights movement. He explained, "In the beginning, the staff people didn't thoroughly understand the whole idea of nonviolence, so I sent out the word to get young people who had been in the South and knew how to struggle nonviolently."[26]

Chavez also called on CORE to send volunteers, due to the civil rights organization's roots in pacifism and Gandhian nonviolent direct action. CORE volunteers taught classes in nonviolent resistance to the farmworkers and joined picket lines at the edges of the grape fields. On picket lines, CORE and SNCC members were especially valued for their experience in dealing with law enforcement. A NFWA leader explained, "You just couldn't have someone who had never been on a picket line before. We needed somebody who could talk to the cops—or who had the confidence to talk to the cops." However, the CORE volunteers soon moved on to other projects. In contrast, SNCC's involvement with the NFWA grew to include additional staff members and volunteers throughout California. This was partly the result of SNCC's loose structure, which encouraged, and even relied on, individual initiative. Offices and field secretaries were expected to develop their own projects that reflected the needs and issues of their communities. When successful, these regional projects became SNCC programs. SNCC field secretaries therefore had tremendous freedom in developing projects, as long as they adhered to SNCC's overall mission. The San Francisco SNCC office was therefore allowed to act as it saw fit on behalf of the NFWA.[27]

One of the first organizers SNCC sent to assist the NFWA was Marshall Ganz, a white staff member originally from Bakersfield, California, thirty miles south of Delano. While a student at Harvard University, Ganz joined the local Friends of SNCC. In 1964 he participated in Mississippi Freedom Summer, during which he worked with Hardy Frye. In September of that year, Ganz dropped out of Harvard to join the SNCC staff. By 1965, Ganz was conducting voter registration work in Amite County, Mississippi and living with E. W. Steptoe, head of the Amite NAACP. Ganz's interest in the NFWA was piqued when the August 1965 issue of *The Movement*, which reported the events of the Tulare County rent strike, arrived at Steptoe's house. Ganz recalled in the introduction to his study of the union,

> Although I had grown up in the midst of the farm worker world,
> I had never really seen it. But Mississippi had taught many of us
> that it was not an exception, but rather a clearly drawn example
> of how race, politics, and power work in America. This gave me
> the "Mississippi eyes" to see where I had grown up in a new way.
> I now saw farm workers who faced challenges not unlike those
> faced by their southern counterparts: no voting power, low wages,
> and, as people of color, subjected to California's own legacy of
> racial discrimination, which began with the Chinese immigrants.
> Now, they too were fighting back with their own movement.

His recognition that the Mexican American farmworkers in California and African Americans in the Deep South were suffering from the same forms of exploitation and discrimination prompted him to return to Bakersfield that

fall. Upon his arrival, Ganz met with LeRoy Chatfield, a former Christian
Brother with whom he had organized a Bakersfield Friends of SNCC chapter the previous year and who was now working as Cesar Chavez's assistant.
Soon afterward, Ganz heard Chavez speak to the Council for Civic Unity
in Bakersfield. Chavez recalled, "After my talk, he came up to say hello, and
someone told me he had just come from Mississippi. I made a point of talking to him some more." Following a weekend spent driving Chavez around
the Bay Area during a fundraising tour, Ganz began working for the farmworkers full time while still a SNCC staff member.[28]

Ganz's position as SNCC's representative in the NFWA points to the
multiracial nature of the coalition between the two organizations. Although
the recognition of common experiences of African Americans and Mexican
Americans was the cornerstone of the alliance, their relationship did not re-
volve around a racial binary. Rather, the alliance was reflective of each group's
commitment to multiracial solidarity. SNCC, while focused on equality for African Americans, included white members from its founding and eventually
included Latinas as well. African Americans, Asians, Puerto Ricans, Arabs, and
whites (mostly "Okies" and their descendants), were among the members of
the majority Mexican American NFWA. Similarly, despite its reputation as a
Mexican American organization, the CSO "was an interracial endeavor" and
had a diverse membership. That white men—Miller, Ganz, Cannon, and Ballis—played central roles in engineering and sustaining the coalition between
the NFWA and SNCC was both indicative of the frequency of cross-racial cooperation in these organizations and inconsequential to the farmworkers.[29]

Indeed, the NFWA welcomed the civil rights activists who came to their
aid—regardless of their race—with open arms. Eliseo Medina, a young farmworker who had broken his piggy bank to join the NFWA when the strike
began, appreciated the skills that SNCC workers brought to the strike. Growing up, he felt that there was no way to challenge the power held by the growers. He attributed the tactics and bravery of SNCC to changing this attitude.
Medina recalled, "I think SNCC people were the only ones that really had
any kind of concept about what to do. Particularly in things like marches
and demonstrations and all those tools of the civil rights movement, hell, we
didn't have a clue." Wendy Goepel Brooks acknowledged that at the beginning of the strike very few farmworkers had a practical knowledge of protesting, which resulted in "the blind leading the blind." She believed SNCC's
greatest contribution was teaching the "not particularly nonviolent" farmworkers about the importance of nonviolence. She recalled that SNCC or-

ganizers who joined the strike "came up with new ideas about non-violent methods to use to convey our message about the strike in Delano. They preached non-violence and supported Cesar's contention that the strike had to remain non-violent or we would all be losers." NFWA meeting minutes reveal that the farmworkers warmly received SNCC's lessons in nonviolent resistance. At one meeting, picket captain Julio Hernandez thanked volunteers from SNCC "for classes in non-violence which they have conducted for other staff members."[30]

Despite the warm welcome that SNCC workers received from most of the farmworkers, some in the NFWA initially cautioned Chavez against recruiting volunteers from the civil rights movement. Those opposed to the NFWA also resented the presence of the SNCC volunteers, particularly those who were white. Al Espinosa, a Mexican American captain in the Delano police department, told journalist John Gregory Dunne, "I abhor those SNCC Anglos coming in here to teach the Mexicans how to be civilized and nonviolent. My people are by nature nonviolent and we don't need Anglos to teach us nonviolence." While Espinosa resented the implication that white SNCC volunteers were instructing the farmworkers in nonviolent resistance, many of the growers used SNCC's presence to deny that the farmworkers wanted to strike and to blame any such activity on outside agitators. The NFWA actively rebuffed such claims in ways that reaffirmed their connection to the civil rights activists. Chavez told Dunne, "They say the farm workers are happy living the way they are—just like the Southern plantation owner used to say about his Negroes."[31]

The involvement of volunteers from SNCC and other progressive organizations also increased the already substantial red-baiting of the union. Southern whites had long accused civil rights organizations and activists of Communism as a way to diminish support for the movement and deflect attention from their complicity in racial discrimination and segregation. Southern business owners also labeled unions as Communist in part to prevent cross-racial unity among black and white workers. Following the same strategies as their southern counterparts, California growers and their allies (including the far right, anticommunist John Birch Society) similarly levied charges of Communism against the NFWA. The alliance with SNCC thus opened the NFWA to further red-baiting because, according to Dunne, "in Delano, such associations were tantamount to taking instructions from Peking." Nevertheless, Chavez was determined to continue working with these new allies because he believed that the benefits to the NFWA outweighed any

negative repercussions. He explained, "If we were nothing but farm workers in the Union now, just Mexican farm workers, we'd only have about 30
percent of all the ideas that we have. There would be no cross-fertilization,
no growing. It's beautiful to work with other groups, other ideas, and other
customs. It's like the wood is laminated." Chavez's commitment to multiracial coalition building stemmed from his experience with the CSO, which
engaged in numerous coalitions with African American, Jewish, and Asian
American groups. CSO leaders believed that such collaboration was necessary—especially in racially and ethnically diverse California—to achieve
progress and reduce discrimination.[32]

The relationship between SNCC and the farmworkers was facilitated by
the fact that the NFWA had positioned itself as a movement, rather than as
a labor union. As such, the farmworkers felt a kinship with civil rights activists and took inspiration from the milestones of the civil rights movement.
For example, a flier advertising a march and rally for the Tulare County rent
strike dubbed the region, "California's Selma." The NFWA newspaper *El Malcriado* editorialized about the situation in Tulare County,

> In the rent strike once again the farm worker is showing what
> he learned from the Negro movement. . . . Each day the working
> people are proving their courage more and more as the Negroes
> do in their movement. The day in which we the farm workers
> apply this lesson with the same courage which has been shown
> in Alabama and Mississippi, this will be the day in which the
> misfortune of the farm workers will end.

When the NFWA joined AWOC in its strike against Delano grape growers,
El Malcriado likened the strike to the 1955 Montgomery bus boycott. *El
Malcriado* elaborated: "This is how a movement begins. This is why the farm
workers association is a 'movement' more than a 'union.' Once a movement
begins it is impossible to stop. It will sweep through California and it will
not be over until the farm worker has the equality of a living wage and
decent treatment."[33]

The members of SNCC also related to the NFWA as a movement. SNCC
frequently had a contentious relationship with some of the leaders of other
major unions. Those in SNCC who did not approve of an alliance with organized labor nonetheless eagerly supported the NFWA on the basis of the
farmworkers' pursuit of racial equality. As Terry Cannon explained, "The

core of the connection [between SNCC and the NFWA] was the similarity in treatment of blacks in the South and Latinos in the West and Southwest." The fact that the union and SNCC combated both economic and racial discrimination enabled the alliance between the two organizations.[34]

*   *   *

This feeling of kinship and common purpose prompted SNCC to rally to the side of the NFWA. However, SNCC's involvement in the Delano strike was initially limited to the activities of the San Francisco staff, as the national organization's headquarters in Atlanta was at first ignorant of the relationship that had blossomed between it and the NFWA. On September 25, 1965, Muriel Tillinghast in the national SNCC office sent a letter to Chavez explaining the organization and asking him for information on the NFWA. The national SNCC office did not appear to be aware of the strike because Tillinghast did not mention it. In the postscript, she informed him that "SNCC folk in San Francisco are working with Mexican-American [sic] and you might want to contact them . . . Mike Miller heads that office." While this must have been confusing to Chavez and embarrassing to the San Francisco SNCC staff, who had been working with the NFWA for several months, it is not surprising due to SNCC's loose structure, which fostered the independence of its offices. However, this loose structure also resulted in disarray and a breakdown in communication within the SNCC staff.[35]

The Movement was instrumental in eliminating the communication gap between the national and San Francisco SNCC offices. The October 1965 issue covered the strike on the front page and featured an interview with Chavez that was conducted on September 25, making it the first interview with Chavez since the beginning of the strike. The issue also included articles explaining the strike in detail, an account of Terry Cannon's firsthand experience on the picket line, and a call for donations for the farmworkers. These articles, particularly one on the harassment and physical assault of the striking farmworkers by growers and the police, demonstrated that the NFWA faced many of the same challenges as SNCC organizers in the South. The October 1965 edition of *The Movement* not only served to increase the national SNCC office's awareness of the issues confronted by the NFWA, but it also prompted the rest of the organization to support the strike. Despite the fact that the SNCC offices outside San Francisco were slower to come to the aid of the NFWA, they were eventually able to embrace the union's cause wholeheartedly because the farmworkers' fight against both racial discrimination and economic oppression fit SNCC's mission and resembled its experiences.[36]

With the approval of the national SNCC headquarters, which distributed funding to local projects, overall SNCC participation in the strike accelerated. The organization supplied the NFWA with two-way radios, which were vital to the strike's effectiveness. The total area of the strike was one thousand square miles, which made it difficult for the NFWA to monitor farm owners' use of scab labor. With the radios, scouts could quickly inform the NFWA office when scabs entered the fields. The union could then send pickets to the fields being worked by scabs. Moreover, as SNCC was well aware, two-way radios could be life-saving apparatus in the face of violence by growers and police. In July 1965 SNCC set up a radio network for the Louisiana chapter of CORE. Three months later SNCC asked Louisiana CORE to return the favor by lending four of the radios to the NFWA. These radios supplemented those sent to Delano from SNCC offices in the South. SNCC not only supplied the radios, but also obtained a business band license for the NFWA to use.[37]

Even though the national SNCC office supported the strike, it initially appeared detached and uninterested, especially in comparison to the involvement of the San Francisco SNCC office. In November 1965, a frustrated Mike Miller wrote to the national office asking why no one had addressed his repeated requests, which included the addition of George Ballis to the SNCC staff and scholarship money for Hardy Frye so that he could continue working for SNCC. Miller also proposed that Chavez be invited to SNCC's national staff meeting at the end of the month and that SNCC chairman John Lewis issue a statement in support of the strike, uniting the plights of Mexican American farmworkers and African American sharecroppers and proclaiming that "we, as a civil rights organization, are concerned with the human rights of all people." Miller received little sympathy from the national headquarters; in a reply sent November 20, a staff member in the national SNCC office, which was responsible for hiring staff, informed him that she did not know who George Ballis was and added, "If we are to request additional salaries, I tend to think that we should take care of the most pressing needs first." She also noted that SNCC executive secretary James Forman thought that attending the SNCC staff meeting would take Chavez away from the strike for too long, but "if Chaves [*sic*] wants to come bring him." No mention was made of a statement from Lewis.[38]

Despite the aloofness of the SNCC headquarters, Miller worked to ensure that its support for the NFWA not only continued, but increased. At Miller's invitation, Chavez and Forman spoke at the statewide meeting of California SNCC and Friends of SNCC groups in November 1965. A few days later, Miller and Marshall Ganz attended the national SNCC staff meeting and gave a presentation on the Delano strike as part of a panel on migrant labor organizing. Although Chavez did not attend the meeting, Miller recalled that the SNCC staff members who were present were "curious, interested, very positive." As a result of their presentation, the SNCC staff voted to give full support to the union and to allow Ganz to represent SNCC on the NFWA staff while still paying him as a SNCC field secretary. The national SNCC office also agreed to provide the farmworkers with extra manpower. In December 1965, a small delegation from SNCC, including Stokely Carmichael, Cleveland Sellers, and Ralph Featherstone, visited Chavez at the NFWA office in Delano to discuss how SNCC could further help the union. After the meeting, the group adjourned to the local hangout, People's Bar, to drink beer and play pool. Ganz recalled, "Cesar was quite a pool player and so was Stokely and I think they surprised each other." As a result of this meeting, SNCC sent Richard "Dickie" Flowers, an African American field secretary from Greenwood, Mississippi, to work with Ganz.[39]

Due to their work in the Deep South, Ganz and Flowers were assigned to organize in Bakersfield, a farming town south of Delano where there were more African American farmworkers than in other parts of the Central Valley. African Americans were a small percentage of farmworkers in both the NFWA and California, but Chavez was committed to organizing them as well. In an attempt to prevent workers from joining together to demand higher wages and better working conditions, growers separated workers by race. Organizing African American farmworkers, then, would create a sense of multiracial solidarity among the farmworkers and reduce strike breaking. Chavez explained, "Discrimination is bad for all the moral reasons, but it is also bad for reasons of unity. It can quickly destroy the Movement." Chavez's commitment to multiracial equality derived from his experience with the CSO. In the early 1950s, most members of the San Jose, California, chapter left after the president, Chavez's sister Rita, attempted to punish a member for not allowing African Americans in his restaurant. Although the chapter nearly dissolved, Chavez stood by his sister's decision: "We had a very strong commitment to civil rights. But if we wanted civil rights for us, then we certainly had to respect the rights of blacks, Jews, and other minorities." The understanding that both Mexican Americans and African Americans experienced discrimination based on race and class thus infused the activities of the NFWA from its founding and predated the involvement of SNCC. The civil rights organization, however, was able to lend its experience in organizing African Americans in the South, many of whom were agricultural workers, to aid the union's cause.[40]

In organizing African American farmworkers in Bakersfield, Ganz and Flowers utilized SNCC's strategies, such as field secretaries working in interracial pairs. When conducting voter registration in Mississippi, for example, SNCC volunteers canvassed in interracial pairs to prevent local African Americans from facetiously agreeing to register to vote just to appease (and get rid of) the white organizer. However, Ganz and Flowers also learned and employed the organizing techniques developed by Chavez, such as the house meeting. By combining the organizing strategies of SNCC and the NFWA, Ganz and Flowers were able to recruit African American farmworkers, as well as white and Puerto Rican ones, to the union. Mack Lyons, a black farmworker who had migrated to Bakersfield from Texas in 1965, first noticed Ganz and Flowers passing out leaflets outside the DiGiorgio Corporation's Arvin Ranch in Bakersfield: "We stopped and talked. I gave Marshall my address, and I asked him if he could come by my house that night. He and Richard Flowers almost beat me there." Although Lyons did not join the NFWA that day, he joined at the next house meeting and went on to become one of the union's foremost organizers.[41]

*   *   *

SNCC's involvement with the farmworkers intensified beginning in December 1965 when Chavez asked Mike Miller to coordinate a national boycott of Schenley Industries, a liquor company that owned one of the largest of the ranches being struck by the NFWA. The boycott had been the idea of Jim Drake, who took his cue from the civil rights movement: "Blacks used to boycott stores that wouldn't hire them. So we decided to try it." Chavez and Drake both recognized the effectiveness of the economic boycott as a weapon for civil rights, which had been employed so effectively during the

Montgomery Bus Boycott and the earlier "Don't Buy Where You Can't Work" campaigns. Although the Schenley boycott addressed the low wages and unsafe working conditions of the farmworkers rather than exclusion from employment, like these earlier examples, it demonstrated the connection between racial and economic inequality and therefore dovetailed with SNCC's civil rights activism. The NFWA's boycott of Schenley Industries took full advantage of SNCC's skills, as well as its network of field secretaries and supporters. In fact, the decision to boycott Schenley came about after Chavez asked SNCC volunteers to research the connections of the Delano growers. The SNCC volunteers discovered that Schenley distributed well-known whiskeys such as Cutty Sark, as well as wine made with Delano grapes. Drake, Chavez, Miller and others recognized that Schenley products would be effective boycott targets because Americans could easily identify the company's brands, as opposed to those of grapes.[42]

Even before the boycott began, SNCC was able to use its notoriety to gain publicity for the farmworkers' fight against Schenley. Two months before the NFWA announced the boycott, SNCC began weekly picket lines in front of the company's San Francisco offices. On discovering the pickets, Schenley executives wrongly assumed SNCC wanted the company to hire more African Americans. They quickly informed various civil rights organizations that they had a "Negro Vice-President." *The Movement* reported, "On learning that the issue was not their treatment of Negroes, but their treatment of Mexican-Americans, they had nothing to say." Once the boycott began, SNCC helped spread it nationwide through publicity in *The Movement*.[43]

The spread of the Schenley boycott nationwide enabled SNCC and Friends of SNCC chapters outside California to participate. The New York SNCC office was particularly helpful to the boycott because Schenley's national headquarters were in that city and the local SNCC office could therefore put constant pressure on the company. In early December, Wendy Goepel Brooks visited New York SNCC and suggested that both SNCC and the local CORE chapter coordinate picket lines at New York and New Jersey grocery stores and schedule a meeting with Schenley executives to urge negotiations with the union. New York SNCC and CORE went into action immediately, organizing a letter-writing campaign and holding meetings on boycott action. They also conducted visits to liquor stores where delegations asked managers to remove Schenley products from their shelves and to display posters acknowledging their support of the strike. If managers did not comply, picket lines appeared outside the stores to inform consumers about the boycott. Twenty liquor stores in Brooklyn complied with the boycott within three weeks. SNCC and CORE were even more successful in Harlem, where all forty-nine stores visited by the activists agreed to cooperate with the boycott. *The Movement* reported on their effective tactics: "One reluctant retailer found himself with 30 or more would-be customers milling around his store but making no purchases. He got the point and joined his fellow merchants in boycotting Schenley." SNCC and CORE's stunning success on behalf of the NFWA in majority African American areas reveals that the organizations' actions educated their constituencies on the connections between the racial and economic oppression experienced by African Americans and Mexican Americans.[44]

Participating in the farmworkers' battle with Schenley allowed SNCC to demonstrate that it could apply its activist philosophy and tactics to oppressed groups other than African Americans. The final issue of *The Student Voice*, the national SNCC headquarters' newsletter, urged readers to boycott Schenley products. The national headquarters also sent a memo to all Friends of SNCC chapters informing them of the strike details and instructing all to support the strike and the boycott. The memo explicitly linked the struggles of SNCC and the NFWA: "The workers have been harassed by strikebreaking tactics reminiscent of the 1930s and with police oppression typical of Birmingham's Bull Connor and Selma's Jim Clark."[45]

*   *   *

Members of SNCC were also involved when the union chose to utilize the march, a long-favored tactic of the civil rights movement and other American social movements. In February 1966 Chavez, Ganz, Dolores Huerta, and other NFWA organizers gathered at a supporter's home near Santa Barbara for a three-day strategy meeting. During a brainstorming session over how to increase the visibility of the Schenley boycott, someone suggested marching from California to Schenley headquarters in New York, likening it to the Selma to Montgomery march of 1965. Realizing that New York was too far, someone else suggested that they march to the Schenley offices in San Francisco. But Chavez questioned whether Schenley would respond, so he recommended marching to Sacramento to put pressure on Governor Edmund "Pat" Brown to intervene. He also reasoned that Sacramento was

Figure 2. Marshall Ganz (on left in white hat, carrying a clipboard) overseeing the Delano to Sacramento march, March 1966. Photo by Jon Lewis. Courtesy of the Farmworker Movement Documentation Project, http://www.farmworkermovement.org.

an appropriate target because the California Fair Trade Act set a minimum price for liquor, meaning that "the California Legislature guaranteed a high price to Schenley for the liquor it made, but denied farm workers the right to a minimum wage." Chavez further argued that since the season of Lent neared, this protest would not simply be a march. Rather, the protest should be a pilgrimage in the tradition of a Mexican *peregrinación* that would arrive in the capital on Easter Sunday. Chavez explained, "This was a penance more than anything else—and it was quite a penance, because there was an awful lot of suffering involved in this pilgrimage, a great deal of pain." Chavez requested that Marshall Ganz coordinate the march and Terry Cannon serve as press secretary. With Miller, Ganz, and Cannon in charge of the boycott and march, SNCC activists were indispensable to the NFWA's protest against Schenley Industries.[46]

The march began on March 17, 1966, the day after the U.S. Senate Subcommittee on Migratory Farm Labor held hearings in Delano, with sixty-eight farmworkers and NFWA staff members, and included Dickie Flowers of SNCC. Over the next twenty-five days, the marchers stopped overnight in nineteen farming communities and passed through many others along the 250-mile route to Sacramento. In each of these places the marchers held public meetings to explain the pilgrimage and the grape strike. At the overnight stops, which the NFWA had carefully selected, association members and other supporters were relied upon to provide food and housing for the marchers. *El Malcriado* noted that this was also calculated to demonstrate the widespread support for the farmworkers: "There is, contrary to public opinion, a community of farm workers—for the marchers never lacked food, shelter, or moral support." Allies also demonstrated their support by marching with the farmworkers for a day or two when they passed through their towns. Throughout the march, the NFWA emphasized the importance of multiracial unity. The union proclaimed in the Plan of Delano, the march's official statement of purpose, "We know that the poverty of the Mexican or Filipino worker in California is the same as that of all farm workers across the country, the Negroes and poor whites, the Puerto Ricans, Japanese, and Arabians; in short, all of the races that comprise the oppressed minorities of the United States."[47]

Although the farmworkers were the heart and soul of the march, the collective organizing experience of the SNCC volunteers proved essential to the success of the march. Riding the length of the march in a panel truck equipped with a typewriter and a primitive version of a wireless telephone, Terry Cannon issued press releases and handled press relations to promote

Figure 3. George Ballis gets his feet tended to on a stop along the march to Sacramento, March 1966. Ballis had been photographing the march. Photo by John Kouns. Courtesy of the Farmworker Movement Documentation Project, http://www.farmworkermovement.org.

the march and boycott, but despite his efforts the march initially received little attention outside California. "When we started, I couldn't get anyone. Nobody was interested. Nobody cared," Cannon recalled. SNCC was one of the few organizations that supported the march from the beginning. In addition to the work of Ganz, Miller, and Cannon, SNCC and Friends of SNCC groups lent assistance to the march by raising money and donating supplies. For example, the Marin Friends of SNCC raised $200 for the NFWA, which the union used to purchase shoes and sleeping bags for the marchers. Other SNCC chapters collected food and clothing, while members of various California Friends of SNCC groups marched themselves. Elizabeth Sutherland Martínez, head of the New York SNCC office and one of two Mexican Americans on the SNCC staff nationwide, traveled to California to participate in the march. At the conclusion of the march, Hardy Frye gave a speech on the Capitol steps that explicitly connected the NFWA to SNCC and the civil rights movement by comparing Governor Brown's refusal to meet with the marchers to Alabama Governor George Wallace's refusal to meet with those who marched from Selma to Montgomery in 1965.[48]

The NFWA march from Delano to Sacramento in spring 1966 was a tremendous success. The march and boycott damaged Schenley's public image. Moreover, since all aspects of Schenley were unionized except for its vineyards, executives worried about the consequences for its relationships with other unions. Therefore, days before the conclusion of the march, Schenley Industries agreed to recognize the NFWA as the union representing its field workers and signed a contract granting a pay increase of 35 cents an hour and union control of hiring. As a result, the union ended its boycott of Schenley products. The march was also successful in that the spectacle of the march itself eventually captured the attention of the national media. Cannon recalled that national news outlets that had ignored the march at the beginning were frantically calling him, begging for an interview with Chavez, as the marchers neared Sacramento. He observed, "I think more than any . . . single event, I think [the march] transformed the relationship of the strike and the union to the rest of the world and it was amazing to watch it happen. So by the time we crossed the bridge, with ten thousand people or however many people there were, it was a national event."[49]

＊　　＊　　＊

While SNCC was intimately involved in the Schenley boycott and Delano to Sacramento march, none of the other major civil rights organizations participated in the protests. The West Coast branches of the NAACP were stymied by their organization's national headquarters in their efforts to support the farmworkers. The Portland branch of the NAACP attempted to issue a resolution in support of the NFWA two days after the beginning of the march, but the NAACP national headquarters prevented this. Because the resolution included a pledge to urge NAACP members to boycott Schenley, the branch president requested approval from NAACP executive director Roy Wilkins. Wilkins did not respond until three weeks later, after the march had concluded and three days after Schenley signed the agreement to recognize the NFWA. In his belated response, Wilkins recommended that the Portland NAACP send a letter to Schenley "commending Schenley for having recognized the union."[50]

Wilkins refused to allow NAACP branches to support the NFWA because he enjoyed a close relationship with Schenley Industries. Early in 1965,

Schenley's founder donated $50,000 to the NAACP, the largest single gift to the organization up to that time. One of Wilkins's advisors recalled, "Wilkins was stunned and almost lost his voice in expressing his appreciation." Schenley also attempted to curry favor with the black community by giving scholarships to African American students and donating large amounts of money to black-owned banks and businesses. When the NFWA ended its boycott of Schenley products in April 1966, Wilkins issued a press release—drafted by the corporation—congratulating Schenley for resolving the strike:

> It is not surprising that the first company in its industry to promote a Negro to an important executive position is also the first company to recognize the legitimate grievances of transient California farm laborers, most of whom are members of minority groups. We commend Schenley Industries, Inc., for signing the union agreement that opens the door to further advancement for the California grape pickers. Schenley's cooperation in California is an omen of hope and progress for migrant farm workers for whose welfare the NAACP has campaigned on the east as well as the west coast of the nation.

At no point did Wilkins congratulate Chavez and the NFWA.[51]

Schenley Industries also used its connections in the black community in an attempt to hinder any potential support for the NFWA from SCLC. Two days before the NFWA began the Delano to Sacramento march, Jackie Robinson, who was the brother-in-law of Schenley vice-president Charles T. Williams and who had been hired to do public relations for Schenley, sent a telegram to Martin Luther King, Jr., asking him to meet with Williams regarding the boycott. Robinson wrote, "I think there are some facts you would like to know which shows both sides of the situation." It is unclear whether the NFWA or its allies had reached out to King to support the farmworkers' cause, but Schenley was concerned enough about the potential consequences of his endorsement that the company dispatched Robinson. It is unknown whether King ever met with Williams, but King did not issue a statement in support of the march and did not urge SCLC members to boycott Schenley products, despite his own use of the boycott as an instrument of social change.[52]

Schenley's ability to influence the national leadership of the NAACP, and perhaps SCLC, was indicative of the importance of corporate ties and donations to middle-class civil rights organizations. The national leadership of the NAACP felt that it was more important to support Schenley Industries than to mobilize on behalf of its exploited workers because of the economic contributions the company could make to the black community. In contrast, SNCC activists were deeply concerned about the plight of workers and were disinterested in cultivating corporate support. Not only did they organize among the rural poor, but many SNCC staff members were themselves of working-class backgrounds. Those SNCC staff members from middle-class backgrounds had rejected middle-class values by dropping out of school and leaving lucrative career paths to work for the organization full time. According to political scientist Emily Stoper, "Other black-advancement groups had tried to secure for their clientele the privileges and amenities of the white middle class; SNCC rejected the middle-class life-style as empty and immoral." Consequently, when the black middle class engaged in civil rights activism, they gravitated to the NAACP and SCLC. In contrast, SNCC chose to work on behalf of the powerless poor, who they saw as marginalized by American society and most in need of organizing. SNCC staff members and volunteers embodied their rejection of the middle class by abandoning the suits, ties, dresses, and cardigans that were the uniform of the sit-ins in favor of overalls and jeans, which they felt united them with the people they attempted to organize. SNCC field secretaries were also able to personally relate to impoverished people because they earned less than ten dollars per week and supplemented their meager earnings by living communally or in the homes of local residents.[53]

The spartan lifestyle of SNCC field secretaries epitomized what Chavez thought of as proper for NFWA organizers. In fact, Chavez believed that such sacrifices contributed to the morality of the cause. He explained, "It's beautiful to give up material things that take up your time, for the sake of time to help your fellow human beings." NFWA organizers were therefore paid five dollars per week, with food and housing provided by the union. However, like in SNCC, organizers' meager pay was augmented by contributions from supporters and the farmworkers themselves. Chavez recalled that when he asked Dolores Huerta to leave her job to become a full-time organizer for the fledging union, she asked him how they would eat and he replied that he did not know: "And I didn't know. But as we later found out, somebody in the Cause would never starve. The people would never let you." The NFWA and SNCC were therefore further united in their mutual commitment to self-sacrifice for the greater good.[54]

SNCC's rejection of middle-class values such as lucrative employment and material comforts was more than a mere act of youthful rebellion. Historian Howard Zinn argued, "They are not playing; it is no casual act of defiance, no irresponsible whim of adolescence, when young people of sixteen or twenty or twenty-five turn away from school, job, family, all the tokens of success in modern America, to take up new lives, hungry and hunted, in the hinterland of the Deep South." By rejecting middle-class values, SNCC was free to openly confront economic inequality. This differentiated SNCC from the NAACP and SCLC, whose leaders were from the middle and upper classes and who sought middle-class gains for African Americans. Although SNCC initially joined the NAACP and SCLC in fighting for the integration of restaurants, schools, and public spaces, its members quickly realized that these achievements were of little value for a constituency that was trapped by their lack of economic and political power.[55]

SNCC's emphasis on economic oppression enabled the organization to pursue equality for all poor people, not just African Americans. Once the barrier of class was eliminated, it was easier for SNCC to then bridge the racial divide because it could recognize the commonalities between poor people of all races and apply its principles and organizational praxis to a freedom struggle that did not involve African Americans in the Deep South. This resulted in the productive and successful coalition that formed between SNCC and the NFWA, which contributed to the farmworkers' victory over Schenley Industries. As Hardy Frye explained, "To work with the farm workers was like an extension of what we had already been doing." This coalition was also due to the understanding of Chavez and others in the NFWA that while the Mexican American farmworkers were discriminated against based on their race, all agricultural workers were economically oppressed. The union therefore championed multiracial equality, enabling it to find common cause with the civil rights movement. The shared commitment to fighting both racial and class inequality was the basis of the alliance between the two organizations, but it was strengthened by their similar organizing strategies and nonviolent resistance.[56]

CHAPTER 2

To Wage Our Own War of Liberation

FOLLOWING the NFWA victory over Schenley Industries, journalist John Gregory Dunne asked veteran organizer Saul Alinsky what he would have done differently had he been in charge of the strike in Delano's grape fields. Alinsky, head of the Industrial Areas Foundation (IAF), was the virtual godfather to the NFWA. In 1947 he hired Fred Ross to organize Mexican Americans in Los Angeles, which led to Ross's discovery and cultivation of Cesar Chavez as a farmworker organizer. Furthermore, Alinsky's model of community organizing served as the blueprint for the organizing philosophy of SNCC's Mike Miller, who initiated the alliance between the civil rights organization and the union. Alinsky recognized the importance of the SNCC/ NFWA alliance, but with significant reservations. He told Dunne, "The farm workers aren't going to win this by themselves. When the SNCC kids and the civil-rights people leave, you're back on page 27 of the newspaper. The money tree stops and who cares." Alinsky, the master strategist, was prophetic: a year later, the once productive relationship between the two organizations was over. Although SNCC's departure did not spell the end of the NFWA, as Alinsky had foretold, it did reveal the limits of multiracial coalition building.[1]

SNCC and NFWA organizers had developed an alliance based on their mutual recognition that African Americans and Mexican Americans experienced similar, intertwined forms of economic exploitation and racial discrimination. They built on these shared experiences of inequality to craft an ideology and praxis that prioritized cross-racial solidarity and cooperation in the pursuit of social change. The organizers believed that by working together and supporting each other, both organizations could more effectively reduce the power of agribusiness, which maintained racial inequities in order to continue to exploit the most vulnerable workers. Accordingly, SNCC organizers believed that supporting the NFWA by participating in picket lines, boycotting a liquor company, or donating food and supplies fit into their broader goal of pursuing racial equality and economic justice for all. Although these coalition politics resulted in an alliance that achieved significant victories for the farmworkers, racial unity proved insufficient in sustaining it. As SNCC evolved, its thinking on racial identity, discrimination, and cross-racial solidarity changed dramatically, which led the organization to shift its priorities to emphasizing race over class rather than addressing the two in tandem. These changes not only caused significant changes within SNCC, but led to the dissolution of its relationship with the NFWA. Furthermore, as the union grew and developed, its ideals, goals, and strategies became incompatible with SNCC's new direction.[2]

*   *   *

Conflicts over race arose within SNCC as early as 1964 during the Mississippi Freedom Summer Project, when hundreds of primarily northern white college students went to Mississippi to conduct voter registration among African Americans in rural areas. Disagreements over the purpose of the project, the impact of white volunteers on local black leadership, and interracial relationships caused deep divisions within SNCC. Continued violence directed against African Americans and SNCC volunteers compounded these tensions. Many in SNCC began to question the value of their work, the practicality of depending on white allies and, in some cases, the wisdom of working with whites at all. As a result, many black SNCC staff members began to consider dismissing white SNCC workers. Initially, however, distance shielded the San Francisco SNCC office—which included several whites—from these conflicts, allowing SNCC members in California to focus on issues of economic inequality, rather than being distracted by the debate over black separatism that began disrupting SNCC's organizing in the South. Furthermore, by working with the NFWA, SNCC was able to continue to apply the organizing principles on which the organization was founded.[3]

Immediately following the victorious Delano to Sacramento march, SNCC organizers continued to work alongside the NFWA in its battles with Delano's grape growers. Four days after the conclusion of the march, the union turned its attention to the DiGiorgio Corporation, the largest of the Delano grape growers that had been struck by the NFWA since September 1965. On April 7, 1966, the day after Schenley Industries recognized the NFWA as the bargaining representative of its grape pickers, DiGiorgio sent letters to Governor Edmund "Pat" Brown, Chavez, and other union leaders informing them that the corporation wanted the California State Mediation and Conciliation Service to conduct elections for union representation on its ranches. While Chavez was in favor of elections, he was adamantly opposed to the conditions that DiGiorgio demanded, including limiting the election to active workers, who were actually scab workers and not the pickers who had previously worked for DiGiorgio. Chavez and the NFWA also objected to DiGiorgio's stipulation that strikes could not occur during contract negotiations or harvest season. In response to DiGiorgio's attempts to hem in its workers' rights to collective bargaining, the NFWA began picketing at DiGiorgio's Sierra Vista Ranch on April 14. Using the experience gained during the Schenley strike, the NFWA chose to boycott S&W Fine Food and Treesweet Juices, DiGiorgio's most popular brands, rather than attempt to boycott DiGiorgio grapes.[4]

The NFWA strike and boycott of DiGiorgio had an immediate effect and union officials began meeting with the corporation to negotiate the terms of an election for union representation of its workers. However, in an attempt to circumvent the NFWA, DiGiorgio began meeting with the International Brotherhood of Teamsters regarding union representation of the farmworkers. DiGiorgio welcomed the intervention of the Teamsters, an overwhelmingly white union that did not truly represent the farmworkers and had no qualms about agreeing to no-strike clauses in its contracts. The company agreed to an election for union representation on the condition that the Teamsters appear on the ballot and then attempted to rig it by restricting organizing on its ranches solely to the Teamsters. The NFWA urged workers to abstain from the fraudulent election and established picket lines around the Sierra Vista Ranch, shouting, "No voten viernes" ("Do not vote Friday"). On the day of the election, June 24, only 84 of 219 eligible workers voted; the few who did so voted for the Teamsters.[5]

SNCC staff members organized many of the protest activities against DiGiorgio. For example, Marshall Ganz and Dickie Flowers recruited African Americans from Bakersfield to join a vigil outside the home of the Rev. R. B. Moore, the African American minister of St. Paul's Baptist Church in Delano and "the only Negro in the Delano Kiwanis Club." Moore was to observe the DiGiorgio election and had spoken out against the NFWA by arguing that farmworkers did not suffer discrimination and that "Delano had the best race relations in America." Ganz, along with organizer Eliseo Medina, also conducted house meetings to educate farmworkers on the issues of the election. Additionally, SNCC co-sponsored the NFWA Student Summer Project. Based on SNCC's Mississippi Freedom Summer Project of 1964, the Student Summer Project brought together eighty students from activist groups such as the National Student Association, Students for a Democratic Society, and Young Christian Students to work for the NFWA from June through August 1966.[6]

Friends of SNCC chapters also continued to support the NFWA by organizing food caravans and hosting fundraisers. For example, the College of Marin Friends of SNCC held two screenings of the movie *Salt of the Earth*, about the Mexican American copper miners' strike in New Mexico in the 1950s, with all proceeds going to the NFWA. In thanking the College of Marin Friends of SNCC, Chavez applauded the choice of the movie and stated, "We hope that you will continue to work beside us in the coming months." Due in part to public pressure, including that from SNCC and other progressive groups, DiGiorgio agreed to conduct new elections for union representation of its workers supervised by the American Arbitration Association and with rules agreed on by the NFWA. In turn, the NFWA ceased picketing at DiGiorgio ranches and called off the boycott of DiGiorgio products. At the August 30 election at DiGiorgio's Sierra Vista and Borrego Springs ranches, 530 field workers voted for the NFWA, 331 for the Teamsters, and 7 for no union representation.[7]

Despite the momentum generated by another SNCC-supported NFWA victory, the decision of the NFWA to officially merge with the Agricultural Workers Organizing Committee to form the United Farm Workers Organizing Committee, AFL-CIO (UFWOC) in August 1966 threatened this productive alliance. Chavez and AWOC leader Larry Itliong believed that the merger was necessary because it created a united front between the two farmworker unions and enabled both to receive financial and logistical support from the AFL-CIO. Moreover, after the long battles against Schenley and DiGiorgio, the NFWA was cash-strapped and had only one foreseeable option—to join AWOC and the AFL-CIO. However, months before the merger, farmworkers and activists worried that the AFL-CIO bureaucracy would kill the farmworkers' movement. One NFWA staff member asked, "If the AFL is so damn great, why couldn't they organize the workers?" Marshall Ganz, however, was more practical: "I think it's inevitable. . . . The Association doesn't stand a chance in competition with the big money unions. The AFL-CIO could kill us by throwing millions of dollars into an organizing campaign. It has nothing to do with how good an organization they are. We have to join them." This did not sit well with SNCC and others on the left because it appeared that the independent NFWA was being co-opted "by one of the giant institutions involved in preserving the status-quo in America." In an analysis of the merger, *The Movement* declared that despite misgivings about the AFL-CIO, SNCC should still support the UFWOC because of "the justice of the cause itself."[8]

The Movement's statement on the merger reflects the complicated nature of the civil rights movement's relationship with organized labor. Civil rights and labor activism shared many commonalities, especially in terms of organizing and protest strategies, guiding ethos, government response, and violent opposition. At a conference of the United Packinghouse Workers of America (UPWA), Congress of Racial Equality executive director James Farmer pointed out that those opposed to civil rights were also in favor of "right-to-work" laws, which greatly limited the power of unions. Moreover, some union members viewed the achievement of racial equality as "a necessary precondition for economic and political equality." Many labor unions were therefore supportive of the civil rights movement. Unions frequently staged sympathy protests around the country in response to civil rights demonstrations in the South, including one organized by the International Longshore and Warehouse Union (ILWU) in San Francisco that drew around 30,000 people in solidarity with the protestors who had been blasted with fire hoses in Birmingham, Alabama, in 1963. Unions also frequently donated money to civil rights organizations, including SNCC. For example, the AFL-CIO funded SNCC's founding meeting in April 1960 and issued public statements in support of Mississippi Freedom Summer. The ILWU, Packinghouse Workers, United Electrical Workers (UE), and other unions made financial contributions to several SNCC projects. SNCC organizer Ekwueme Michael Thelwell recalled after receiving a significant donation from representatives of the UE, "Two class-conscious workers—and a strong union—are worth a thousand students."[9]

Labor's support of the civil rights movement came only from northern unions, however. Southern unions did not offer support to SNCC or other civil rights organizations and occasionally donated to segregationist organizations instead. Numerous polls confirmed that southern white workers overwhelmingly did not support the struggle for black equality. In addition to their antagonistic relationship with southern unions, many in SNCC were wary of the compromises that came with northern unions' support. For example, in October 1960 SNCC held a second conference in Atlanta, partly funded by a grant from the UPWA, to establish itself as a permanent organization. The union threatened to withhold the money unless Bayard Rustin, a noted civil rights activist and advisor to Martin Luther King, Jr., was disinvited as a keynote speaker. Rustin had formerly been a member of the American Communist Party, and therefore the UPWA—reflecting the liberal anticommunism of organized labor during the Cold War and attempting to distance themselves from the historical communist influence within the union—believed he was an "inappropriate" choice. SNCC field secretary Cleveland Sellers wrote in his autobiography that "the students decided that they needed the Packinghouse Workers' grant more than they needed to hear Bayard Rustin." Although SNCC acceded to the union's demand and disinvited Rustin, Sellers noted that many conference participants later regretted this decision. This event also planted the seed of distrust for organized labor among those in SNCC, despite the Packinghouse Workers' continued donations of bail money, food, and even college scholarships. James Forman, who later became SNCC's executive secretary, reflected in his autobiography that the Packinghouse Workers' "success in preventing Rustin from speaking must have suggested that it was indeed possible to influence if not control the student movement."[10]

Forman's reservations about organized labor were reflected in his perceptions of the March on Washington in August 1963. The march was originally conceived of by black trade unionists and coordinated by Rustin and A. Philip Randolph, founder of the Brotherhood of Sleeping Car Porters, to draw attention to the economic inequality experienced by African Americans, particularly in rates of unemployment, and its connection to racial discrimination. Despite the fact that unions took the lead in providing logistical and financial support for the march, Forman remained deeply suspicious of the involvement of organized labor. He recalled, "Everywhere there were large groups from labor unions and especially the United Automobile Workers, all with prominent signs. We had asked them for financial help and they refused. We felt that not only the UAW, but many other so-called liberal forces were shamming and this was just another march." Forman was particularly wary of UAW president Walter Reuther, who had helped convince organizers not to incorporate direct action protests into the march and who later joined the planning committee mere weeks before the march occurred. But for many civil rights activists, Reuther's participation was less troubling than AFL-CIO president George Meany's refusal to endorse the march at all. Meany did not support it both because he was concerned that such a demonstration would lead to additional charges of communist influence in the labor movement and, as a member of an all-white plumber's union, he opposed "any hiring preferences for blacks that might undermine union seniority systems."[11]

SNCC's relationship with organized labor was further strained during the Mississippi Freedom Democratic Party (MFDP) attempt to unseat their state's regular delegation at the Democratic National Convention in Atlantic City in 1964. The MFDP was formed during Freedom Summer and represented an alternative to the segregationist Mississippi Democrats, who systematically disenfranchised black voters. According to historian Clayborne Carson, "The hopes of the MFDP delegation were based on the belief that they, rather than the regular, all-white delegation, represented the expressed principles of the national Democratic party." Moreover, the MFDP supported the election of Lyndon Johnson, as opposed to the regular Mississippi Democratic Party, who actually supported Republican candidate Barry Goldwater. Regardless, Johnson was determined to not alienate white southern Democrats and thus did not want the MFDP to be seated. Johnson's forces therefore offered the MFDP two at-large seats, with the rest of the delegation as "guests" of the convention. The MFDP refused the compromise and viewed the entire situation as a betrayal by the Democratic Party leadership, including its allies in organized labor, especially those who had originally supported seating the MFDP and then urged them to accept the compromise. Stokely Carmichael later reflected,

> The lesson, in fact, was clear at Atlantic City. The major moral of
> that experience was not merely that the national conscience was
> unreliable but that, very specifically, black people in Mississippi
> and throughout this country could not rely on their so-called
> allies. Many labor, liberal and civil rights leaders deserted the
> MFDP because of closer ties to the national Democratic party.

Following the convention, SNCC began to question the wisdom of working with the Democratic Party, which was not seen as representing the interests of African Americans. By extension, organized labor was increasingly not viewed as sincere in its support of the civil rights movement.[12]

Thus by the time that SNCC formed an alliance with the NFWA in 1965, the civil rights organization was already becoming disenchanted with labor unions. It was therefore due to the pioneering work of SNCC field secretaries like Mike Miller and George Ballis, whose ties to organized labor predated their civil rights activism, that the alliance with the farmworkers even occurred. Miller later explained,

> I grew up with the idea that unions were a good thing. Nothing in my college education or the student movement persuaded me otherwise. At the same time, as the Student Nonviolent Coordinating Committee (and I) learned in the civil rights movement, most of organized labor was deeply intertwined with the Democratic Party's established leadership.

Miller therefore believed that a careful "balancing act" was required in working with organized labor, but that doing so was worthwhile. The NFWA also alleviated SNCC's reservations about organized labor by having conceptualized itself as a movement connected to other crusades for social change, making it far more palatable to SNCC than a union.[13]

The NFWA's identity as both a union and a social movement caused considerable tension among members, supporters, growers, and fellow unions. In response to writer Eugene Nelson's question about whether the NFWA strike was a civil rights issue, a volunteer explained, "Of course it's a civil rights issue. Civil rights means equality of opportunity. . . . And farm workers don't have equality of opportunity." It was that line of reasoning that caused activists of the New Left to flock to support the NFWA. But this identity also caused problems for the farmworkers. White officials in AWOC at first resisted working with the NFWA because of its movement-centered identity and links to civil rights organizations. Chavez explained, "They just couldn't make us out. . . . The NFWA didn't speak the proper language, you know, worker solidarity, the union above all." The Teamsters felt justified in representing field workers because they believed that the NFWA was not a legitimate union. Teamster official William Grami proclaimed, "They're not even a union. They're a civil rights organization." Growers were alarmed by the NFWA's popularity as a movement, prompting one to declare, "This isn't a strike, it's a revolution." But despite the NFWA's efforts to position *la causa* as a movement and the willingness of others to view it as such, it was still a labor union whose most basic goal was representation of its workers. By joining the AFL-CIO, the NFWA made it more difficult for SNCC to think of it as a social justice movement rather than part of organized labor. As one NFWA volunteer told John Gregory Dunne, "The romance is gone."[14]

Although SNCC was critical of the NFWA for joining the AFL-CIO to become the UFWOC, it continued to support and assist the union in its struggles with Delano grape growers. Soon after the victorious DiGiorgio election, workers at A. Perelli-Minetti & Sons, almost all of whom were UFWOC members, went on strike September 9, 1966 to obtain wages and benefits similar to those guaranteed in the union's contract with Schenley Industries. Perelli-Minetti was a small wine grape grower in Delano that was not struck in September 1965 because it did not grow table grapes. The forty-eight workers asked the UFWOC to represent them in negotiations with the growers and the union immediately agreed. SNCC was intimately involved in these negotiations; Marshall Ganz and Dolores Huerta met with the owners of Perelli-Minetti and proposed an election for union recognition. Less than a week later, while the UFWOC waited for Perelli-Minetti to decide on its proposal, the Teamsters crossed the picket line to sign a "sweetheart" contract (one more beneficial to the employer than to the workers) with the ranch. The involvement of the Teamsters served to escalate, rather than end, the conflict between Perelli-Minetti and the UFWOC. Although the striking workers numbered fewer than fifty, the UFWOC decided that it had to act in order to prevent the Teamsters from establishing a solid foothold in the grape-growing industry. Consequently, the UFWOC declared a nationwide boycott of Perelli-Minetti products on September 20.[15]

Although the Perelli-Minetti strike was gaining momentum, the boycott could not get underway for another two months. The labor dispute with DiGiorgio had not been completely resolved, and because of the UFWOC's limited resources the union could not afford to be involved in both conflicts at the same time. The issue at hand was now DiGiorgio's Arvin Ranch in Bakersfield, which had not previously been struck. Most Arvin workers had wanted elections the previous August, during the early harvest season, but DiGiorgio refused. The Arvin workers therefore pushed for elections in October during another peak in harvesting and before many migrant workers left to work in other areas. SNCC was particularly helpful in organizing the workers at Arvin for the UFWOC because many were African American or white migrants. Mack Lyons, an African American farmworker who had been recruited to the union by SNCC members Ganz and Dickie Flowers,

Figure 4. DiGiorgio workers line up to register to vote in the election for union representation. Photo by Jon Lewis. Courtesy of the Farmworker Movement Documentation Project, http://www.farmworkermovement.org.

was elected to represent the Arvin workers to the company. In recruiting Lyons, Flowers and Ganz succeeded in applying SNCC's organizing principles of identifying and cultivating local leadership.[16]

SNCC was also involved when UFWOC organizers, including Lyons, traveled to DiGiorgio's San Francisco headquarters to personally demand that company President Robert DiGiorgio agree to an election. The protest at DiGiorgio headquarters revealed that the relationship between the union and SNCC was still quite close. While UFWOC organizers waited inside to meet with DiGiorgio, a picket line of over 200 supporters marched outside the building and El Teatro Campesino, a theater group affiliated with the UFWOC, performed strike songs. During the demonstration someone unfurled a sixty-two-foot banner from the roof of the building that employed a SNCC slogan: "DiGiorgio—One Man One Vote—Workers Demand Elections." Inside, police arrested Terry Cannon, editor of *The*

Movement, along with Lyons and six UFWOC and AFL-CIO officials for entering the DiGiorgio offices and refusing to leave until they were granted a meeting with the president of the corporation. The arrests of Cannon and the labor leaders were broadcast from San Francisco stations on that evening's news. Rather than risk additional bad press, DiGiorgio agreed to an election when UFWOC organizers returned to the DiGiorgio offices the next morning (including those arrested, who had posted bail). The next day the Teamsters announced it would withdraw from the Arvin election. On November 4 the UFWOC won the right to represent the Arvin workers and negotiate a contract on their behalf. SNCC participation in the demonstration at DiGiorgio headquarters was crucial to this victory, as was its success in organizing African American farmworkers at Arvin. Huerta later asserted, "We wouldn't have won the Arvin election if it hadn't been for the Okie and black votes."[17]

With the victory at DiGiorgio's Arvin ranch, the UFWOC could proceed against Perelli-Minetti. Beginning in November, the union called for boycotts of Tribuno Vermouth, Eleven Cellars Brandy, and other Perelli-Minetti products. The Teamsters attempted to mobilize a counteroffensive in response to the boycott, but they were unable to rally the kind of support that the farmworkers had from SNCC and other progressive activists. According to Ganz, "For many in the cities, for whom the grape strike had been framed as the struggle of an 'oppressed minority fighting for its freedom,' the Teamsters were a powerful and corrupt white union conspiring with powerful white growers to deny the rights of powerless earnest Mexican farm workers." The Teamsters' violent behavior toward farmworkers and their supporters, such as the beating of UFWOC organizer Eliseo Medina during the DiGiorgio campaign, strengthened this image. This dynamic of the minority farmworkers versus white growers and Teamsters demonstrated the parallels between the UFWOC's struggle and that of African Americans; it also facilitated SNCC staff members' continued support of the union's fight against racial discrimination and economic oppression. Therefore, SNCC expressed support for the union and participated in its boycott of Perelli-Minetti products in New York, Chicago, and Milwaukee. The boycott proved so financially damaging that Perelli-Minetti signed a contract with the UFWOC in July 1967.[18]

*   *   *

The multiracial solidarity that characterized SNCC's protest activities against DiGiorgio and Perelli-Minetti became increasingly limited to the San Francisco SNCC office and its supporters. These organizers remained committed to multiracial solidarity and cooperation. Moreover, their understanding of the link between racial discrimination and economic exploitation enabled them to recognize that the Mexican American farmworkers had much in common with African Americans in the Deep South. However, shifts in ideology, priorities, and tactics among SNCC's other members eventually destroyed its alliance with the UFWOC. For those in SNCC whose ideas about race were becoming increasingly nationalistic and separatist, the fact that the organization's alliance with the farmworkers was cross-racial made it untenable.[19]

The evolution of SNCC's ideology occurred within broader developments in the black freedom struggle. Some black activists and intellectuals, particularly in the urban North, rejected (or at least questioned) the integrationist goals of the southern civil rights movement. They believed that integration privileged whiteness by demanding proximity to it and did not result in true equality for African Americans through the sharing of resources and power. Moreover, the massive white resistance to the desegregation of schools and public accommodations in the South demonstrated that the complete incorporation of African Americans into American institutions was unfeasible. Rather, the common experience of racism proved that African Americans (and all people of African descent throughout the diaspora) were part of a distinct black "nation" with common issues and struggles. Black nationalist and minister in the Nation of Islam, Malcolm X, explained in 1963 in his speech, "Message to the Grassroots,"

> What you and I need to do is learn to forget our differences. When we come together, we don't come together as Baptists or Methodists. You don't catch hell 'cause you're a Baptist, and you don't catch hell 'cause you're a Methodist. . . . You don't catch hell because you're a Democrat or a Republican. You don't catch hell because you're a Mason or an Elk. And you sure don't catch hell 'cause you're an American; 'cause if you was an American, you wouldn't catch no hell. You catch hell 'cause you're a black man. You catch hell, all of us catch hell, for the same reason.

Although there was much variation among black nationalists, they shared ideals of black pride, racial unity, and self-determination. Some black nationalists, in developing a positive conception of "blackness" as the center of community identity, called for racial separatism as a more empowering alternative to integration. As such, multiracial coalition building was an impractical and unappealing strategy for racial separatists.[20]

Black nationalism became increasingly popular among black SNCC staff members during Mississippi Freedom Summer, the end of which did nothing to dispel the racial tensions that the project had introduced. Instead, tensions increased when many of the white volunteers decided to stay in Mississippi after the conclusion of the project, greatly increasing the proportion of white members in the organization. Furthermore, the outcome of the MFDP's challenge at the Democratic National Convention left many in SNCC disenchanted with any strategy that required them to rely on white liberals or the federal government for assistance. In response to the disappointments and resentments caused by Freedom Summer and its aftermath, many black SNCC staff members were attracted to the ideology of black nationalism, particularly its call for self-determination in the pursuit of racial equality and economic justice. However, this was not simply a negative reaction to the presence of whites in the movement. Rather, SNCC organizers were deeply impressed with the independence, racial pride, economic power, and solidarity demonstrated within the rural, southern black communities in which they organized. Black nationalism thus evolved in SNCC in response to members' growing awareness of the limitations of interracial cooperation and, simultaneously, the potential for black self-determination. Some in SNCC took black nationalism to its extreme and called for complete racial separatism. Clayborne Carson revealed that these individuals "began to see racial separatism as an ideal that would awaken the consciousness of black people and begin a new phase of the black struggle." Despite the organic evolution of black nationalism within SNCC, some viewed it as a dramatic departure from SNCC's original "dream of an interracial movement of the poor," which deeply divided the organization.[21]

The centerpieces of SNCC's activities in the two years following Mississippi Freedom Summer reflect the organization's turn away from multiracial coalitions and toward black nationalism. Following the march from Selma to Montgomery, Alabama in 1965, Stokely Carmichael and other SNCC organizers helped African Americans in neighboring Lowndes County to form the Lowndes County Freedom Organization (LCFO), an independent black political party. The LCFO was founded on the idea that gaining the vote was useless if it meant that African Americans were forced to vote for white candidates who were determined to keep them oppressed. Carmichael argued, "Once the black man has knocked back centuries of fear, once he is willing to resist, he then must decide how best to use that vote. To listen to those whites who conspired for many years to deny him the ballot would be a return to that previous subordinated condition. He must move independently." The LCFO therefore ran a slate of black candidates for public office, which inspired African Americans across the country.[22]

Carmichael discouraged white organizers from working with the LCFO, mostly due to concern for their safety. SNCC organizer Ruby Sales explained, "One of the things that we were very conscious of is that sometimes in that kind of situation, white presence would incite local white people to violence." Indeed, white organizers had been the targets of violence during both Freedom Summer and the Selma to Montgomery march. Lowndes County also demonstrated its reputation for extreme violence in August 1965, when a police deputy shot and killed Jonathan Daniels, a white seminary student working with SNCC. However, the lack of white organizers also enhanced the sense of pride and self-sufficiency among blacks in Lowndes County by eliminating the potential for black deference to white leadership. Carmichael and others therefore began to envision independent black politics as the focus of SNCC organizing.[23]

SNCC's gradual shift away from cross-racial organizing initially did little to affect its relationship between it and the UFWOC because the SNCC members working with the union were so geographically removed from the epicenter of these developments in the South. However, the events of the SNCC staff meeting in December 1966—no matter how distant—managed to destroy the successful coalition between SNCC and the farmworkers. Held at the home of black entertainer "Peg Leg" Bates in upstate New York, the meeting was dominated by a faction within SNCC who worked in Atlanta and had been calling for the expulsion of whites from the organization since 1964. Since there were few whites to expel from SNCC by the end of 1966, James Forman was concerned about the underlying reasons for this push. According to Forman, "The cause sprang from SNCC's unresolved disagreement about the nature of the problems that black people faced: Did our oppression spring from exclusively racial causes or from a combination of racial and class factors?" The same question had been discussed that May at another staff meeting in Kingston Springs, Tennessee. Forman was dissatisfied with the discussion at both meetings because they did not incorporate revolutionary theory and therefore did not include an understanding of how class affected race relations. Forman explained the debates over the presence of whites in SNCC in his autobiography: "We were clearly victims of racism, and the most visible manifestation of that racism was white people. Lacking a clear understanding of the economic basis of racism and exploitation, black people will flail out against the most visible manifestation—white people." To support his argument, Forman pointed out that those in SNCC who would not address class in relation to racial discrimination were from middle-class backgrounds and thus had difficulty relating to working-class African Americans.[24]

Despite their myopic focus on race, the members of SNCC who were calling for the expulsion of whites were able to dominate the discussion at the Peg Leg Bates meeting. After several days of agonizing debate, a vote on dismissing whites was held at 2 a.m. By one vote, SNCC decided to expel whites. However, most staff members had gone to bed before the vote: of 100 staff members present at the retreat, only 19 voted for the expulsion. The nature of the vote caused considerable confusion the next morning and created divisions within the organization. Mike Miller, who attended the meeting, recalled that Fannie Lou Hamer, a black former sharecropper who had become one of SNCC's most iconic organizers, cried after the vote: "She came up to me and said, 'Mike, I just don't understand what's going on with them.'" Enraged, Forman, who was not present for the vote, recommended that SNCC dissolve and that all its assets be sent to newly independent countries in Africa, which, as Elizabeth Sutherland Martínez recalled, "was a provocative proposal and made people stop and think." After further debate, a compromise was reached that whites were still allowed to be staff members of SNCC, but they were urged to restrict their organizing to white communities and were no longer allowed to vote within the organization.[25]

Even though Forman had attempted to mitigate the situation, to most of the whites in SNCC, the damage had been done. While some whites continued their work, others accepted the outcome of the vote and left SNCC. Miller recalled, "Forman says that the motion was reconsidered and tabled, so that technically they weren't voted out. But most people think of that as the meeting when whites were voted out of the organization." However, Terry Cannon did not feel he had been expelled from SNCC: "I was there at the meeting when we were all kicked out of SNCC and to my dying day, we were not. But nobody believes it." Rather, through his work dispensing news to the radical community as editor of *The Movement*, Cannon was already organizing in the white community. It was not until the following year, when few whites were still associated with the organization, that it was decided whites were no longer staff members but "technical assistants."[26]

Some white organizers, detecting the changes in SNCC ideology and questioning their role in the movement, voluntarily withdrew from the organization even prior to the December 1966 staff meeting. Others left shortly after the fateful vote. In late 1966, Mike Miller had accepted an offer to work as an organizer for Saul Alinsky's IAF in Kansas City, Missouri, on the condition that he could continue to work for SNCC through the end of the year. Following the SNCC staff meeting, he withdrew from SNCC in order to begin his career with the IAF. Miller's departure spelled the end of San Francisco SNCC. In December 1966, *The Movement*, which was published out of the San Francisco office, informed its readers that it was no longer being published by SNCC and was incorporating separately as the Movement Press. The change was supposedly a legal one that would prevent SNCC from being sued for anything published in *The Movement*. However, by separating itself from SNCC, *The Movement* would be able to avoid the turmoil that was pervading the organization. A year later, an FBI agent reported, "A staff member of 'The Movement' stated that SNCC has no official staff members in San Francisco area, SNCC is not active in the San Francisco area."[27]

Marshall Ganz simply transitioned from being a SNCC field secretary working with the UFWOC to being a full-fledged union staff member. Chavez had asked Ganz to join the staff in 1965, but Ganz declined because he "wanted to be SNCC's person there because at that point one of the possible SNCC futures was a network of organizers working with things like the farm workers all over the country." But since Ganz worked solely with the UFWOC, which came to rely on his organizing skills, it seemed only natural that he would eventually work for the union full time. SNCC never officially dismissed Ganz. Instead, after not being in contact with the headquarters in Atlanta, he eventually stopped receiving paychecks from SNCC.[28]

With the exception of Ganz's transition to union organizer, the expulsion and withdrawal of white organizers from SNCC deprived the UFWOC of the resources and support of the San Francisco SNCC office, one of its earliest allies. Without the leadership of the field secretaries in the San Francisco office, the relationship between SNCC and the UFWOC rapidly deteriorated because no other SNCC office prioritized the farmworkers' cause. In fact, the members of the San Francisco SNCC office were uniquely suited to forge a coalition between SNCC and the UFWOC. The staff members—particularly Miller, Cannon, and George Ballis—had experience in the labor movement and were committed to the fight for economic justice. Unlike many in SNCC elsewhere, they also had an overall positive opinion of organized labor. The San Francisco SNCC office was also influenced by the unique racial and ethnic diversity of the area. Although there were fewer African Americans in the West than in the South and Northeast, the West had much higher populations of Latinos, as well as American Indians, Asians, and Pacific Islanders. San Francisco was especially remarkable in its diversity, with a 40 percent nonwhite population in 1970, which led the movements for racial equality there to prioritize multiracial solidarity and cooperation. These dynamics led SNCC field secretaries in California to pursue both labor organizing and multiracial coalition building as integral and essential to their movement praxis. That the relationship between SNCC and the UFWOC dissolved when these individuals left SNCC reinforces the importance of personal relationships and individual initiative in sustaining multiracial coalitions.[29]

*   *   *

SNCC's adoption of black nationalism and the expulsion and withdrawal of white organizers demonstrated a shift in the organization's position toward multiracial solidarity that negatively affected its relationship with the UFWOC. An unforeseen consequence of the vote taken at the Peg Leg Bates meeting was that nonblack racial minorities were expelled along with whites. This meant that María Varela and Elizabeth Sutherland Martínez, two Mexican Americans who had been on the SNCC staff since the period prior to Freedom Summer, were also forced out. Varela had been a field secretary in Alabama and Mississippi, developing adult literacy projects in some of the most dangerous areas of the South. By 1966 her role evolved to include photography, film production, and the manufacture of promotional material for SNCC, which was funded by outside sources. She contributed to the alliance between SNCC and the UFWOC by making a film of the Delano grape strike, which she later showed to African American farmworkers and sharecroppers in the South. Martínez was the director of the New York SNCC office. She kept the New York press informed of events in the South, edited Stokely Carmichael's book *Black Power*, and conducted fundraisers. During Mississippi Freedom Summer, she worked in the state testing public accommodations legislation. Never having identified as white, Varela and Martínez were shocked to learn that many African Americans wanted them out of SNCC.[30]

At the December staff meeting, Varela did not protest the decision to bar whites from voting in SNCC: "Coming to terms with my own identity, I wasn't going to ask permission or seek approval of what I knew I was inside. And anyway, my work, supported by my own fundraising, would go on no matter how anyone voted in SNCC." However, after the vote, when the whites present stood and left the room en masse in a display of both solidarity and acquiescence, Varela remained. After the meeting, she returned to the South to continue her work. But she discovered that how her colleagues viewed her Mexican American heritage determined how they treated her: "Some in SNCC didn't consider Mexican Americans white and therefore didn't include me in the exclusion. Others were working with me at the local level and ignored the policy. Still others stopped speaking to me. In the darkroom, the hurt and anger was pushed to the edges and work went on."[31]

When whites were finally expelled from SNCC the following year, Martínez attempted to confront the issue directly by sending a position paper entitled "Black, White and Tan" to the Atlanta SNCC office, where the conflict over whites in SNCC had originated:

> From time to time, the question of whether I was to be classified as white or Mexican (i.e., non-white) has come up in SNCC. People talked about me, but never asked me what I considered myself. . . . One day I found myself unable to vote in SNCC because I was "white." When I was a child, the girl next door wasn't allowed to play with me because I was a Mexican; remembering this and other experiences, something seemed mixed up. But I wasn't going to fight that classification; that would have been only half-truthful and I didn't want to claim exceptional status, honorary "blackness."

Martínez's description of the confusion over her racial identity within SNCC reveals that the majority of the organization, for all its groundbreaking philosophy and activism, continued to view race through the lens of black/white and therefore still had difficulty grappling with Latino identity by 1967. Varela recalled that when she went to organize in Selma, Alabama, part of her activities included educating her SNCC colleagues—a mix of rural southerners and students from Howard University—on her identity as a Mexican

American: "We'd start getting in these discussions about, you know, identity and . . . I guess I grew in my identity by having to explain it to people that had never really met anybody who was Mexican American." Although these discussions were generally positive experiences that helped Varela develop her racial consciousness and complicated her colleagues' understanding of race, they did not prevent her from experiencing discrimination within SNCC. In fact, Varela began going by "Mary" instead of María after a fellow SNCC staff member snapped, "Speak English!" when she introduced herself with a Mexican accent. She also remembered a Mexican American SNCC volunteer who was assigned to Laurel, Mississippi, but left after a short period because she resented being treated as white by others in the organization.[32]

Despite its alliance with the UFWOC, the racial ideology of many in SNCC did not develop to fully include Mexican Americans as oppressed minorities. While the members of the San Francisco SNCC office challenged the organization to think of race in terms beyond black and white, the expulsion of Varela and Martínez indicates that some in SNCC did not recognize the connections between African Americans and Mexican Americans and the potential for cross-racial solidarity, which undermined the basis of its relationship with the UFWOC. When Varela and Martínez were pushed out of SNCC for being "white," it was clear SNCC no longer saw that Mexican Americans and African Americans experienced similar kinds of racial and economic oppression. And if SNCC considered Mexican Americans white, then black nationalists in the organization could no longer work with the farmworkers.

SNCC's fluctuating ideas about racial classification were representative of Mexican Americans' experiences in the United States. White interactions with Mexicans during the course of nineteenth-century westward expansion caused changes to the American racial hierarchy, which previously only addressed whites, blacks, and American Indians. The Treaty of Guadalupe Hidalgo, which ended the war between the United States and Mexico in 1848 and ceded the territory that is now the southwestern states, defined Mexicans "as a 'white' population and accorded the political-legal status of 'free white persons.'" However, historian Neil Foley has demonstrated that during this period, whites "did not regard Mexicans as blacks, but they also did not regard them as whites. Neither black nor white, Mexicans were usually regarded as a degraded 'mongrel' race, a mixture of Indian, Spanish, and African ancestry, only different from Indians and Africans in the degree of their inferiority to whites." Mexican Americans in the Southwest were therefore the victims of racial violence—including lynchings—and endured segregation in housing, education, and public accommodations, mirroring the experiences of African Americans in the Southeast. Due to these experiences, most Mexican Americans viewed themselves as belonging to a separate race, neither black nor white. But beginning in the 1930s, they began to fight discrimination by arguing that they were in fact white and were thus deserving of civil rights, reflecting their belief that claiming whiteness—the quintessential American identity—would strengthen their claims to citizenship.[33]

By the early 1960s, however, the civil rights movement's successes demonstrated to Mexican Americans that whiteness was not a prerequisite for equality. The influence of the movement, combined with other factors such as the war in Vietnam and increased student activism, led a younger generation of Mexican Americans to articulate a new racial identity: Chicano. Historian Ignacio M. García defines Chicanos as "those who fought for the rights of Mexican Americans and fought against Anglo-American racism." The ethos of *chicanismo* included the concept of *la raza*: racial pride and solidarity with other peoples of color, rather than attempting to claim whiteness. Or as García put it, "It became okay to be brown." SNCC's decision that Mexican Americans were white therefore came at the very moment when they decided for themselves that they were not.[34]

SNCC's changed view of Mexican Americans curiously also came at a time when the organization was seeking to identify itself with movements in the Third World. Although SNCC had long expressed solidarity with African liberation movements, by 1967 it also found inspiration in the anticolonial struggles in Latin America and Asia. Stokely Carmichael explained, "Our struggle in Mississippi or Harlem was part and parcel of this great international and historical motion." In response to decreased financial support from white organizations following the expulsion of white staff members, SNCC reconceptualized itself as part of the international movement against Western imperialism. SNCC therefore declared itself a human rights organization, established an International Affairs Commission, and published statements supportive of foreign revolutionary movements. SNCC members also traveled to foreign countries in an effort to establish personal connections with international movements. In July 1967, Carmichael traveled to Havana, Cuba, to attend the meeting of the Organization of Latin-American Solidarity (OLAS). In his speech to the conference, Carmichael proclaimed, "We speak with you, comrades, because we wish to make clear that we understand that our destinies are intertwined. Our world can only be the Third

World; our only struggle, for the Third World; our only vision, of the Third World."[35]

As Clayborne Carson asserts, Carmichael's trip to Cuba and other Third World countries (and, by extension, his speech to OLAS) "demonstrated SNCC's lack of a common set of political principles to guide its efforts to build alliances." In his speech, Carmichael stressed the connections between African Americans and Latinos and called for cooperation. He proclaimed, "Our destiny cannot be separated from the destiny of the Spanish-speaking people in the United States and of the Americas. Our victory will not be achieved unless they celebrate their liberation side by side with us, for it is not their struggle, but our struggle together." But Carmichael gave this speech after Martínez and Varela had been expelled from SNCC and the organization's alliance with the UFWOC had deteriorated. In his autobiography, Carmichael explained, "I was not representing SNCC. . . . Nor was I representing black America or *any* America. It was a personal analysis and a call to struggle." Moreover, Carmichael's speech did not convey his thinking on black/Latino relations because Martínez was actually the author. Therefore, Carmichael's visit to Cuba, though well-intentioned, did not reflect SNCC's ideology and did not indicate that the organization had renewed its commitment to multiracial coalition building.[36]

Carmichael's attendance at the OLAS conference also did not influence SNCC philosophy or programs upon his return to the United States. In fact, the segment of Carmichael's four-month trip to Third World countries that was most influential to him was the time he spent in Africa; he was therefore determined to establish closer ties between SNCC and African nations. Carmichael's Pan-Africanism was in line with the priorities of many others in SNCC. However, this Pan-Africanism undermined the establishment of alliances with American minority groups by exclusively focusing on similarities between Africans and African Americans. María Varela recalled that when she attempted to interest SNCC in forming coalitions with Latinos, she became frustrated by the organization's inability to recognize the significance of other minority group struggles. She was particularly disappointed with the speech Forman delivered at the National Conference for New Politics (NCNP) over Labor Day weekend 1967. The purpose of the convention was to gather progressive activists from diverse backgrounds, but Forman only discussed the experiences of Africans and African Americans. He argued, "Here in the United States, we are the lowest class on the economic ladder. We suffer the most from racism. What does this mean? This means that we and we alone have the responsibility to wage our own war of liberation as we see fit to do that, and no one who has not suffered as we have has the right to dictate to us the forms of our struggle." Varela attended the convention and met with the other Latino activists present, who were upset that Forman seemed to discredit the movements of other minority groups. In response, Varela wrote Forman a five-page letter explaining discrimination against Latinos. She also scolded, "When you fight racism and oppression Jim, you cannot just fight a part of it. The same racism that brutalizes your people brutalizes our people." Forman's speech reveals that not only did SNCC's leaders no longer recognize the commonalities between African Americans and Mexican Americans, but they also deemed that the struggles of other groups were not comparable to those of blacks. Moreover, in championing Pan-Africanism, SNCC downplayed class differences in favor of racial solidarity, which weakened any chance for multiracial alliances. Although the organization was intensely interested in liberation struggles of people of color around the world, its members largely ignored the growing movements of American minorities.[37]

SNCC's emphasis on Pan-Africanism also revealed different understandings of the Third World—which were rooted in personal relationships and lived experiences—within the organization. To SNCC in the South, the Third World was comprised of anticolonial movements in other countries, particularly those in Africa. The international focus was the product of some members' upbringings and familial ties in the Caribbean, and acquaintances with college students from newly independent African countries. However, the San Francisco SNCC office, which had masterminded the alliance with the farmworkers, and the Friends of SNCC chapters on the West Coast, prioritized the domestic Third World—African Americans, Asian Americans, Latina/os, and American Indians who viewed themselves as part of an international movement against oppression. Ethnic studies scholar Jason Ferreira argues that the idea of a "Third World within" was incredibly empowering to these groups: "No longer were communities of color in the United States simply a domestic 'minority,' instead they were conceived of as part of a global 'majority.'" This concept was an outgrowth of the tremendous racial and ethnic diversity of the San Francisco Bay Area and other parts of the West. Conceiving of themselves as part of the Third World enabled these groups to form alliances based on shared experiences and multiracial solidarity. In San Francisco, these forces facilitated the formation of the Third World Liberation Front, which orchestrated a strike at San Francisco State College in 1968–1969 that led to the creation of the first

Black Studies and Ethnic Studies departments. The atmosphere of domestic Third Worldism in the San Francisco Bay Area activist community helps to explain why Mike Miller and the San Francisco SNCC office were able to form a relationship with the UFWOC so easily and why this alliance was viewed as a natural course of action. Moreover, San Francisco SNCC's support of the UFWOC demonstrates Ferreira's argument that "a Third Worldist orientation enabled activists to speak to the multiple facets of oppression experienced by racialized 'peoples' and therefore was grounded in grassroots community organizing." SNCC offices in the Southeast, though inspired by the international Third World, did not share this domestic Third Worldist philosophy and were therefore not fully committed to the alliance with the farmworkers or to other American minority groups.[38]

*   *   *

SNCC's shifting racial philosophy magnified other differences between it and the UFWOC, which eventually undermined its alliance with the union. Although the alliance had been based on shared values, ideologies, and tactics, the divergent evolution of SNCC and the UFWOC created insurmountable divisions between the two organizations.

By the end of 1966, each organization had developed different conceptions of their role in national politics. The outcome of the 1964 Democratic National Convention and the success of the Lowndes County Freedom Organization convinced many in SNCC that their organizing should be focused on independent black politics. The UFWOC, on the other hand, had become more closely tied to the Democratic Party. Before forming the union, its leaders had participated in Viva Kennedy Clubs, which rallied Latino support for Massachusetts Senator John F. Kennedy's 1960 presidential campaign. Soon after the union's founding, New York Senator Robert Kennedy became a strong ally, endearing himself to the farmworkers by championing their cause as a member of the Senate Subcommittee on Migratory Labor. Kennedy and his wife Ethel also supported the union's strike in Delano and participated in fundraisers for the farmworkers. Later, Kennedy was by Chavez's side when he ended his fast in 1968, and Chavez in turn endorsed his presidential campaign. The union also endorsed other Democratic candidates who were deemed friendly to farmworkers, and campaigned for or against legislation regarding farm labor. Aligning themselves so closely with the Democratic Party was directly at odds with SNCC's new political philosophy. Furthermore, the concept of independent politics championed by SNCC was impractical and unappealing to the UFWOC.[39]

The location of struggle also became a divisive point between the two organizations. At the beginning of their alliance, SNCC was able to connect to the union because it recognized the similarities between African American sharecroppers in the South and Mexican American farmworkers in California. By the end of 1966, however, SNCC had turned its attention away from rural areas and had come to believe that cities were the most fertile areas for organizing. Cleveland Sellers explained,

> We were all very conscious of the fact that the axis of the struggle appeared to be shifting away from the rural South to the cities in the North. The totally unexpected rebellions in Harlem, Watts, Chicago, and Philadelphia made a big impact on our thinking. They motivated us to begin a search for ways in which we could mold the discontent in the urban ghettos to revolutionary advantage.

The fields of California were therefore far from the areas on which SNCC had set its sights. Moreover, the turn to urban areas meant that the organizing of agricultural workers was no longer a priority. SNCC's indifference to reforming agricultural labor is reflected in the fate of the Mississippi Freedom Labor Union (MFLU), which was founded by cotton choppers and pickers in January 1965 and grew to over one thousand members by the summer of that year. In June, the MFLU went on strike to force growers to comply with the federal minimum wage of $1.25 per hour. Many MFLU members had been active in the MFDP and their struggle shared much in common with the civil rights movement, but SNCC did not lend significant support. Although mechanization in cotton was the primary reason for the strike's rapid failure, SNCC's lack of support was another contributing factor.[40]

The UFWOC's rural agricultural character was also at odds with the lives of most Mexican Americans. In 1967, Saul Alinsky remarked, "The problem of the Mexican-Americans is an urban problem." As of the 1960 census, 79.1 percent of the Spanish surname population in the Southwest lived in urban areas. By 1970, that number had increased to 85.5 percent. The census also revealed that fewer Mexican Americans were working as farm laborers. Although the trend would continue, the union did not address that reality. Alinsky explained, "In ten years, mechanization will make the historical farm worker obsolete. So what you've got to do is retrain the Mexican-Americans for urban living. Cesar doesn't understand this, any more than he understands that the majority of the AFL-CIO is middle class now." Although the UFWOC worked to improve wages and working conditions, it did not encourage the farmworkers to become the landowners themselves. This position was too conciliatory to many and was in conflict with Black Power's emphasis on self-determination and economic empowerment.[41]

During this phase of SNCC's evolution, the organization explored alliances with those who appeared to more closely share its ideals than the UFWOC. The commitment to self-determination and racial pride were factors in the formation of an alliance between SNCC and the Alianza Federal de Pueblos Libres in 1967. Led by Reies López Tijerina, the Alianza sought to regain lands in the Southwest that had been awarded by the Spanish and Mexican governments to early settlers, but had been lost after the 1848 U.S. takeover of the region. The Alianza appealed to advocates of Black Power because of both their cause and their militancy. Tijerina and the Alianza became infamous in June 1967 when they attempted to place the district attorney of Rio Arriba County, New Mexico, under citizen's arrest at the courthouse in Tierra Amarilla, which ended in a violent confrontation. Tijerina and the leaders of SNCC first encountered each other at the Chicago NCNP convention over Labor Day weekend 1967. Former SNCC communications director Julian Bond asked Varela to act as hostess to Tijerina at the convention "so he would feel more at home." Deeply impressed with SNCC, Tijerina asked Varela if she could amass a SNCC delegation to participate in the annual national convention of the Alianza that October in New Mexico. Although Varela had long hoped to connect SNCC with the Chicano movement, she approached this alliance with some trepidation. She wrote to SNCC staff member Ethel Minor,

> One of the things that most impressed Reies was that SNCC had two Chicanos working for it. It was hard for him to understand when I explained a little of the reality of that—that some black people still see us, Chicanos and Puerto Ricans—as white—and still do not trust us, and perhaps would not trust him. He says, "but don't they read about what we are doing to the anglo?" and I explained that east of the Mississippi very little news is carried about his struggle.

Figure 5. SNCC representative Ralph Featherstone (second from left) with Hopi leader Thomas Banyacya, US founder Maulana Karenga, and Reies López Tijerina at the annual convention of the Alianza Federal de Pueblos Libres, Albuquerque, New Mexico, October 21, 1967. PICT 000-093-0017, Peter Nabokov Photograph Collection, Center for Southwest Research, University Libraries, University of New Mexico.

Due to her experience with SNCC, Varela knew that the organization's racial ideology and lack of understanding of the issues facing Mexican Americans could easily hamper any attempt at coalition building. By October 1967, however, SNCC had alienated many of its former allies and lost the majority of its funding sources. When the lack of support became so dire that SNCC began losing visibility, legitimacy, and relevance, Varela succeeded in convincing its leaders to attempt a coalition with the Alianza. Therefore, a delegation comprised of Varela, Ralph Featherstone, Willie Ricks, Freddie Greene, Ethel Minor, and Muriel Tillinghast traveled to Albuquerque to attend the convention.[42]

SNCC was one of several African Americans organizations invited to the Alianza convention. In fact, Tijerina also invited Martin Luther King, Jr., and Muhammad Ali, though neither attended. One reason Tijerina invited such diverse black leaders was that in Albuquerque, African Americans had joined with poor whites to attack Mexican Americans, and he wanted the organizations at the conference to sign a multiracial peace treaty. Reflecting on the ideology of the SNCC delegation, Varela remarked that, "it was really interesting because, you know, within that delegation of people were various opinions in terms of who was more oppressed than who." SNCC program director Ralph Featherstone demonstrated his sympathy with the Alianza and interest in coalition building when he addressed the convention on October 21. As he approached the podium, Featherstone chanted, "Poder Negro" (Black Power), which was echoed by the audience. In his speech, Featherstone declared, "We have things common to our struggles. We have a common enemy." At least at the convention, a few SNCC members appeared once again to recognize the similarities in the experiences of African Americans and Mexican Americans.[43]

Despite SNCC's message of solidarity and the positive reception Featherstone and the rest of the delegation received, cooperation between SNCC and the Alianza was limited. Following the convention, SNCC spoke out in defense of the Alianza when it was targeted by law enforcement agencies. In January 1968, SNCC chairman H. Rap Brown sent a telegram in support of the Alianza to David Cargo, governor of New Mexico, when several Alianza members were arrested on murder charges. SNCC also printed articles on the Alianza in its occasional newsletter and issued press releases through the Aframerican News Service. The relationship between the two organizations, however, never reached the scope of that between SNCC and the UFWOC. For example, SNCC's support for the Alianza never included the lending of staff or resources as it did with the union (although by that time SNCC had little staff and few resources to lend). Neither SNCC nor the Alianza was committed to multiracial solidarity or coalition building. In February 1968 Tijerina expressed reluctance at appearing at a rally with Carmichael and other black militants: "We signed that treaty but that was for the future, to assure that we would be at peace with those people. But I'm not sure it's wise to be tied in with them. We have a different struggle even though they are fighting for their rights too." Both SNCC and the Alianza understood themselves as the victims of racism, but did not appreciate the commonalities between them nor see the need to fight discrimination together.[44]

∗   ∗   ∗

The multiracial alliance that had formed between SNCC and the UFWOC in 1965 was the result of bridge leaders who recognized the parallel ideologies and praxis of the organizations. These individuals also understood that both African Americans and Mexican Americans experienced racial discrimination and economic exploitation and therefore believed SNCC and the UFWOC needed to work together in their pursuit of equality and justice. However, the evolution of the organizations along different trajectories ended their alliance. In February 1967, a donation to the UFWOC by East Bay Friends of SNCC marked the last time SNCC supported the farmworkers financially. *The Movement* continued to publish news of the farmworkers, but the newspaper was no longer affiliated with SNCC. Thus, after a fruitful coalition that lasted two years, the only connection the UFWOC had to SNCC was its continuing relationship with former staff members, such as Marshall Ganz, whose commitment to the farmworkers outlasted their careers in SNCC.[45]

Cesar Chavez was dismayed that SNCC no longer supported the farmworkers. For him it represented a larger pattern of early union supporters moving on to other causes. In an April 1967 interview, Chavez lamented, "The labor movement is by and large our biggest help. And we've been able to keep the church help. But we're getting very little help from the student groups or the civil rights groups—well, some, but not anywhere what we were getting before. Even our correspondence with our contacts in these groups is almost nil." Although SNCC had criticized the UFWOC for coming under the fold

of the AFL-CIO, the merger proved even more important and necessary once
SNCC ended its support.[46]

Following the end of its relationship with the UFWOC, some in SNCC
again attempted to reach out to Mexican Americans, recognizing that their
experiences indeed overlapped. In a letter to Varela in January 1968, Carmichael admitted, "We can't take the honkie by ourselves and since he messed
over everyone we might as get everybody to help wipe him out once and
for all." One month later while announcing that a chapter of SNCC in Texas
was forming a youth organization in San Antonio, Larry Jackson confessed,
"SNCC is a Black people's organization. But as Public Relations Director of
Texas SNCC, I recognize that Mexican-Americans are suffering the same
kind of discrimination and oppression as Black people in America." Without
the presence of determined bridge leaders, however, the feeling that Mexican
Americans and African Americans were victims of similar oppression did
not become widespread among SNCC's staff and did not lead to the formation of any multiracial coalitions. The relationship between SNCC and the
UFWOC thus demonstrates the key role of individual leadership in setting
priorities and forging multiracial coalitions. The leaders who orchestrated
the alliance between the organizations chose to focus on the commonalities rather than their differences, which increased as each evolved. SNCC's
prioritization of black nationalism over class-based multiracial solidarity, in
prompting the departure of these bridge leaders, thus hastened the end of an
important and rewarding multiracial coalition.[47]

CHAPTER 3

Consumers Who Understand Hunger and Joblessness

ESPERANZA Fierro Lopez was surprised by the minister's reaction to her protest. After much discussion and debate with the other members of the UFWOC boycott committee in Philadelphia, Lopez had decided to fast in front of an A&P supermarket to draw attention to the plight of the farmworkers and persuade the store to remove California grapes from its shelves. She and the committee chose the A&P store at Progress Plaza, the first black-owned and operated shopping center in the United States, for her May 1969 fast because they believed its African American patrons would be supportive. As Lopez explained to the committee, "I want to speak to consumers who understand hunger and joblessness." This strategy had worked in the union's past; the boycott of Schenley Industries in 1965–1966 had been especially successful in African American neighborhoods such as Harlem. Similarly, African American organizations on the West Coast were some of the farmworkers' most vocal supporters of the national boycott of California grapes, which had begun in 1968. In Oakland and Los Angeles, members of the Black Panther Party joined UFWOC picket lines at grocery stores.[1]

Lopez therefore had good reason to believe that the A&P grocery store at Progress Plaza would be an appropriate place to begin her fast. And true to her prediction, the African American customers in the working-class neighborhood in North Philadelphia were receptive and promised to boycott grapes. But it soon became apparent that the city's middle-class black leadership did not appreciate her protest. On the fourth day of her fast, the host of an African American radio show berated Lopez for protesting at Progress Plaza, scolding, "This place is a mess with you people and your posters all over." Later that night, Lopez received a call from Reverend Leon Sullivan, member of the Philadelphia NAACP Executive Board, founder of the clergy-led civil rights organization the 400 Ministers, and mastermind behind Progress Plaza. She recalled,

> Mr. Sullivan informed me that Progress Plaza was no easy venture, it had taken time to come to its successful conclusion. He assured me that the Black Community was and had been in support of the farm workers from the onset. . . . This was followed by the inevitable However. "You and your committee are doing this all wrong Mrs. Lopez. . . . You have brought your cause to the doors of Progress Plaza. . . . You are at the wrong door."

Instead, Sullivan suggested that Lopez move her fast to A&P's administrative offices, which she recognized as a "diplomatic approach to getting rid of me."[2]

Whereas SNCC was one of the few civil rights organizations that supported the farmworkers during the Schenley strike and boycott, the UFWOC's ambitious national boycott of California grapes attracted the attention and support of a diverse spectrum of African American civil rights organizations, including the National Urban League, the NAACP, and the Black Panther Party. By taking the union's fight outside of California and into urban areas and demonstrating *la causa*'s simultaneous fight against economic exploitation and racial discrimination, the grape boycott led many civil rights activists to recognize and act on the relevance of the farmworkers' struggle to African Americans. However, the level of support that these organizations gave to the UFWOC and their boycott of California grapes varied according to class identity, organizational praxis, and geographic location. For many middle-class civil rights organizations, the grape boycott presented a challenge: support the farmworkers, who took inspiration from the victories of the civil rights movement, or maintain their carefully cultivated ties with the business community that exploited them. In contrast to the youthful activists of SNCC, whose rejection of the ideals and trappings of middle-class American life facilitated their coalition with the UFWOC, the dependence of the NAACP and NUL on patronage from white corporations served as a barrier to the formation of multiracial alliances with the Mexican American farmworkers. The support of some middle-class civil rights organizations for the UFOWC grape boycott was therefore tepid at best. However, geographic proximity served to mitigate the limitations of class; middle-class civil rights organizations on the West Coast were significantly more supportive of the boycott because of their intimate knowledge of Mexican American issues. Place was therefore as important as racial and class-based solidarity in multiracial coalition building. Furthermore, personal connections and individual leadership were also instrumental in forging coalitions during the grape boycott. The BPP combined its geographic proximity, identification with the working class, and strong leadership to become the farmworkers' strongest ally in the black freedom struggle during the grape boycott.

*   *   *

The UFWOC's nationwide boycott of California grapes demonstrates both the challenges and possibilities of grassroots organizing and multiracial coalition building. Immediately following the victory against A. Perelli-Minetti & Sons in 1967, the union continued its successful tactic of targeting one grape grower at a time. The UFWOC decided to focus next on the Giumarra Vineyard Corporation: one of the largest table grape growers in the Delano region with 6,000 acres of vines, and one of the growers that had been struck since September 1965. On June 26, 1967, Cesar Chavez sent a letter to Giumarra requesting a meeting "to establish procedure for settling our labor dispute with you in keeping with the democratic process." The UFWOC also asked the California State Conciliation Service for assistance in negotiating elections with Giumarra. Although corporation president Joseph Giumarra and other executives met with representatives from the UFWOC on July 10, it soon became clear that the corporation did not have any interest in negotiating an election with the union. The industrial relations representative for Giumarra admitted, "We did meet Monday with the union people, but only because we were invited by the State Conciliation Service and only out of courtesy to that state service." After Chavez's repeated requests for elections at Giumarra's ranches were ignored, the UFWOC declared a renewed strike on August 3.[3]

Buoyed by the UFWOC's previous victories, Giumarra's farmworkers felt confident in striking.On the first day of the strike, 150 farmworkers picketed at Giumarra's ranches. The pickets had their desired effect; only four days after the strike began, the workforce in the fields was reduced from 1,200 to 50. The workforce was further decreased when the U.S. Department of Labor

certified the strike against Giumarra, which made it illegal for the corporation to use Mexican nationals with green cards as strikebreakers. In an effort
to stem the UFWOC's increasing power in the strike, Giumarra obtained an
injunction against the union that limited the number of pickets to three in
front of any entrance to its ranches. In response, the UFWOC began a nationwide boycott of Giumarra grapes.[4]

From the beginning, the boycott of Giumarra grapes did not go as
smoothly as the union's earlier actions. According to Cesar Chavez, "Between August and December, we experienced a lot of frustration and abso-
lutely no progress." In early January 1968 the UFWOC decided to focus the
boycott in New York City, the largest market for Giumarra grapes and 20
percent of the total grape market. Another reason for focusing the boycott
in New York was to target Victor Joseph & Son Company of New Jersey, Giumarra's most successful agent. Not only was the company responsible for
selling Giumarra grapes in New York and New Jersey, but Fred Ross also
faulted it for not using its influence to end the dispute between Giumarra
and the union. Furthermore, the union's previous boycotts in New York,
such as the one against Schenley Industries, had been extremely successful.
Those boycotts had been conducted by volunteers, many from civil rights
organizations. During the Giumarra boycott, however, the volunteers felt
that their actions were not sufficiently effective because "they were obvi-
ously not farm workers" and thus were less successful in gaining the public's sympathy and persuading them to participate in the boycott. At their
request, Chavez asked farmworkers to volunteer to assist with the boycott
in New York City. Fifty farmworkers and UFWOC volunteers, as well as
Ross and Dolores Huerta, left Delano for New York on January 5 in a donated school bus, "carrying sleeping bags and warm clothes," to organize
the boycott there.[5]

The farmworkers and volunteers sent to New York relied on the contributions of their supporters. As they traveled across the county, they obtained
lodging and food from churches and progressive organizations, including
the Alianza Federal de Pueblos Libres in New Mexico. When they arrived in
New York, they were housed in the dormitory of the Seafarers International
Union (SIU) in Brooklyn and given meal tickets to use in the union dining
hall. As they spread word of the boycott and set up pickets at grocery stores,
the UFWOC received support from a variety of people and organizations.
In fact, Fred Ross assigned each organizer a group—whether religiously or
ethnically affiliated, a student organization, or union—with whom to make

contact. Volunteer Mark Silverman reflected, "New York was one of the easiest places to do a boycott. Groups that didn't get along with each other all supported the boycott—liberals, unionists, Puerto Ricans, blacks, Jews, and others." Supporters boycotted grapes, donated food and money, and participated in picket lines. Some of the farmworkers' allies were especially helpful by conducting shop-ins, during which people seemingly unconnected to the farmworkers filled their shopping carts with small items and then left them at the registers without paying (costing the stores money in labor spent restocking the items from the carts) after loudly criticizing the store for selling California grapes.[6]

Organizers in New York made a concerted effort to appeal to African Americans because they viewed the black community's participation in and support of the boycott as essential to its success. Forty-nine stores in Harlem had cooperated with the Schenley boycott, which contributed to the union's victory. But the UFWOC organizers discovered that African American participation helped the boycott in areas beyond black neighborhoods. In September 1968 Dolores Huerta reported to fellow organizers, "Richard had a swinging, loud, noisy, super-militant picket line going in a middle class area of the Bronx (white) and boy did it hurt. From this we have come to the conclusion that a brown or black line in an all white area is extremely effective." In order to appeal to the black community and demonstrate the relevance of the grape boycott, union organizers played on the racial discrimination and economic exploitation suffered by both African Americans and Mexican Americans. For example, the boycott committee distributed fliers that juxtaposed photos of Mexican American farmworker children with photos of urban African American children.[7]

In appealing to African Americans, the New York boycott attracted the support of middle-class civil rights organizations that had not supported or participated in the earlier UFWOC boycotts. One of the first of these to come to the aid of the farmworkers was the National Urban League, founded by black and white reformers in New York City in 1910 in response to the mass migration of African Americans to that city from the rural South. From the beginning, the League's members were primarily professionals who were committed to inculcating the working poor with middle-class values. Its founders and members were heavily influenced by the Progressive Era interest in the use of social work as a solution for urban conditions. Accordingly, the Urban League's activities were based on the belief that decent housing and employment opportunities for African Americans could both reduce

YOUR GROCER PROMOTES POVERTY BY SELLING CALIFORNIA GRAPES

In an effort to secure rights that most Americans have long enjoyed, Farm Workers in California have been on strike for three years, seeking simple justice and dignity which they cannot obtain through other means.

The Farm Workers are asking for recognition of their Union, for decent wages, and for an end to degrading working conditions. They seek such basic decencies as **toilets in the fields, hand-washing facilities, cool drinking water in hot weather** and **elimination of racial discrimination in hiring.**

Grape growers have responded to these simple demands by refusing to negotiate with the Union. They have answered peaceful picketing with violence and terror tactics, and by running down workers with their trucks.

Illegal recruitment of alien strike-breakers from Mexico has made it impossible to win justice in the fields. Farm Workers are forced to bring their cause to YOU, the Consumers of this City.

YOU CAN HELP:
(1) Refuse to shop in stores that sell California grapes.
(2) Urge others to support this boycott.
(3) Let your grocer know that you will not shop in stores that handle products of farm sweatshops.

BOYCOTT STORES THAT SELL CALIFORNIA GRAPES!

UNITED FARM WORKERS ORGANIZING COMMITTEE, AFL-CIO

1300 South Wabash Ave., Chicago, Illinois 60605,
Phone Contacts: (312) 427-7078 or 427-4357.

Figure 6. Flier distributed by the UFWOC. Courtesy of Walter P. Reuther Library, Wayne State University.

racial animosity and remedy the problems of urban living, such as crime, overcrowding, and poverty. One of the League's main functions was therefore to provide job training and serve as an employment agency.[8]

The Urban League focus on employment issues led it to support the UFWOC boycott of Giumarra grapes. Although the NUL had not engaged in multiracial coalition building with other minority groups, preferring to form alliances with powerful whites, it acted upon the similarities that it recognized between the experiences of Mexican American and African American agricultural workers. In July 1965, two months before the UFWOC began its first strike against Delano's grape growers, NUL executive director Whitney Young, Jr., criticized California growers for exploiting *braceros* (temporary Mexican agricultural workers) in his nationally syndicated column, "To Be Equal . . .": "The big growers take the same attitude toward the migrants that they do toward the braceros; the same taken by Mississippi cotton planters down in the Delta country now experiencing their first strikes. Their claim is that they would have to close down if they quit working men and women 12 hours a day in the fields at skinflint rates." In likening the experience of braceros to that of African American migrant workers in the East, Young revealed that he understood that workers, regardless of race, faced the same kind of exploitation. Despite this recognition, he had not spoken out in support of the union's earlier boycotts. When the union brought the Giumarra boycott to New York, however, Young took a more active interest in the UFWOC and decided that it was appropriate for NUL to support the Mexican American farmworkers. With his encouragement, members of New York Urban League chapters wrote letters to Joseph Giumarra informing him that its members would boycott grapes until he signed a contract with the union. This further demonstrates the importance of place in cross-racial coalition building. To Young and the NUL, when the UFWOC brought the boycott to New York, the presence of the farmworkers and the publicity surrounding the boycott made *la causa* personal and immediate rather than abstract. Through geographic proximity, the UFWOC was able to foster the personal connections and mutual understanding that are essential to forming alliances across race.[9]

Personal relationships were central to the Urban League's operation, particularly in the area of employment. The NUL industrial relations department worked directly with corporations and managers to secure employment for black job seekers who applied directly through the League. This strategy required the cooperation and support of employers, so NUL leaders strove to maintain positive relationships with business leaders and corporations. Furthermore, the NUL relied on substantial donations from major corporations and philanthropic foundations for the majority of its funding. The NUL leaders therefore had carefully cultivated relationships with the white elite. This was especially true of Whitney Young, who, through his friendships with the heads of America's wealthiest companies and foundations, had secured substantial funds for programs benefitting African Americans.[10]

The NUL strategy of increasing black employment through personal diplomacy had led it to acquire by the 1960s the reputation as the most conservative of the civil rights organizations. Instead of engaging in the direct action protest tactics that characterized the era, the NUL continued to focus on "corporate sponsorship" to effect social change. This not only put the NUL at odds with groups like SNCC, but also revealed the wide ideological and tactical gulf between it and the UFWOC. The union's goal of collective bargaining gave workers power and control over their labor. The NUL, on the other hand, willingly ceded that power to the employers; although the League obtained job opportunities for African Americans, it was the white managers and executives who decided who (if anyone) would be hired, how much they would be paid, and whether they would be promoted. African Americans outside of the organization frequently criticized the NUL for depending on powerful whites to bestow favors on the black community. Moreover, the League's prioritization of the white elite limited its influence among the black working class.[11]

However, Young and NUL officials were committed to obtaining employment for African Americans and sincerely believed that the League's program would lead to black equality. Despite the differences between its strategies and that of the UFWOC, the situation of the Mexican American farmworkers resonated with Young and prompted his support when the Giumarra boycott was launched in New York. Furthermore, Young believed that it was his responsibility to communicate the issues and concerns of the oppressed to powerful whites and convince them that it was in their best interest to act on behalf of the black freedom struggle. As such, in critiquing the treatment of Mexican American farmworkers in his syndicated column and directing League members to write protest letters to Giumarra, Young applied his organizational praxis to the UFWOC's struggle.[12]

The UFWOC's move of the Giumarra boycott to New York City also gained the support of the NAACP, but with much more difficulty. The NAACP was founded by a group of black and white reformers in 1909 in the aftermath of the devastating race riot in Springfield, Illinois the previous year. The NAACP fought for the complete integration of African Americans into American civic and political life, as guaranteed by the Fourteenth and Fifteenth Amendments to the Constitution, primarily through legal means. The association's headquarters were in New York City, a deliberate move based on the belief that an organization committed to African American equality could not survive in the Jim Crow South. However, the NAACP grew quickly and expanded its influence nationwide. By the end of 1968, there were 450,673 members in 1,730 units (which included branches, college chapters, and youth councils). The overwhelming majority of both the membership and leadership came from the ranks of the middle class, including doctors, teachers, lawyers, business owners, and government employees.[13]

The integrationist goals and legalistic methods of the association were direct reflections of its middle-class orientation. For the black elite and upper middle class, who were educated and financially successful, their race was the only obstacle to full acceptance into American society. Integration was therefore the surest path to true citizenship and equality. The organization was thus frequently at odds with working-class African Americans, whose marginalization was the product of both their race and their lower economic status. For this group, whose lives were shaped by exploitation by white employers, racial integration did not seem to be a goal worth pursuing. Rather, many working-class African Americans preferred the development of an independent black community and "freedom from white interference in black affairs." Accordingly, opinion polls in the early 1960s revealed that working-class African Americans were far more concerned with economic issues such as increased wages than the integration that the NAACP so actively pursued.[14]

The NAACP further distanced itself from the working class by cultivating relationships with corporations and foundations, whose cooperation was considered to be essential to the pursuit of integration in American institutions and upon whose financial support the association increasingly relied. The association's reliance on financial contributions from corporations both inhibited its potential support for the UFWOC and became a point of tension between its national office and its branches. During the UFWOC's earlier actions, the West Coast branches of the NAACP had wanted to support the farmworkers, but were hindered by the national office because of the association's corporate ties. Executive Director Roy Wilkins had prevented the association's branches from participating in the union boycott of Schenley Industries because of the liquor company's $50,000 donation to the NAACP and significant financial contributions to black-owned businesses. After the union signed a contract with Schenley and began its strike and boycott of the DiGiorgio Corporation (which had not donated to the NAACP) in 1966, Wilkins reluctantly allowed the NAACP to support the farmworkers. In direct contrast to Wilkins, West Coast Regional NAACP Director Leonard H. Carter stridently directed all branches in his region to support the DiGiorgio strike and participate in the boycott, reminding them that "the problems of farm workers have always been an important concern of the National Association for the Advancement of Colored People." He also directed the branches located in the strike region to work to halt the use of black strikebreakers, recalling Resolution 42 of the 1965 NAACP convention: "We reiterate our stand, adopted in past conventions against Negroes acting as strikebreakers, and in support of collective bargaining by democratic trade unions which do not discriminate in membership and apprentice training." The West Coast branches of the NAACP heeded Carter's call to action, issuing resolutions in support of the strike, holding fundraisers, and conducting food and clothing drives for the striking farmworkers. The West Coast NAACP's determination to assist the farmworkers in opposition to the national leadership's appeasement of corporate interests demonstrates the importance of grassroots activism among the association's branches.[15]

The West Coast branches' actions on behalf of the UFWOC were illustrative of the regional association's history of cooperation with Mexican Americans. The pronounced and distinctive racial and ethnic diversity of the West put African Americans, whose population in the region was low prior to World War II, into frequent contact with Latinos and Asian Americans. For example, African Americans in Los Angeles in the 1940s lived either in racially mixed neighborhoods or adjacent to ethnic enclaves. The close proximity of African Americans and Mexican Americans in the West produced significant cultural exchanges in their neighborhoods, as well as spaces of work and leisure. In nightclubs, young African Americans and Mexican Americans learned, embraced, and borrowed from each other's music, dances, and fashion. The intimate familiarity of African Americans and Mexican Americans in the West also caused both groups to recognize that they shared common experiences of discrimination, in addition to cultural and artistic forms.[16]

The home front World War II experience prompted minorities in the West to acknowledge the urgent need for multiracial cooperation. The internment of Japanese Americans, in particular, forced activists to confront the racism and xenophobia of the region. The war therefore produced several alliances between Mexican American and African American groups, including the NAACP. For example, Los Angeles NAACP president Thomas Griffith, Jr., was outspoken in his condemnation of the ten days of "Zoot Suit Riots" in June 1943, during which white sailors preyed upon and beat Mexican American youths wearing the popular clothing in Los Angeles. During the riots Griffith sent telegrams of protest to California Governor Earl Warren and President Franklin D. Roosevelt. Following the riots, Griffith testified in a grand jury investigation, served on the multiracial Council for Civic Unity, and continued to urge NAACP and government officials to work to prevent a repeat of such racial violence. Also in Los Angeles, the NAACP Youth Council and the Mexican Youth Defense Committee formed an alliance to combat racial discrimination in that city.[17]

Following World War II, multiracial coalitions characterized much of the fight for civil rights in the West. Civil rights activists used many of the same tactics as their counterparts in the South in their pursuit of racial equality, such as sit-ins, picket lines, and selective buying campaigns. However, the racial and ethnic diversity of the West necessitated the development of a movement that conceived of and fought for racial equality in terms beyond black and white. Accordingly, multiracial cooperation became a standard practice among civil rights organizations in the region. For example, the leaders of the University of New Mexico NAACP worked with Latino organizations to write "the first civil rights ordinance in the intermountain West," passed by the Albuquerque city council in 1952. Although interracial coalitions occurred less frequently in Texas, the state NAACP supported Henry B. Gonzalez, who championed the civil rights of both Mexican Americans and African Americans as a San Antonio city council member and then state senator throughout the 1950s. In addition to coalition building, Mexican Americans also joined the NAACP in the West. Rey Franco, a Mexican American who joined the Long Beach, California branch in 1951, actively participated in NAACP demonstrations "because he felt strongly that when discrimination was challenged, other third-world groups were helped in their quest for equality."[18]

In contrast to the NAACP branches in the West, the leadership of the national headquarters in New York was generally unfamiliar with Mexican American experiences. In 1970 Hispanics accounted for 8 percent of the population of the entire state of New York, but Mexican Americans were only 1.6 percent of that number. New York City was 16.2 percent Hispanic, but the majority were Puerto Rican, who had some similarities with Mexican Americans but also significant differences in demographics, history, and culture. Therefore, bringing the boycott to New York, as in the case of the NUL, introduced the national NAACP to the Mexican American farmworkers and their issues, reinforcing the importance of place in cross-racial coalition building.[19]

The NAACP national leadership was also reluctant to participate in the union's boycotts because of its historic aversion to nonviolent direct action protest strategies. Nonviolent direct action, including boycotts, troubled the NAACP because the dramatic nature of such protests drew public attention away from the association's legal endeavors. In fact, the Montgomery Bus Boycott was particularly threatening to the NAACP because, although the boycott's leaders were NAACP members and the NAACP legal team brought the suit of *Browder v. Gayle* that ended segregation on the buses, the daily operation of the boycott shifted power and attention to the grassroots and away from the association. Boycotts also worried the national leadership because they alienated allies in the business community. Although the NAACP had participated in some boycotts early in its history, most notably against the film *Birth of a Nation*, the association preferred to engage in voter registration instead of boycotts and other nonviolent direct action tactics because they believed that it was both more effective and more in keeping with the association's emphasis on the political process.[20]

The NAACP branches, on the other hand, were much more receptive to using boycotts, occasionally doing so without the approval of the national leadership. Like the UFWOC organizers, NAACP members understood that, in demonstrating the collective economic power of consumers, boycotts were particularly effective when linked to issues of employment. Furthermore, the NAACP branches paralleled the UFWOC in using picket lines to draw attention to their boycotts. For example, in 1959 the Harlem branch organized a picket line at a liquor store in the neighborhood to gain employment opportunities for African American liquor salesmen. The branch's actions appalled Wilkins and the national leadership, who vocally condemned both the boycott and the picket line. NAACP members who had become impatient with ineffective Fair Employment Practice laws and agencies believed the boycott to be a useful tactic in combating discrimination in employment. Rather than be patient with lengthy legal suits favored by the NAACP leadership, these branches organized boycotts and picket lines to create immediate employment opportunities for African Americans. Carter's support of the UFWOC boycotts is partly explained by his organization of campaigns for Fair Employment Practice laws in five states as a field secretary prior to his appointment as director of the West Coast Regional NAACP.[21]

The determination of NAACP branches to engage in boycotts and other direct action protests in direct opposition to the wishes of the national leadership demonstrates the importance of grassroots politics in social movement organizations. Moreover, the eagerness of NAACP members and branches to support the UFWOC in spite of the national organization's corporate ties is further proof of the importance of individual initiative and leadership in coalition building. Defying the entrenched bureaucracy of the NAACP was no simple feat, but many members were willing to do so to push the association in the direction that they believed it needed to go.

The tensions between the conservative national office and the increasingly militant branches of the NAACP resulted in the formation of an insurgent group led by Chester Lewis of the Wichita, Kansas, branch. Referring to themselves as the "Young Turks," these members sought to push the association in a more radical direction and depose some of the older leadership, including executive director Wilkins. Lewis and the Young Turks especially criticized the NAACP for relying on corporate donations, which they saw as compromising the association's actions. Although the majority of the membership did not agree with the Young Turks and many of its leaders left the association, their critiques did force a discussion of the NAACP's priorities, actions, and directions. It was in this atmosphere that Carter was finally able to persuade the national NAACP to express support for the farmworkers. At the NAACP 58th annual convention in Boston in July 1967, the association passed its first resolution regarding the UFWOC after the union's victory against Perelli-Minetti Winery:

> We hail the partial victory, won against great odds and with the substantial support of the UAW, by the Farm Workers Organizing Commission, AFL-CIO, under Cesar Chavez. We support fully the efforts of migrant farm workers to organize unions throughout the United States and to win, through collective bargaining, more nearly decent pay and decent housing. . . . We urge our branches, state conferences, and the National Office to take part in these organizing efforts wherever possible, and to support them by selective buying and otherwise.

This resolution marked the first time the national organization spoke out on behalf of the UFWOC. It may have been a direct attempt to stem the complaints
of the Young Turks, who were particularly popular among NAACP branches in
the West and Midwest (many of which supported the UFWOC), who felt that
the national leadership did not share their concerns and priorities. For example,
the Palo Alto-Stanford, California branch supported the actions of the insurgents
and was one of the earliest advocates of the farmworkers in the NAACP.[22]

The resolution facilitated the NAACP's cooperation when the Giumarra
boycott went to New York, where Wilkins personally met with Dolores Huerta.
With the national leadership of the NAACP finally behind the farmworkers,
the individual chapters were free to work on behalf of the boycott. The director
of the NAACP's labor program urged every NAACP branch to write letters to
Joseph Giumarra and Victor Joseph & Son informing them that all members
would boycott grapes until a contract was signed with the UFWOC. NAACP
branches across the country accordingly sent letters from such far-flung locations as Homestead, Pennsylvania, and Cape Cod, Massachusetts.[23]

The NUL and NAACP letter-writing campaigns brought the organizations
into the UFWOC boycott of Giumarra grapes. However, their chosen protest
strategy reflects the middle-class orientation of both organizations. By the
1960s, civil rights organizations frequently conducted mass letter-writing campaigns to sway public opinion, demonstrate their collective power, and influence politicians. However, it was a tactic most often employed by the middle
class because such standing was accompanied by high rates of literacy and educational attainment necessary to conducting such a campaign. Thus, members
of middle-class organizations wrote most protest letters from African Americans during the civil rights era. The act of writing letters also reflected the
middle class's cautious and gradual approach to social change. Writing letters,
after all, did not require personal confrontation nor generally put one at risk of
arrest or reprisals. Letters also usually did not produce rapid and decisive actions from the recipients. Writing letters on behalf of the UFWOC Giumarra
boycott was therefore a way for the Urban League and NAACP to support the
farmworkers that was not only in keeping with their middle-class orientation,
but did not jeopardize the writers or require a significant commitment beyond
a modicum of time and energy. Similarly, unless one participated in a picket
line or shop-in, boycotting a product or store preserved anonymity and allowed one to protest without taking personal risks. The NUL and NAACP's
middle-class standing consequently served as a barrier to fuller support of and
participation in the union's protest activities.[24]

*   *   *

Despite the newfound support of allies such as the NAACP and NUL, the Giumarra boycott in New York was not as successful as UFWOC organizers had hoped. A few weeks after arriving in New York, Ross and Huerta discovered that the reason the boycott was progressing so slowly was that consumers were having difficulty identifying Giumarra grapes. The union's earlier targets were processors, or companies that used grapes to make other products such as wine, but Giumarra grew table grapes whose brands were not household names. Furthermore, Giumarra had obtained the labels of seventy other growers and affixed them to their crates, which compounded the problem of identifying Giumarra table grapes. Ross and Huerta realized that as long as consumers could not tell the difference between Giumarra grapes and other grapes whose labels it was using, a boycott specifically against Giumarra would fail. They called Chavez in late January 1968 and advised him that the UFWOC should organize a boycott of all California grapes. Chavez agreed and later explained, "It was the only way we could do it—take on the whole industry. The grape itself had to become the label."[25]

When it was decided that all California table grapes, regardless of the grower, would be the target of the boycott, most of the farmworkers and volunteers in New York were dispatched to Boston, Chicago, Detroit, and Los Angeles, all cities that were large markets for California grapes. Farm workers and volunteers were also sent from Delano to help organize the boycott in other cities. As in New York, interacting with the farmworkers created personal connections that enabled the UFWOC to obtain support from people who were geographically distant from the fields of California and had little knowledge of Mexican Americans. For example, the farmworkers who went to organize the boycott in Pittsburgh were some of the first Mexican Americans that many residents had met. A supporter of the boycott in Pittsburgh later noted that he enjoyed getting to know the farmworkers and their families, who joined them in the boycott cities. He recalled, "It made the issues very human to me. It was not just a theoretical thing or just somebody's job or anything. It really felt good to be part of this family's effort to marshal interest and support for them and the people they were advocating for."[26]

The nationwide spread of the grape boycott escalated the involvement of the NUL. The League's support for the farmworkers was rooted in its faith in organized labor. From early in the organization's history, the leadership of the NUL saw organized labor as a vehicle to improve both the lives of African American workers and race relations more generally. The NUL maintained its confidence in organized labor, despite its frequent discrimination against African American workers. For example, although the American Federation of Labor claimed to have a policy of nondiscrimination, its locals often excluded African Americans. However, since the AFL controlled access to jobs in closed shops, in which employment was contingent upon union membership, the NUL believed that it was worthwhile to pursue a relationship with the AFL. At its 1918 conference on the "Negro in Industry," the NUL officially encouraged its members to affiliate with the AFL, while it passed resolutions urging the AFL to treat African American workers equally. The League also established an alliance with the CIO—which actively attempted to enlist black participation—on its founding in 1935. Whitney Young's support for the AFL-CIO-affiliated UFWOC therefore invigorated the Urban League's historic relationship with the labor movement and was part of his own attempts to create a bridge between organized labor and the civil rights movement.[27]

Supporting the UFWOC also gave Young the opportunity to come to the defense of organized labor, which had come under intense scrutiny and criticism by the late the 1960s for red-baiting, endorsing the war in Vietnam, and discriminatory practices. Furthermore, some civil rights organizations, such as SNCC, had come to believe that the labor movement was not sincere in its support for racial equality. To Young, however, the support of the farmworkers by the AFL-CIO and its member unions—especially the UAW, the International Longshore and Warehouse Union, and the SIU—was evidence of organized labor's commitment to the fight for equality. In December 1968, he wrote in "To Be Equal . . . ,"

> I believe that, when we look at the whole picture, labor is strongly
> on the side of social justice and equal rights. . . . Organized
> labor has backed the strike of the California farm workers,
> predominantly Mexican-Americans suffering from the same
> discrimination blacks know so well. . . . It's just too glib to talk
> about union discrimination and anti-civil rights activity without
> taking into account the fact that just the reverse is true for the
> mainstream of the labor movement.

Supporting the UFWOC boycott of Giumarra grapes therefore enabled Young and the NUL to work alongside organized labor to refute the criticism directed at it.[28]

The nationwide expansion of the grape boycott also increased the West Coast NAACP's activities on behalf of the farmworkers. The alliance between the West Coast NAACP and the UFWOC was yet another example of the regional association's coalitions with Mexican Americans based on common interests. In April 1968, members of the NAACP and the UFWOC joined together to picket a fundraising dinner in Fresno, California for Congressman Bernice "Bernie" Sisk, who opposed the fair housing section of the 1968 Civil Rights Act and prevented it from being voted upon by the House of Representatives by delaying it in the House Rules Committee for three weeks. Sisk represented Fresno and Madera counties in California's Central Valley and had sided with growers in labor disputes, defending their practice of importing Mexican green card workers to serve as strikebreakers. The UFWOC editorialized in *El Malcriado*, "Sisk's vote against Civil Rights is not inconsistent with the vicious campaign he has waged against the poor people and Mexican-Americans in California. . . . His latest vote against the civil rights bill is one more proof that he is an enemy of the Negroes and Mexican Americans and poor people."[29]

The shared concerns of the NAACP and UFWOC prompted Leonard Carter to pursue a meeting with Chavez "to extend the fullest possible support" to the UFWOC. On July 24–25, 1968, Carter traveled to Delano with NAACP staff members to meet with Chavez. Carter also arranged for a press conference and photo session to inform the public of the organization's support because he understood that the NAACP's national prominence would be beneficial to the union and boycott. At the press conference concluding the meeting, Carter explained that the NAACP's unequivocal support for the UFWOC was due to the fact that both African Americans and Mexican Americans experienced racial discrimination and economic exploitation, especially the members of both groups who were agricultural laborers. Furthermore, Carter felt that the NAACP's historic role in fighting discrimination made it well-suited to challenge the forces in agribusiness and government that were keeping the farm workers oppressed. He remarked,

> Fifty-nine years ago the NAACP started its long battle against racial discrimination. Manifestations of racism have been exhibited most dramatically in the area of economic exploitation. Twentieth century quasi-slavery of farm workers in the South and North is a contributing factor to the plight of the California farm worker today.[30]

Figure 7. Cesar Chavez with Leonard H. Carter, NAACP West Coast regional director, Delano, California, July 25, 1968. Courtesy of Walter P. Reuther Library, Wayne State University.

Following the press conference, Carter directed the 104 branches and nineteen youth chapters of the West Coast NAACP to support the union by boycotting California grapes, donating food to the striking farmworkers, distributing leaflets and posters in favor of the boycott, conducting meetings with civic leaders and other organizations, and assisting the farmworkers sent to West Coast cities to organize the grape boycott. West Coast NAACP branches eagerly obeyed Carter's directive. For example, members of the Portland, Oregon and Mt. Angel College chapters were arrested and jailed on Thanksgiving 1968 for picketing grocery stores that sold California grapes. A member of the Mt. Angel College chapter fasted for two weeks to gain publicity for the grape boycott. These actions were not without consequences for the association; the newly reformed NAACP branch in Delano, the center of strike activity, faced harassment and reprisals from the growers and their allies because of its support of the boycott, but the president of the branch assured field director Virna Canson that they were "holding their own."[31]

Working with the NAACP among the racial and ethnic diversity of the West Coast had led Carter to appreciate that other minorities experienced similar employment discrimination to African Americans. He also understood that farmworkers were of diverse racial and ethnic backgrounds and that the activities of the predominantly Mexican American UFWOC would ultimately benefit them all. During the NAACP's press conference in Delano, he reminded his audience, "Every minority in California is included among the farm workers. Some fifteen to twenty percent of them are Negroes." Carter therefore recognized that assisting the union and participating in the California grape boycott was ultimately beneficial to African Americans. He also believed that supporting the UFWOC aided the plight of African Americans in urban areas. He explained at the press conference in Delano, "Many families have been driven from the lands by this exploitation. They have come to the cities—the ghetto with its degradation and despair. Thus the impact of our efforts to join with our brothers in the United Farm Workers Committee in their efforts toward equality will surely be felt in the cities."[32]

Carter's view of the potential urban benefits to the union's success was identical to that of Chavez. In an interview with Peter Matthiessen, Chavez reflected,

> As one looks at the millions of acres in this country that have been taken out of agricultural production . . . and at the millions of additional acres that have never been cultivated; and at the millions of people who have moved off the farm to rot and decay in ghettos of our big cities; and at all the millions of hungry people at home and abroad—does it not seem that all these people and things were somehow made to come together and serve one another?

Chavez's solution was to relocate the urban poor onto surplus land, where they would be taught to farm. Carter and Chavez both believed that the success of the UFWOC in gaining higher pay and better working conditions would stem the migration of the rural poor to already overcrowded inner cities. Thus, both leaders recognized that the importance of the grape boycott to both Mexican Americans and African Americans surpassed its relevance to agricultural workers.[33]

Carter informed the national NAACP leadership of his regional branches' support of the grape boycott and the press coverage it received. Although the West Coast NAACP actively supported the UFWOC, Carter had to continuously urge the national leadership of the NAACP to demonstrate the association's support for the farmworkers. In a letter to Wilkins and Gloster Current, the NAACP director of branches, Carter implored,

> I would like for you to give consideration of having the National Board of Directors formally adopt a statement of support to Cesar Chavez and the farm workers and more importantly endorse the grape boycott. Mr. Chavez is a truly outstanding man who merits the fullest possible support in this endeavor from across the nation.

However, no such statement ever came from the national office of the NAACP. Furthermore, the NAACP national magazine, *The Crisis*, did not include any mention of the UFWOC grape boycott or the association's participation in it. The June–July 1968 issue mentioned in its regular "Freedom Notes" column, which cited the activities of NAACP branches, that the Scituate, Massachusetts branch enclosed pre-addressed postcards to Giumarra in its newsletter for members to sign and mail in protest of the company's treatment of its workers. However, the article curiously failed to mention the UFWOC or the grape boycott. *The Crisis* also never reported on Carter's meeting with Chavez or the support activities of the West Coast branches. The NAACP's involvement with the UFWOC was therefore due to Carter's role as bridge leader rather than the actions of the national leadership.[34]

Unlike Carter and the West Coast Regional NAACP, the national NAACP office and some branches on the East Coast did not recognize their common interests with the UFWOC. In addition to its reliance on corporate donations, the NAACP had a complicated relationship with organized labor that affected its attitude toward the UFWOC. Like other civil rights organizations, the leaders of the NAACP were convinced that allying with labor was necessary to pressure the federal government to act in matters of racial equality. At the same time, the NAACP used its legal apparatus to challenge racial discrimination in unions. During the 1930s and 1940s, the NAACP used New Deal legislation and the Fair Employment Practices Commission (FEPC) to demand that federal protection only be given to unions that did not discriminate based on race. After the passage of the 1964 Civil Rights Act, the NAACP filed thousands of complaints against discriminatory unions with the Equal Employment Opportunity Commission (EEOC) under Title VII. The NAACP was also vocal in its criticism of racism within organized labor. In 1961 NAACP Labor Secretary Herbert Hill drew the wrath of the

AFL-CIO for publishing a report entitled, "Racism Within Organized Labor, 1955–1960," which condemned labor for failing to eliminate discrimination in unions. Supporting the UFWOC, which was affiliated with the AFL-CIO but lacked power to influence the federal government, was thus unappealing to the national leadership of the NAACP.[35]

The NAACP's strained relationship with organized labor and the national leadership's disinterest in the UFWOC led to missed opportunities for coalition building between the two organizations. A striking example is the New York State NAACP's program to provide social services to African American migrant farmworkers in Wayne County, an apple-producing region between Rochester and Syracuse in upstate New York, in the midst of the California grape boycott. Members of the New York City NAACP branch volunteered their time to the program, dubbed "THRESH" (Transportation, Health, Registration, Education, Social Services, and Housing), in July–October 1968. In describing the issues confronting the migrant farmworkers, *The Crisis* noted that "the living conditions of these families, mostly southern-born, have been described as 'appalling,' 'intolerable,' 'sickening,' and worse," but did not mention their striking similarities to the highly publicized living conditions of Mexican American farmworkers in California. The volunteers and leaders of THRESH also did not reach out to the UFWOC farmworkers and volunteers who were organizing the grape boycott in upstate New York and who had obtained the endorsement of the mayor of nearby Rochester.[36]

The inability of the New York NAACP to make connections with the UFWOC around the plight of agricultural workers indicates that geography, class, and organizational ideology and praxis combined to inhibit the possibility of forming multiracial coalitions. Unlike the NAACP branches on the West Coast, who were intimately familiar with the oppression of Mexican Americans, the New York NAACP did not act on the relevance of the UFWOC's activities to African Americans. Moreover, the THRESH program volunteers, many of whom were professional social workers, sought to improve migrant workers' living conditions without addressing growers' exploitation of those same workers, which was at odds with the strategy and objectives of the UFWOC. The THRESH program illustrated both the NAACP's middle-class predisposition toward philanthropy—based on W. E. B. Du Bois's early twentieth-century belief that the top 10 percent of the black community should work to uplift the less fortunate—and aversion to organized labor. This was incompatible with the UFWOC aim for the farmworkers themselves to organize and obtain union recognition in order to improve their situation. The potential for an alliance between the New York NAACP and the UFWOC was therefore limited.[37]

*   *   *

Although the UFWOC boycott of California grapes had attracted consider-able attention nationwide, gained the union new allies, and resulted in sig-nificant financial losses for the grape industry, California growers persisted in denying union representation for the farmworkers. Therefore, in early 1969 Fred Ross decided that the UFWOC should also conduct a secondary boycott of the Safeway grocery store chain, which was the largest buyer of California grapes next to the U.S. Department of Defense; Safeway annu-ally bought grapes from Giumarra totaling one million dollars in sales. In addition, most of Safeway's directors served as the heads of large agribusi-ness corporations. UFWOC leaders also believed that a boycott of Safeway would serve to galvanize racial minority groups. As the union was prepar-ing to embark on the boycott, Chavez wrote to Robert Magowan, CEO of Safeway Stores, Inc., "Blacks, Filipinos, and members of all minorities will express their solidarity against all oppression by joining their neighbors in supermarkets other than Safeway."[38]

The Urban League's Whitney Young continued to support the UFWOC when it began its boycott of Safeway stores. On May 14, 1969, Young met with Chavez and the UFWOC Executive Committee in Delano, who educated him on the issues of the grape strike and the role of Safeway stores. Young was particularly struck by the dangerous and unsanitary working conditions and the plight of child laborers. Two days later he wrote a lengthy, impassioned letter to Magowan, who had supported the NUL in the past and who Young considered to be "a personal friend." Despite his relationship with Magowan, Young felt compelled to express his dismay over Safeway's involvement in the oppression of the farmworkers: "I was deeply depressed by what I actually saw, in terms of working and living conditions for these people; and I was not aware until then of the key role which Safeway now plays in the resolution of this problem." Magowan responded that he felt that Safeway was stuck in the middle of the dispute between the growers and the farmworkers and that customers should be able to decide whether to purchase grapes. Magowan at-tempted to sound neutral, but he admitted, "We think the secondary boycott is an evil weapon." In light of Magowan's response and his history of supporting the NUL, Young neither discussed the Safeway boycott publicly nor directed League members to participate in it.[39]

In his syndicated column on the grape strike and his visit with Chavez, Young revealed the tension inherent in balancing the NUL's tradition of support for organized labor and cultivation of positive relationships with industry. He explained in sympathetic terms the farmworkers' poor working conditions and the reasons for the strike. Young championed the right of workers to organize and compared the farmworkers' struggle to that of African American hospital workers who were at that time on strike in Charleston, South Carolina. He also continued to emphasize the potential of the grape strike in enhancing the reputation of the labor movement:

> But beyond the needs of justice and fair play, perhaps the most significant aspect of these strikes is the opportunity they provide for the labor movement to regain its crusading role. The AFL-CIO and other unions have supported Cesar Chavez, and they have backed other organizing efforts, too. Labor, by organizing the poor and friendless, can help end poverty by protecting low-wage workers, and it can give the lie to those who so happily proclaim the selfishness and prejudice of some unions.

Young also informed his readers, "I haven't bought California grapes since the boycott started, and millions of other Americans have refused to buy them, too." As this statement reveals, Young's support of the boycott was cautious, falling short of explicitly directing his readers to boycott grapes. He then hinted, "Many concerned people are putting pressure on their local supermarkets to bar these grapes until the union is recognized." He did not, however, mention Safeway. Young's determination to maintain the historic relationship between the business community and the NUL hampered the organization's support for the UFWOC. This demonstrates the compromises the NUL was forced to make in exchange for the patronage of the white elite; the corporations and foundations upon which the League relied for financial support wielded tremendous influence over Young and the NUL's programs, often at the expense of African Americans and workers.[40]

The West Coast Regional NAACP was much more supportive of the UFWOC's secondary boycott of Safeway grocery stores. The region's newsletter promptly educated its members on the issues behind the boycott and directed all branches "to continue to support the grape boycott and *withdraw your patronage from Safeway stores*, until they discontinue handling grapes that are picked by strike breakers." The branches promptly complied and publicized their actions in support of both boycotts in their own newsletters and press releases. For example, UFWOC assistant director Philip Vera Cruz was guest speaker at the NAACP Northwest Area Conference in Klamath Falls, Oregon, in May 1969. Conference attendees passed a resolution that reaffirmed their support for the grape boycott and declared that they would henceforth refuse "to shop at Safeway Stores until the strike and boycott of table grapes has been successfully resolved by the United Farm Workers Organizing Committee, AFL-CIO."[41]

In explaining why its members should boycott California grapes and Safeway stores, the NAACP branches on the West Coast cited the connections between African Americans and Mexican Americans. The Tucson, Arizona branch was particularly cognizant of these links because the UFWOC had begun to organize farmworkers—including African American migrant workers—in the area. Therefore, in addition to publishing regular boycott updates, the branch's newsletter discussed the relevance of the farmworkers' struggles to African Americans. For example, the Tucson NAACP newsletter editorialized in May 1969,

> Why do we support the struggle of some farm workers in
> California when we have our own jobs and our own lives to
> consider? Perhaps, that's just the reason. Our own jobs and our
> own lives aren't really too secure as long as America's farm workers
> are being paid starvation wages and forced to live in sub-human
> surroundings because they are powerless. Or perhaps we really do
> care about them because they are human beings.

The members of the Tucson branch recognized that the discrimination and exploitation suffered by Mexican American farmworkers could easily be directed at African Americans and that supporting the UFWOC was therefore necessary. Furthermore, according to the 1970 census, African Americans were 3.5 percent of the population of Tucson, and Hispanics 23.1 percent. The formation of alliances between African Americans and Mexican Americans was therefore a practical strategy in the pursuit of civil rights in Arizona and other parts of the West.[42]

NAACP branches in the West were also impressed that the UFWOC sought to organize all farmworkers, regardless of race. To counter NAACP members' perceptions of labor unions as exclusionary of African American workers, the Tucson branch newsletter reminded its readers, "UFWOC, the farmworkers' union, is one union that *does not discriminate* against black members." For many NAACP members, this was sufficient reason to support the union. A member of the Palo Alto, California branch wrote, "Cesar Chavez has always resisted the temptation to limit the benefits to his own people. The Farm Workers' newsletter, *El Malcriado*, frequently stresses the brotherhood of workers . . . NAACP members should be supporting their brothers." Participating in the grape and Safeway boycotts therefore became a way for NAACP members to encourage nondiscrimination and multiracial cooperation in the labor movement.[43]

NAACP branches in the West also recognized that participation in the grape and Safeway boycotts provided a vehicle for the formation of multiracial coalitions around other civil rights issues. For example, in 1969 judge Jerald S. Chargin of the Superior Court of San Jose, California, made racist statements against Mexican American defendants, including referring to them as "animals," and declaring, "maybe Hitler was right," prompting protests from Latino organizations. Leonard Carter pledged the West Coast NAACP's support and worked to remove Chargin from the bench. Following protests from Mexican American and civil rights organizations, Chargin was publicly censured and resigned his seat.[44]

The national office of the NAACP, however, remained deeply uncomfortable with participating in boycotts, especially those directed against businesses. The national office required all branches and youth councils to obtain advanced written permission to participate in a boycott from the association's legal office. However, reflecting the tension within the organizational structure of the association, branches frequently engaged in boycotts of their own accord. This prompted Roy Wilkins to remind all NAACP members,

> A favorite device is the coalition, consisting of several organizations, most of which have good goals, but no assets. Usually, the NAACP Branch or Youth group is the only organization of standing, with a national organization—and a national treasury—to back it up. Our local Branches and Youth groups should not allow themselves to be sucked into coalitions which are formed to press a boycott campaign.

Wilkins had denied the West Coast NAACP permission to participate in the UFWOC boycott of Schenley Industries in 1965–1966 because of the national NAACP office's stance against boycotts and coalitions. However, the groundswell of support for the grape and Safeway boycotts among NAACP members forced the association's leadership to condone the union's protests. Statements of support for the UFWOC were therefore among the resolutions passed at the NAACP's national convention in July 1969: "WHEREAS, many branches of the National Association for the Advancement of Colored People have actively supported the grape boycott, NOW THEREFORE BE IT RESOLVED, that the NAACP reaffirm its full support of the boycott." All association members were also encouraged to participate in boycotts of stores, including Safeway, which sold California grapes.[45]

The NAACP resolution in support of the UFWOC, however, was largely an empty gesture. NAACP members nationwide continued to participate in the union's boycotts. The involvement of some branches outside of the West also increased, most notably the Detroit branch, whose president was also president of the local AFL-CIO, and the Pittsburgh branch, where local grape boycott committee member Jim McCoy was an officer in both the NAACP and the United Steelworkers. However, no mention was made of these actions—or of the grape and Safeway boycotts—in *The Crisis* in 1969. And although the conference resolution stated that NAACP members nationwide were participating in these boycotts, the NAACP's annual report for 1969 claimed that only the West Coast branches were supporting the farmworkers. Furthermore, aside from the conference resolutions, the national leadership did not issue any public statements in support of the UFWOC. It is therefore apparent that, despite the popularity of the farmworkers' struggle among the NAACP members, the more conservative national leadership remained uncomfortable with participating in their fight and uninterested in forming multiracial coalitions.[46]

*   *   *

The UFWOC's boycott of California grapes and Safeway grocery stores also attracted the attention of the Black Panther Party, which differed fundamentally from the Urban League and the NAACP in its approach toward multiracial coalitions and therefore in its relationship with the farmworkers. The

UFWOC and the BPP appeared to be unlikely allies; the BPP was African American, militant, urban, and socialist and therefore differed in nearly every way from the largely Mexican American, nonviolent, rural, and Catholic UFWOC. But despite their differences, Chavez and the farmworkers welcomed the support of the Party and its leaders, and supported them in turn, beginning in 1968. Over the years, the two organizations came together because they saw each other as commonly oppressed victims of the ruling class. It was this willingness and ability to find class-based commonalities across racial lines that enabled the UFWOC and the BPP to form a successful, mutually beneficial alliance that exceeded the union's coalitions with the NUL and the NAACP.

The BPP was founded in Oakland, California in October 1966 by Bobby Seale and Huey Newton in an effort to confront police brutality in that city. Soon after the Party's founding, its leaders expanded its aims to include issues of poverty, employment, education, housing, and legal rights. From its inception, the Party addressed these issues on behalf of all oppressed groups, not just African Americans, and advocated multiracial solidarity. This stemmed from the BPP's socialist ideology that class, not race, was what defined a group and its concerns. Seale explained the BPP's objectives in his 1970 memoir, *Seize the Time: The Story of the Black Panther Party and Huey P. Newton*: "In our view it is a class struggle between the massive proletarian working class and the small, minority ruling class. Working-class people of all colors must unite against the exploitative, oppressive ruling class . . . .We believe our fight is a class struggle and not a race struggle." Therefore, the Party formed alliances with several progressive organizations, regardless of race, including the Young Lords, a Puerto Rican nationalist organization; the Young Patriots, a group of young, white Appalachian migrants in Chicago; and the Red Guard, a radical Chinese organization based in San Francisco's Chinatown. The BPP formed these coalitions because they recognized early on that they could not combat the power structure on their own and that camaraderie across racial lines was imperative for obtaining justice and equality. Seale explained, "Racism and ethnic differences allow the power structure to exploit the masses of workers in this country, because that's the key by which they maintain their control."[47]

Like the San Francisco SNCC office, the BPP was motivated to pursue multiracial solidarity and coalitions due to the racial and ethnic diversity of the Bay Area. Party members in Oakland grew up around Latinos, Asian Americans, and American Indians who shared their experiences of police brutality, unequal education, and discrimination in housing and employment. Oakland Panthers' lifelong cross-racial interactions, relationships, and friendships shaped the Party's development. Oakland's multiracial milieu led the Party to prefer coalition building as a more practical and desirable strategy than the racial separatism called for by other advocates of Black Power elsewhere in the United States. BPP Chief of Staff David Hilliard later reflected on the diversity of Oakland,

> It is a misnomer to talk about the "black community" because the black community is a multicultural mix of Asian and Latinos and white people, gays, seniors, etc. . . . That's why we were so involved in the politics of coalition—unlike the North or the South where it was pronounced segregation, it was a bit different here in the 1960s.

Historian Robert Self also points out that "African Americans in the East Bay spoke of the 'white power structure' and 'the people' or 'the community' more often than they spoke of 'black power.' Their language was equally filled with references to 'rights,' 'revolutionary struggle,' 'colonialism,' 'liberation,' 'control,' and 'the poor,' among others." The Party's slogan of "all power to the people" reflected the inclusiveness and emphasis on multiracial solidarity typical of the black freedom struggle in the Bay Area.[48]

Although Chavez and the UFWOC practiced nonviolence and enjoyed close ties to the Democratic Party and the Kennedy family, the BPP sympathized with the farmworkers' struggle against exploitation. Members of the BPP participated in rallies in support of the striking farmworkers at the nearby University of California, Berkeley. In October 1968 the first article on the grape boycott appeared in the Black Panther, the organization's weekly newspaper, which was distributed throughout the country and internationally. The Party leadership viewed its newspaper as an educational tool essential to raising the political consciousness of the community. They explained, "The consistent reporting of all news and information relevant to the interests of Black people, workers, oppressed peoples, youth and the aged provides readers with a built-in interpretation of the news that is in their interests and consequently raises their understanding of the nature and condition of our society." Therefore, the BPP sought not only to inform, but to educate its readers about the farmworkers' issues and their political and economic connections to other groups victimized by economic and racial oppression. After the publication of the first article on the

Figure 8. Black Panther Ducho Dennis with UFWOC members Dan Martínez and Joaquin Ramirez, Delano, California, 1968. Courtesy of It's About Time: Black Panther Legacy & Alumni, http://www.itsabouttimebpp.com.

UFWOC, the *Black Panther* kept its readers informed about the progress of the boycott with regular updates.[49]

In addition to the multiracial character of the Bay Area, the BPP support stemmed from the rural backgrounds of its members. Many members of the BPP in California, including founders Newton and Seale, had migrated from the rural South as children with their families; others were descendants of migrants. Historian Donna Murch argues that "for West Coast migrants, less than a generation removed from southern agrarian struggles, Maoism and land-based insurgencies held a special appeal." *La causa* therefore resonated with the BPP because its members could relate to the struggles of rural agricultural workers.[50]

Other southern migrants to the Bay Area were skilled craftsmen who supported and joined industrial unions. The migrants' history of labor activism infiltrated the BPP. For example, Panthers in Detroit belonged to the Dodge Revolutionary Union Movement (DRUM) and Ford Revolutionary Union Movement (FRUM), radical organizations of black workers that fought racism in both the auto industry and the UAW. Panther Kenny Horston organized a Black Panther Caucus at the General Motors plant in Fremont, California, thirty miles south of Oakland. These activities were in keeping with the Marxist philosophy of the BPP because the leaders conceived of the Panthers—and the larger black community—as workers. This sense of working-class identity and tradition of labor activism further strengthened the Party's relationship with the UFWOC. In 1968, for example, Panthers Ducho Dennis and Wilbert Poe, who were also municipal bus drivers, visited Delano to demonstrate solidarity with the farmworkers on behalf of both the BPP and fellow union members.[51]

The leadership group of the BPP, known as the Central Committee, spearheaded the organization's support for the UFWOC. One of the Central Committee's first actions in support of the farmworkers was to ban the consumption of "Bitter Dog," the official drink of the BPP. Bitter Dog was made by pouring filtered lemon juice into Italian Swiss Colony red wine and refrigerating it; it was the favorite drink of Bobby Hutton, the first Party recruit. After Hutton was gunned down by Oakland police in April 1968, Panthers nationwide drank Bitter Dog to honor his memory. In late 1968, the Central Committee declared that Panthers were no longer to drink Bitter Dog "out of solidarity with the farmworkers." The hundreds of Panthers nationwide immediately stopped drinking what had been the official drink of the Party because, as Panther Bill Jennings explained, "You don't challenge stuff that comes out of the Central Committee. That's law." In December 1968, Minister of Information Eldridge Cleaver gave a speech at the Berkeley Community Center in which he voiced his support for the striking farmworkers and explained the ban on Bitter Dog:

> We used to get that Italian Swiss Colony Wine, put lemon juice off into that and dig it. But from now on, we're not drinking any more of that because DiGiorgio is fucking over our brothers, the Mexican Americans with those grapes, and that's all being done for the Bank of America and Mayor Alioto—that's the Mafia: (1) The Italian Mafia—Al Capone powers; (2) the Irish Mafia— machine gun Kelley.

The flamboyant Cleaver admitted at the beginning of his speech that he was high (a violation of Party rules), but it is unknown whether sober he was aware that the UFWOC had ended its boycott of DiGiorgio more than two years prior, before the BPP was even founded, and that the current boycott was against California table grapes. Regardless, it is significant that the Party leadership saw the need to take a firm stand in support of the farmworkers. Furthermore, in referring to the Mexican American farmworkers as the Panthers' "brothers," Cleaver expressed the Party's position that "to be progressive was to be beyond nationalism."[52]

The BPP's support for the UFWOC escalated when the union announced its boycott of Safeway grocery stores because the Party had reasons of its own for taking action against the company. In announcing the boycott in the *Black Panther* newspaper, the leaders emphasized that Safeway stores had consistently refused to donate food to its Free Breakfast for Children Program. Developed by Bobby Seale and others in October 1968, the Free Breakfast for Children Program was launched at St. Augustine's Episcopal Church in Oakland in January 1969, and was used to combat academic underachievement among poor, hungry children. The program, which eventually provided a hot, nutritious breakfast to 20,000 school-aged children in nineteen cities, depended on the donations of local stores and businesses. Store owners and managers were asked to donate food or money to support the children's breakfast program. In order to secure donations, Party members sometimes put pressure on store owners through tactics of harassment and intimidation. The *Black Panther* newspaper listed the names of the stores whose owners refused to make donations, and readers were urged to boycott those businesses. Due to the repercussions of not complying, numerous grocery stores donated food and money to the Free Breakfast for Children Program, but all Safeway grocery stores refused. As the largest grocery store chain in the West, and the second largest in the country, Safeway was not as vulnerable to pressure by the BPP as small, local stores. When the BPP found in Safeway a common enemy with the UFWOC, the Party became one of the most vocal supporters of the union's boycott. The *Black Panther* contained regular reminders for its readers to support the farmworkers: "The Black Panther Party urges all consumers to support the farmworkers' boycott and to do everything possible to bring victory to them in their struggle for survival here in fascist America." But Panthers supported the UFWOC with both their words and their bodies; when union organizers planned to picket a Safeway store or hold a press conference, they would call the local BPP office and the "officer of the day," who administrated activity at the Party office, would then dispatch however many Panthers were requested to assist the farmworkers.[53]

The BPP boycott of Safeway stores was a tremendous contribution to the UFWOC boycott efforts. When the Panthers set up pickets at Safeway stores, they were an intimidating presence. UFWOC organizer Gilbert Padilla recalled that when he organized the grape boycott in the Los Angeles area, Panthers on the picket line deterred police harassment because the Panthers "scared the hell out of them." Organizer Rudy Reyes similarly recalled that the UFWOC occasionally used the intimidating image of the Panthers to their advantage. When calling Los Angeles grocery stores to ask them not to stock grapes, an organizer might say to a store manager following a shop-in, "We know where your other stores are, and we have lots of supporters, so tell your general manager what happened at your store. In fact we have a hard time asking our friends, the Black Panthers, to keep it cool. But you'll be cooperating with us, right, sir?"[54]

The Panthers contributed to *la causa* in more substantial ways than intimidation. The Party's boycott of Safeway was well organized and innovative. Seale, like many other Panthers, had served in the military. Drawing on his experience in the United States Air Force motor pool, Seale created a motor pool for Party use which was employed in the Safeway boycott. In the evenings when people went grocery shopping after work, Party members would not only explain to shoppers why they should not shop at Safeway, but they also took the boycott a step farther by providing transportation to Lucky's grocery stores, which donated to the Free Breakfast for Children Program and had agreed not to sell California grapes. Seale explained,

> In the evening we'd get the kids who lived in the community to come get in the picket line and when people would come walk into the store, we'd say, "Lucky supermarket donates to the Black Panther Party Free Breakfast for Children Program. And therefore we would like you to go to Lucky stores to do your shopping. . . . We have cars here. We will drive you to the Lucky store and drive you home."

By using the motor pool to aid in the UFWOC-BPP boycott, the Safeway across the street from St. Augustine's at 27th and West Streets in Oakland was quickly shut down.[55]

The Panthers' support for the UFWOC was not limited to its activities in California. When Gilbert Padilla conducted boycott activities in Philadelphia, the Panthers "had an open door for us." In fact, Padilla believed that the Party was supportive of the UFWOC nationally. "I [sought] them [out] whenever I went somewhere. I looked for them." UFWOC organizer Eliseo

Medina worked with Fred Hampton and the Panthers in Chicago. The Party's widespread support for the UFWOC was reciprocated when the BPP was the victim of a series of beatings, murders, and raids by law enforcement. In the late 1960s the FBI had unleashed COINTELPRO—a counterintelligence program aimed at destroying African American civil rights and progressive leaders and organizations—on the BPP. As a part of COINTELPRO, FBI agents infiltrated the Party, many Panthers were murdered, and even more were imprisoned. Following the murders of Chicago Party leaders Fred Hampton and Mark Clark in their apartment in a pre-dawn attack by Chicago police on December 4, 1969, and the violent raids on BPP offices in Los Angeles four days later, the UFWOC took decisive steps to help defend the Panthers against such attacks, while still utilizing nonviolent tactics. Two weeks after the murders of Hampton and Clark, the UFWOC began discussions with the BPP on how they could be of service. A UFWOC spokesman explained, "We felt it was not just enough to pass a resolution saying that what happened in Chicago and Los Angeles was not right. We discussed ways and means of making our bodies available to place between the police and Panthers."[56]

UFWOC boycott committees in the Pacific Northwest were particularly willing to come to the defense of the BPP chapters in the region, with whom they had developed close and productive relationships. In January 1970, the Portland, Oregon boycott committee announced, "The United Farm Workers four weeks ago voted unanimously to support the Black Panther Party in an effort to stop the killing and jailing of Panther members." In Seattle, Washington UFWOC members participated in a rally in defense of the Party after it was revealed that the Alcohol, Tobacco and Firearms Division of the U.S. Treasury Department asked Seattle Mayor Wes Uhlman for permission to raid the Party office. Uhlman, however, refused and prevented the raid. He recalled that the Panthers "did have some guns, but they did not pose a threat to anyone in this city." In fact, the Seattle Panthers were highly regarded in the city because of their community survival programs, which included a food bank, a Free Breakfast for Children Program that served 2,000 children per day, and a tremendously successful medical clinic. Following a local reporter's revelation of the aborted ATF raid, a massive rally was held on February 28, 1970 to demonstrate support for the Panthers. A UFWOC representative at the rally proclaimed, "We will not sit in silence while the enormous fire power of government is used in attempt to annihilate a group of Black People who have felt the same sting of racism, job discrimination, and exclusion that we have felt."[57]

The UFWOC's support of the BPP caused no small amount of disagreement, both inside and outside of the union. Some farmworkers did not agree with the union's declarations of solidarity with an organization that did not follow the philosophy of nonviolence. Other unions that did not support the Panthers were also concerned about the UFWOC's position. For example, a representative of the local of the International Woodworkers of America in Klamath Falls, Oregon, wrote to Cesar Chavez requesting that he clarify the UFWOC's position on the Party. In response, Chavez reasserted the solidarity between the farmworkers and the Panthers and replied, "We may not agree with the philosophy of the Black Panther Party, but they are our brothers, and non-violence extends to standing up for whomever is being persecuted."[58]

That Chavez considered the Panthers to be the "brothers" of the farmworkers reveals that, despite their differences, the UFWOC and the BPP saw each other as partners in the struggle. The farmworkers and the Panthers had successfully crossed racial lines to form a coalition based on the alignment of their interests. This coalition was also facilitated by the Party's socialist philosophy and working-class identity, which positioned the farmworkers as victims of the same capitalist forces that had exploited African Americans. In turn, the strong feeling of class solidarity caused the UFWOC to come to the aid of the BPP when it was under attack by law enforcement, creating a multiracial coalition that was truly mutually beneficial.

*   *   *

The support of the grape boycott from the UFWOC allies in the black freedom struggle—including the NAACP, the NUL, and the BPP—kept the farmworkers in the national spotlight and put constant pressure on the grape growers. The participation of civil rights organizations in urban centers such as Chicago, New York, Detroit, Pittsburgh, Seattle, Tucson, and Oakland ensured that the farmworkers' struggle was not confined to the farming communities of California. The constant pressure by these civil rights organizations, together with other supporters of the UFWOC, nationwide took a mounting toll on California's table grape growers. Furthermore, the UFWOC's secondary boycotts of grocery stores that sold California grapes—in which the involvement of civil rights organizations was instrumental—was the most damaging tactic and the one that proved to be the final straw for the growers.

On April 1, 1970, David Friedman Company in Coachella, California, became the first table grape grower to sign a contract with the union. Gradually other grape growers followed suit. On July 29, Giumarra and twenty-five other table grape growers arrived at UFWOC headquarters and signed contracts. The day after the UFWOC signed contracts with the grape growers, Leonard Carter sent Chavez a telegram:

> Congratulations to you of United Farm Workers Organizing Committee upon your great victory in organizing most farm workers in California. It will be good to eat grapes again. The NAACP renews its support to your organization in its continued struggle to represent and improve economic conditions of all farm workers.[59]

Although the NAACP, NUL, and BPP all contributed to the UFWOC victory, their level of support varied according to class orientation, historic relationship with organized labor, and knowledge of Mexican Americans due to geographic proximity. The middle-class leadership of the NUL and the NAACP supported the UFWOC based on their pursuit of employment equality, but their support for the farmworkers was limited because of their own financial ties to corporations and reluctance to engage in direct action. The activities of these organizations were therefore restrained—limited to letter-writing campaigns and boycotting grapes. However, place played a significant role in multiracial cooperation, as the West Coast NAACP sought to aid the UFWOC based on its familiarity with Mexican Americans' experiences with discrimination. Moreover, the bridge leadership of Carter facilitated the regional association's relationship with the UFWOC. Accordingly, their support ranged from writing letters and passing resolutions to nonviolent direct action. However, the national leadership of the thoroughly bureaucratic NAACP limited the effectiveness of its West Coast branches. Of these three organizations, the BPP gave the most substantial support to the farmworkers. The Party supported the UFWOC because of its belief in multiracial equality and cooperation that was the product of its working-class orientation and base in California. The Party was consequently not content to write letters of protest (and in fact, never did so) and instead committed the combined forces of its nationwide organization to assist the farmworkers. In doing so, the BPP and the UFWOC established a highly successful, multiracial coalition based on class solidarity.[60]

CHAPTER 4

More Mutual Respect Than Ever in Our History

I N the winter of 1968, when agricultural employment was scarce and farm-workers and their families in the California's Central Valley began to go hungry, many UFWOC members became frustrated with the slow progress of the union's strike against Delano grape growers, which had been underway for two and a half years. Cesar Chavez recalled, "There was demoralization in the ranks, people becoming desperate, more and more talk about violence." Minor acts of violence had already occurred, such as the arson of a few packing sheds, and he knew that if he did not act, the level of violence would only escalate. He had built the UFWOC around the nonviolent resistance of primarily Mexican American farmworkers who, against all odds, had won important victories against the powerful forces of agribusiness. If he was going to prevent *la causa* from self-destructing, he had to do something drastic. In February Chavez therefore decided to fast as an act of penance in order to reaffirm the union's commitment to nonviolence. He later explained, "I had to bring the Movement to a halt, do something that would force them and me to deal with the whole question of violence and ourselves . . . I was going to stop eating until such time as everyone in the strike either ignored me or made up their minds that they were not going to be committing violence."[1]

Chavez's fast brought national attention—both positive and negative—to the UFWOC and its boycott. Inspired by his act of nonviolent resistance, Martin Luther King, Jr. sent a telegram of support to Chavez on March 5. He declared,

> I am deeply moved by your courage in fasting as your personal
> sacrifice for justice through nonviolence. . . . You stand today as a

living example of the Gandhian tradition with its great force for
social progress and its healing spiritual powers. My colleagues and
I commend you for your bravery, salute you for your indefatigable
work against poverty and injustice, and pray for your health
and your continuing service as one of the outstanding men of
America.

Despite their mutual use of Gandhian nonviolent resistance, King's telegram
to Chavez was a tepid expression of support that did not indicate a genuine
interest in forming an alliance between the Southern Christian Leadership
Conference and the UFWOC. Less than a week after Chavez ended his fast,
King traveled to Los Angeles (a two- to three-hour drive from Delano), but
declined an invitation to meet with Chavez.[2]

Although both the UFWOC and SCLC practiced nonviolent resistance to
achieve social change, their common ideology did not result in cooperation
during King's presidency of SCLC. Continued discrimination within labor
unions left King wary of aligning with organized labor. Furthermore, because
SCLC focused on African Americans in the urban South, the relevance of
Mexican American struggles in the rural West was unclear. The changes that
occurred within SCLC in the wake of King's assassination, however, opened
the door to a relationship with the UFWOC. Changes in American society
also brought the two organizations together. The racist violence, urban rebellions, and assassinations of the late 1960s left some activists disillusioned, while
others became more militant, calling for the use of self-defense or—among
extremists—urban guerrilla warfare, strategies at odds with the nonviolent
resistance advocated by King and Chavez. Many liberal activists had moved
on to other causes that had arisen in the late 1960s, inspired by the victories
of the civil rights movement. Moreover, the increasingly conservative mood
of the country, as evidenced by the election of Richard Nixon as president in
1968, resulted in calls for equality and justice frequently being met with apa-
thy and resistance, rather than sympathy, from whites. These dramatic changes
led SCLC to view the possibility of coalitions with labor unions and Mexicans
Americans in a considerably more positive light. In this changed atmosphere,
working with the UFWOC was much more appealing to the SCLC leadership
than it had been during King's tenure. But forming an alliance with the farmworkers did not only provide SCLC with new partners in struggle; it allowed
SCLC leaders to demonstrate the organization's evolution and incorporation of
economic justice and multiracial equality into its mission.

*   *   *

Although the UFWOC strikes and boycotts had obtained the support of a variety of civil rights organizations—including SNCC, the NAACP, the NUL, and the BPP—SCLC was much slower to connect with the farmworkers. For instance, the organization did not support the farmworkers' protests against Schenley Industries, in which members of SNCC participated. However, in September 1966, officers of SCLC in Texas joined local UFWOC-affiliated farmworkers as they marched through downtown Austin. The farmworkers had marched 387 miles from Starr County in South Texas to the state capital to call on Governor John Connally to enact minimum wage legislation. The march concluded on Labor Day, September 5, with a rally of over 8,000 people on the steps of the capitol building, during which a telegram from Senator Robert F. Kennedy was read to cheers. Andrew Young, SCLC secretary treasurer, joined the organization's delegation for the rally. In response to SCLC participation in the conclusion of the march and Kennedy's support, King sent a congratulatory telegram to Chavez:

> As brothers in the fight for equality, I extend the hand of
> fellowship and good will and wish continuing success to you
> and your members. The fight for equality must be fought on
> many fronts—in urban slums, in the sweat shops of the factories
> and fields. Our separate struggles are really one—a struggle for
> freedom, for dignity and for humanity.

Up to this point, King and SCLC had not shown any interest in the union's actions. It should be noted, however, that while King privately expressed his support to Chavez and the UFWOC, he never issued a public statement in support of the union and did not urge SCLC members to participate in any UFWOC boycott.[3]

King's relationship with James Hoffa, president of the International Brotherhood of Teamsters, prevented him from publicly supporting the UF-WOC. Their relationship originated with the murder of Detroit housewife Viola Liuzzo as she shuttled marchers following the Selma to Montgomery march in 1965. Because Liuzzo's husband was an official in Teamsters Local 247, Hoffa arranged for her body to be flown from Montgomery to Detroit in his private plane. That same day, Hoffa announced that the Teamsters were donating $25,000 to SCLC. King and Hoffa met in person a few days later at Liuzzo's funeral. In late 1966, as contributions to SCLC began to dwindle, King's advisors urged him to ask Hoffa for another donation from the Teamsters. Although King was concerned about the propriety of meeting with Hoffa, whose 1964 convictions for mail fraud and jury-tampering were under appeal at the time, a meeting was scheduled for November 1966. King's concern increased as the media reported on their scheduled meeting, which the FBI leaked to the press in an attempt to discredit King and SCLC. Nevertheless, at a meeting on November 10, King agreed to support a Teamsters effort to organize hospital workers in Chicago and Hoffa pledged a $50,000 donation to SCLC.[4]

The Teamsters' substantial donation to SCLC came less than two weeks after the union had lost the election to the UFWOC to represent grape pickers employed by the DiGiorgio Corporation. This donation also hindered King from supporting the UFWOC in its strike against A. Perelli-Minetti & Sons, which had signed a sweetheart contract with the Teamsters two months previously in September 1966. Although the Teamsters were publicly accused of violent attacks on the nonviolent farmworkers and their supporters during the protests against Perelli-Minetti, King remained silent. King's relationship with the Teamsters was curious, especially since their oppressive behavior led SNCC and other progressive organizations to support the UFWOC and draw parallels between *la causa* and the civil rights movement. Marshall Ganz argues, "The farm worker struggle enacted a narrative in which growers, Teamsters, and local law enforcement were on one side, and farm workers, churches, and their supporters were on the other." King found himself on the wrong side. This was the second time the Teamsters' $50,000 contribution had put King in an uncomfortable situation; when he attempted to support the union's efforts to organize Chicago hospital workers as he had promised, he found himself in the middle of a fight between the Teamsters and the Building Services Employees International Union.[5]

The influence of the Teamsters prevented King from acting on behalf of the UFWOC, despite his and Chavez's shared commitment to nonviolent resistance. Furthermore, both King and Chavez were forced to contend with elements of their own movements that preferred more militant action to nonviolent protest. Inspired by the rise of Black Power, urban rebellions, and more militant leaders of the Chicano movement, young members of the UFWOC became disenchanted with nonviolence by early 1968. According to journalist Ronald B. Taylor, "For some within the farm worker movement, the nonviolence of Cesar Chavez was a tactic that had been tried and found wanting; these young men and women felt it was time to return to the tactics of Pancho Villa and Emiliano Zapata." Older farmworkers, who had been instructed in nonviolent philosophy and resistance by volunteers from SNCC and CORE during the union's first strike in 1965, also began to question its practicality. On February 19, four days after he had begun his fast, Chavez gave a speech to the union members wherein he likened the move away from nonviolence to that which had occurred in the civil rights movement, pointing out that "its recourse to violence had made black people suffer; black homes, not white, were being burned, and black sons killed."[6]

The debate over the use of nonviolence in the farmworkers' movement paralleled that in the civil rights movement. Like the Mexican American farmworkers, African Americans in the rural South, who were constantly under siege by local law enforcement and the Ku Klux Klan (who were often one and the same), had to be convinced of the utility of nonviolence. Gradually, King's brand of nonviolence became more acceptable as nonviolent protests achieved significant victories over segregation in such places as Montgomery, Alabama and Nashville, Tennessee. However, the practicality and morality of nonviolent resistance was questioned as the violent responses to peaceful protests not only escalated, but went largely unpunished. Events such as the 1963 bombing of the Sixteenth Street Baptist Church, the murders of three volunteers during Mississippi Freedom Summer in 1964, and the violence surrounding the 1965 Selma to Montgomery March hastened the rejection of King's nonviolence and the acceptance of the self-defense advocated by groups such as the Deacons for Defense. Finally, the urban rebellions during the summers of 1964 to 1967—and the rapid federal response—appeared to prove that nonviolence as both a philosophy and a tactic had failed. As MFDP delegate Hartman Turnbow famously told King at the Democratic National Convention in Atlantic City in 1964, "This nonviolent stuff ain't no good. It'll get ya killed."[7]

The debate over nonviolence created divisions between the civil rights organizations that continued to champion the use of nonviolence and those that began to advocate for self-defense. For continuing to emphasize nonviolent resistance, organizations like SCLC were criticized for being out of touch by young, urban African Americans. Chavez's fast, however, was a clear demonstration that nonviolent resistance could be tremendously successful. By the time Chavez ended his fast on March 11, he had strengthened the UFWOC's commitment to nonviolence, as well as attracted significant publicity that resulted in increased donations to the union and participation in the boycott. UFWOC organizer LeRoy Chatfield later told Chavez biographer Peter Matthiessen, "We never organized so many people in such a short time, before or since. The fast gave the lie to the growers' claim that we have no following."[8]

The relevance of Chavez's fast to King's own dedication to nonviolence and increasing difficulty in maintaining a nonviolent direction to the civil rights movement may have led King to send Chavez his telegram. However, King biographer Taylor Branch has suggested that his expression for support was motivated less by a sense of common purpose than as an attempt at solidarity with Robert Kennedy, who was at Chavez's side when he broke his fast and announced his presidential candidacy a week later. That King sent a telegram to Chavez following the UFWOC march in Texas in 1966 only after Kennedy had expressed his support for the farmworkers gives credibility to Branch's assertion. Moreover, journalist John Gregory Dunne argued that Kennedy's endorsement had "legitimized Chavez": "For the first time Chavez became fashionable, a national figure registering on the nation's moral thermometer." Due to Chavez's close association with Kennedy, it was politically expedient for King to support the farmworkers. However, King sent the telegram two weeks after Chavez had begun his fast and did not take advantage of the opportunity to visit him when King was in Los Angeles just days after Chavez ended the fast.[9]

King's decision not to visit Chavez was strange in light of the fact that King was attempting to gain Chavez's support for his latest endeavor, the Poor People's Campaign. In January 1968 SCLC announced that for its next project it would focus on the grievances of the nation's poor. Although King had long been deeply concerned with economic inequality, his actions following the Montgomery bus boycott had prioritized racial integration and national civil rights legislation. Rev. C. T. Vivian, SCLC director of affiliates, noted that "it was Martin Luther King who removed the Black struggle from the economic realm and placed it in a moral and spiritual context." King eventually acknowledged that integration was insufficient and that economic power was necessary to achieve true equality. The Watts rebellion of August 1965—what historian Thomas Jackson deemed both "a class revolt . . . and a racial rebellion"—and SCLC's failed movement for school integration and open housing in Chicago in 1966 led King to acknowledge that racial integration and "civil rights movement gains were irrelevant to the economic needs and racial resentments of big-city blacks." In both Watts and Chicago, King was criticized by the African American community for not understanding the economic nature of their oppression and for assuming that integration held the same importance for them as it did for blacks in the South. A 1968 SCLC interior statement of purpose revealed that King and his organization were ready to change their focus and tactics: "We can now see ourselves as the powerless poor trapped within an economically oriented power structure." SCLC therefore intended to apply its expertise in mobilization to the overwhelming task of eliminating poverty. As King envisioned it, the campaign would bring poor people from across the country to Washington, D.C., to lobby politicians and federal agencies in order to "pressure the government to fulfill the promise of the War on Poverty" by providing employment and financial support.[10]

King realized that in order to effectively address poverty on a national scale, he would have to involve other racial groups. SCLC had not previously worked with any non-black racial group other than whites, so the organization hastily called a meeting with leaders of progressive race-based organizations. On March 14, 1968, over seventy representatives of black, white, Chicano, Puerto Rican, and American Indian groups attended a conference with SCLC leaders in Atlanta. Baldemar Velásquez, president of the Farm Labor Organizing Committee (FLOC), a farmworkers' union in Ohio, attended the meetings and recalled, "It was a listening session, a learning session, learning about each other. Most of the Mexican Americans who were there, we were very aware of the civil rights movement, but we felt that the civil rights movement was not very aware of us." Indeed, the leaders of SCLC had been so unaware of the burgeoning Chicano movement that it relied on third parties such as the American Friends Service Committee to identify and put them in touch with Mexican American activists. Taylor Branch also noted that King was so ignorant of Mexican American issues that during introductions at the beginning of the meeting, SCLC program director Bernard Lafayette "whispered to King what he had gleaned about basic differences among Puerto Ricans, as distinct from Mexicans (Chicanos)." Even more problematic for the future of the Poor People's Campaign was the fact that many SCLC staff members were openly hostile to forming multiracial coalitions. Some were concerned that such alliances would undermine black unity, but others admitted that they were not comfortable with Mexican Americans or other minorities in leadership positions of the campaign.[11]

SCLC's lack of familiarity with Mexican Americans can partly be explained by the fact that the organization's presence was limited to the Deep

South, which had an almost negligible Latino population. According to both the 1960 and 1970 census, "persons of Spanish heritage" made up only 0.6 percent of the population in Georgia, where SCLC was based. In Alabama, where SCLC also operated, the Latino population was 0.4 percent. Gene Guerrero, the Mexican American leader of the Southern Students Organizing Committee (SSOC), a civil rights organization that sought to organize students on white college campuses, moved to Atlanta when he was in high school in the late 1950s. He recalled that he was treated as white because people in Atlanta were unfamiliar with Mexican Americans: "As far as people in Atlanta were concerned, for the most part I was no different from somebody who had an Italian last name." Due to its base in Atlanta, SCLC had not been exposed to the oppression of Mexican Americans. Moreover, if Mexican Americans like Guerrero were treated as white in Atlanta, SCLC may have been surprised by—or disagreed with—the UFWOC claims of racial discrimination.[12]

SCLC only saw racism as the problem of blacks and whites because it operated solely in a black and white world. In a response to a woman's 1961 letter regarding racism in Southern California, King revealed that he had limited understanding of the oppression faced by anyone other than African Americans when he wrote, "There is possibly more discrimination against Mexicans and Indians in your area." He also claimed in a January 1965 interview with *Playboy*, "The Negro . . . is ostracized as is no other minority group in America by the evil of oppressive and constricting prejudice based solely upon his color." Until the Poor People's Campaign, SCLC had not addressed the issues of Mexican Americans in part because it had not occurred to them to mobilize on behalf of anyone other than African Americans.[13]

Although Chavez was invited to the multiracial conference in Atlanta, he did not attend because he was weakened as a result of his fast. He voiced his support by telephone, but was unimpressed with King and SCLC's overdue attempt at multiracial coalition building. Furthermore, King's conception of the campaign focused on the unemployed poor instead of the working class and thus few unions or union members participated. These factors perhaps caused Chavez to resist SCLC's repeated attempts to enlist the UFWOC in the Poor People's Campaign, including a personal visit from Andrew Young. According to Chavez, "Primero viene el boycoteo" ("The boycott comes first"). In a letter to Marcos Muñoz, coordinator of the UFWOC grape boycott in Boston, Chavez explained that the union could not participate in the Poor People's Campaign, or anything else, until they were victorious against Giumarra because they needed to harness all their strength for the boycott.

LeRoy Chatfield told Peter Matthiessen that Chavez became so exasperated with the frequent requests from the organizers of the Poor People's Campaign that he finally explained, "'It's not that we're not sympathetic or don't endorse you, but what you're asking me to do is exactly the same thing as asking the Memphis garbage men to put aside their strike and come to Delano to help the farm workers.'" However, the fact that the Poor People's Campaign did not address UFWOC interests and King and SCLC did not publicly support the farmworkers may have contributed to Chavez's refusal to participate in the campaign.[14]

*   *   *

The alliance that eventually developed between the UFWOC and SCLC came in the wake of King's assassination. On April 4, 1968, Chavez was in Sacramento stumping for Robert Kennedy, whose presidential campaign the UFWOC had endorsed. Chavez was preparing to speak on behalf of Kennedy at Our Lady of Guadalupe Church when he received word of King's death. After watching some of the news broadcasts, Chavez went to the church and turned what was supposed to be a political meeting into a prayer vigil. He and most of the audience then joined a candlelight vigil held at a local park. Two days later, Chavez sent a telegram of support to King's widow. He proclaimed, "It is my belief that much of the courage which we have found in our struggle for justice in the fields has had its roots in the example set by your husband and by those multitudes who followed his non violent leadership." The members of the UFWOC shared Chavez's sentiments and had looked to King as a source of inspiration. Chavez and the farmworkers were particularly moved by King's commitment to nonviolence. An editorial in *El Malcriado* expressed the influence King's nonviolent philosophy had on the farmworkers: "Dr. King proved that the only road we can walk is that of non-violence and love. It was his example that inspired and continues to inspire us as we confront the obstacles on that road, and overcome them." The farmworkers also likened their own struggle to the work of SCLC. Eliseo Medina recalled,

> I know as a farm worker that we really felt a very close relationship
> to King and SCLC and what they were doing because it really just

rang exactly true to what we were trying to accomplish. Because
for us, even though we were talking about a farm workers union,
it really was more than that. It was more than just being paid more
and getting wages and benefits. It really was about a people that
were just sick and tired of being mistreated and ignored, and so
for us it was a movement as well.

In the wake of King's death, the UFWOC made a conscious effort to connect
his memory to *la causa*. For example, when the New York boycott committee
flew to Memphis (paid for by the New York Labor Council) to participate in
the march that King would have led, they presented the UFWOC efforts to
African American churches.[15]

Although the members of the UFWOC were inspired by King and his
use of nonviolent resistance, and were saddened by his death, Chavez had
been privately critical of the civil rights leader. In the extensive interviews
that Jacques Levy conducted with Chavez for the book, *Cesar Chavez: Autobiography of La Causa*, Chavez confided that while he was influenced by
the Montgomery bus boycott, he was disappointed that King had accepted
the Nobel Peace Prize in 1964. Chavez explained that as a "servant of the
people," Gandhi would not have accepted such recognition and that therefore King should not have, either. Chavez also criticized King's strategy
of pursuing civil rights legislation. He informed Levy that he would not
have focused on legislation because it "comes from the establishment. . . .
They'll give it to you to stop you one way or the other." Chavez believed
that the achievement of legislation stopped the momentum of activism
and that after the passage of the various civil rights laws, "the civil rights
movement fell flat on its face because they didn't have anything after that."
And even though Chavez shared King's commitment to nonviolence, he
disapproved of King's attempts to force the philosophy on others. Reflecting on the riot in the Watts area of Los Angeles in 1965, after which King
traveled to the city to attempt to give a nonviolent direction to the rebellion, Chavez told Levy,

If they are rioting in East L.A. I couldn't go there and tell them,
ask them to stop the rioting. Because I haven't done anything all
these years when they were getting their heads busted by the cops.
. . . When the riots were going on and they called on the Negro
leadership to go out and pacify it you didn't have any control or

leverage. It is just like somebody coming [and] trying to counsel
us to stop the strike or boycott.

Finally, Chavez disapproved of King's public criticisms of U.S. involvement in
Vietnam because he did not want to risk alienating the pro-war forces both
among his allies in organized labor and within the UFWOC membership.[16]

Despite his critiques, Chavez was deeply moved by King's death and used
the occasion to make tentative overtures to the leaders of SCLC. Although
Chavez had refused to participate in the Poor People's Campaign and did
not allow UFWOC members to do so—even after King's assassination, which
had prompted many who had previously been skeptical or critical of the campaign to participate—Chavez and UFWOC assistant director Larry Itliong
sent a telegram of support to SCLC when the march began. Four months
later, Chavez wrote to SCLC again, this time requesting a poster of King to
display in the UFWOC headquarters. Shortly after Chavez made these overtures, Ralph Abernathy, King's hand-picked successor as SCLC president, announced in November 1968 that the organization would support the union's
boycott of California grapes.[17]

When Chavez reached out to SCLC, Abernathy was in dire need of an ally.
The Poor People's Campaign had not come close to achieving its lofty goals of
obtaining employment and economic aid for millions of the nation's poor, leaving the organization—and its reputation—badly damaged. Many both inside
and outside SCLC began to doubt that Abernathy, who had dwelt in King's
shadow for so long, could be an effective leader in his own right. But support
for SCLC had begun to decline years earlier when King was still at the helm.
Abernathy reflected in his autobiography, "When I took over from Martin, I
did so after the civil rights movement had peaked and the SCLC had already
begun to decline in influence." The ill-fated movement in Chicago and King's
vocal criticism of U.S. involvement in Vietnam cost SCLC many of its former
allies, including those from other segments of the civil rights movement. New
organizations that championed Black Power also frequently stole the spotlight
from SCLC, especially among young African Americans in the urban North.
Abernathy explained, "Not only did we fail to recruit the supporters that we
once did, but our contributions began to dwindle, because some of what we
used to get went to more militant groups." From the beginning of his presidency, then, Abernathy saw the need to forge new alliances.[18]

In his effort to gain allies, Abernathy sought to improve the relationship
between SCLC and organized labor, which had become increasingly strained

by 1968. Despite King's commitment to economic justice, he was deeply ambivalent about organized labor. King excoriated organized labor for failing to cease discriminatory practices against African American workers in union locals. He also blamed unions for the racism of white members. Overlooking the role of employers in the maintenance of racial divisions between workers, King wrote in *Stride Toward Freedom: The Montgomery Story*, "In every section of the country one can find local unions existing as a serious and vicious obstacle when the Negro seeks jobs or upgrading in employment." At the same time, he recognized that organized labor could be a potentially valuable source of social change and support for the civil rights movement. He therefore frequently spoke to labor unions, both in an attempt to compel them to rid their locals of discrimination and to obtain financial contributions for SCLC. For example, in a speech at the Constitutional Convention of the AFL-CIO in 1961, during which he repeated verbatim his criticisms of organized labor from *Stride Toward Freedom*, King offered the federation a chance at redemption: "If you would do these two things now in this convention—resolve to deal effectively with discrimination and provide financial aid for our struggle in the South—this convention will have a glorious moral deed to add to an illustrious history."[19]

Labor unions responded to King's appeals with substantial donations. Furthermore, in the 1960s the number of workers who sympathized with the civil rights movement increased annually. But King did not believe that he needed to actively support unions in return and thus did not speak out against anti-labor legislation or pledge SCLC support for union organizing drives in the South. However, in 1964 King and SCLC supported striking workers from Scripto, Inc., a pen and pencil manufacturer in Atlanta. The workers had organized the previous year with the International Chemical Workers Union (ICWU) and were seeking equitable pay for skilled and nonskilled workers. SCLC became involved with the strike at the urging of C. T. Vivian, whose experience as a civil rights activist in Illinois led him to believe that unions were essential for black economic equality. SCLC actively supported the strike and organized a national boycott of Scripto products. King once participated in the striking workers' picket line. But in contrast to Vivian, King and SCLC did not support the Scripto workers because of a desire to cooperate with organized labor. Rather, many of the black Scripto workers were members of King's church, Ebenezer Baptist, which was located a few blocks from the Scripto factory. In supporting the Scripto strike, King was therefore ministering to his flock more than demonstrating his support for organized labor.[20]

Moreover, King's involvement in the Scripto strike eventually under-mined the power of the union to represent its workers. Unwilling to negotiate with the ICWU, Scripto President Carl Singer negotiated with King with-out the knowledge of the union organizers. Despite having no authorization from the ICWU organizers or the workers, King agreed to call off the SCLC boycott of Scripto products if workers would be paid their Christmas bo-nuses (which the union had already demanded in their contract). A Scripto executive present at one of the meetings between King and Singer recalled that King said that SCLC needed to end the Scripto boycott so that it could "get on with plans for the Selma campaign which were about a month behind schedule." King's settlement with Singer was a direct violation of federal labor laws because, as the official representative of the workers, Scripto was obli-gated to bargain exclusively with the ICWU, not with King.[21]

The ICWU organizers resented King's interference in the negotiation process. Furthermore, King's mere involvement in the strike angered both the white business community and the older black leadership who felt that his actions threatened "their carefully nurtured equilibrium" of gradual, controlled civil rights progress in Atlanta. Some on both sides also felt that Scripto, which was one of the first factories in Atlanta to hire African Ameri-cans and represented an escape from domestic labor for black women, had been unfairly targeted. Perhaps due to this negative reaction, labor issues did not become a significant aspect of SCLC's program, despite the successful resolution of the Scripto strike. Thomas Jackson argues that "King remained ambivalent toward labor and unwilling to spend time or resources support-ing labor union organizing." In fact, King did not become deeply involved in a labor dispute again until the Memphis sanitation workers' strike in 1968, but he only did so at the request of his colleague Reverend James Lawson. By the time that King joined the strike effort, it had been underway for five weeks and a cross-class coalition from Memphis's black community had al-ready mobilized behind it. King's lack of support for the UFWOC was there-fore characteristic of his disinterest in labor organizing.[22]

In contrast to King, Abernathy was determined to incorporate labor or-ganizing into the mission of SCLC. Moreover, Abernathy was committed to continuing the fight for economic equality that was the mission of the Poor People's Campaign. Abernathy and SCLC therefore pursued alliances with unions and ethnic minorities, a shift from the organization's previous em-phasis on obtaining the support of white liberals. In October 1968 Aberna-thy announced that nationwide "economic withdrawals" would be a central aspect of the SCLC program to draw attention to the needs of the poor. The UFWOC's nationwide boycott of California grapes fit perfectly with Abernathy's renewed focus; less than a month later, he announced the SCLC endorsement of the grape boycott.[23]

Immediately after SCLC endorsed the boycott, SCLC subsidiary Operation Breadbasket announced that it would follow Abernathy's lead in supporting the farmworkers. Rev. Jesse Jackson, national director of Operation Breadbasket, declared to the press, "We will not eat the grapes of wrath . . . and we are urging all decent Americans to join us. We greet Cesar Chavez and his fellow workers—Viva La Huelga until we again see harvests of abundance." Launched in Atlanta in 1962 and expanded to Chicago in February 1966, Operation Breadbasket was based on the selective buying campaigns coordinated by Rev. Leon H. Sullivan in Philadelphia as a means to address the economic inequality of African Americans. Operation Breadbasket targeted those companies that conducted business in the black community, but refused to hire African American employees. The ministers of Operation Breadbasket conducted research on companies' hiring practices and then attempted to negotiate for the hiring of African Americans. If a company refused, Operation Breadbasket then coordinated a boycott of the company's products until African Americans were hired. Using the power of the boycott, or "not-buying power," Operation Breadbasket had successfully—and nonviolently—created hundreds of jobs for African Americans in Chicago, Atlanta, and elsewhere. Abernathy later reflected that Operation Breadbasket was the perfect venue for Jackson's skills: "Nobody could do more with a crowd of potential supporters waiting to be told what to do. He instinctively knew their hearts, and he was a master of the right phrase to bring out their passion." Immediately after Jackson's announcement, Operation Breadbasket members and supporters boycotted California grapes and picketed stores in the black community that stocked them.[24]

Operation Breadbasket's support was indispensable to the UFWOC grape boycott in Chicago. Jackson invited Eliseo Medina, who was responsible for coordinating the boycott in Chicago, to a number of Operation Breadbasket's weekly mass meetings where the organization presented and discussed their projects. Medina recalled, "I remember the first time I went. [Jackson] says, 'Brother, if you know how to preach, get out there and preach! . . . So I got out there and did what I thought I could." Medina found a receptive audience in the members of Operation Breadbasket because they shared adversaries with the farmworkers; the grocery stores that persisted in carrying California grapes had earlier been targeted by Operation Breadbasket for discriminatory hiring practices. For example, the UFWOC focused its protest efforts against the Jewel Food Stores, the largest grocery store chain in Chicago. In April 1967, Operation Breadbasket had convinced Jewel to agree to increase its recruiting and hiring of African Americans. As a result, Jewel hired over 660 African Americans by spring 1968. Jackson and the rest of the organization thus recognized that the UFWOC was a useful ally in its fight against discriminatory businesses in the black community.[25]

Jewel valued its improved reputation in the black community. Consequently, when Operation Breadbasket supported the UFWOC in its call for Jewel to remove California grapes from its shelves, the grocery chain acted immediately. Medina reported to Chavez in December 1968, "Jewel got pressure from Operation Breadbasket and pulled the grapes from all the black and Spanish speaking areas." When Jewel then tried to unload its California grapes in its stores in white neighborhoods, a member of Operation Breadbasket who was a manager at Jewel helped the farmworkers from the inside by spreading false information about the union's protest plans to the company executives and "convinced them that this was going to result in a lot of adverse publicity." As a result, Jewel announced it would remove California grapes from all 220 of its stores in the Chicago area.[26]

The involvement of Operation Breadbasket in the grape boycott produced rapid results for the farmworkers. With the help of Operation Breadbasket, the Jewel, A&P, National Tea, Hillman's, Dominick's, High-Low, and Kroger grocery store chains in Chicago all stopped selling California grapes. By late December 1968, it was impossible to buy California grapes in Chicago. The president of the Market Service Association, an organization of 200 fruit and produce merchants in the Chicago area, confirmed that "the boycott is successful. There is no interest in grapes whatsoever in Chicago." The role of Operation Breadbasket in helping the UFWOC rid Chicago of California grapes demonstrates the importance of mutual interests in coalition building. By uniting against common adversaries that discriminated against and contributed to the exploitation of both the African American and Mexican American communities, the two organizations formed a powerful and effective alliance.[27]

Operation Breadbasket's participation in the grape boycott brought the SCLC and the UFWOC closer together. Both Chavez and Abernathy were determined that their newfound coalition would not only continue, but become stronger. They therefore highlighted the connections and commonalities between the two organizations. For example, Chavez demonstrated their shared philosophy by celebrating King's memory when addressing the topic of nonviolence. On April 4, 1969, which was both Good Friday and the first anniversary of King's assassination, Chavez sent a letter to E. L. Barr, Jr., president of the California Grape and Tree Fruit League, refuting Barr's public accusations that the UFWOC had used violent tactics during the boycott. In contesting Barr's claims and maintaining the union's commitment to nonviolence, Chavez evoked King's memory when he wrote,

> Today on Good Friday 1969 we remember the life and sacrifice of Martin Luther King, Jr. who gave himself totally to the non-violent struggle for peace and justice. In his *Letter from Birmingham Jail* Dr. King describes better than I could our hopes for the strike and boycott: "injustice must be exposed, with all the tension its exposure creates, to the light of human conscience and the air of national opinion before it can be cured."

Chavez emphasized his connection to King by publishing the letter in the magazine *Christian Century* under the title, "Letter from Delano," echoing King's famous "Letter from Birmingham Jail."[28]

But by 1969 nonviolence was not the only connection between the UFWOC and SCLC. Rather, SCLC increasingly turned to labor organizing as a means to obtain equal rights for African Americans and the poor of all races. In spring 1969 SCLC became involved in a hospital workers' strike in Charleston, South Carolina. A group of black women employed as nonprofessional workers at the South Carolina Medical College Hospital attempted to organize as Local 1199B of the Retail, Wholesale, and Department Store Workers, AFL-CIO. The workers wanted to organize so they could combat race-based wage differentials at the hospital. However, the state of South Carolina was staunchly antiunion and had fought to prevent unions from organizing there by passing "right-to-work" laws and prohibiting all government agencies from negotiating with unions. Therefore, in March the hospital fired twelve workers for union activity. In response, 450 other hospital workers went on strike, and were joined a week later by sixty workers at Charleston County Hospital. Local 1199B then called on Abernathy and SCLC to come to Charleston to mobilize the black community in support of the striking workers. Andrew Young recalled in his autobiography,

> We were as eager to participate in the Charleston strike as
> Local 1199 was to have us; the hospital workers' strike, like the
> garbage workers' strike in Memphis, fit perfectly into our desire
> to combat fundamental economic inequities and was consistent
> with the long-term aims of the Poor People's Campaign as we had
> originally conceived it in 1968.

Abernathy also envisioned SCLC participation in the hospital workers' strike as a way to solidify the relationship between the organization and organized labor. He explained, "We needed to win something big in order to reestablish the credibility of nonviolence as a means of social change, and the unionization of Charleston, South Carolina, would be something big, not only to blacks but also to labor unions around the country."[29]

The hospital workers' strike lasted 100 days and brought national attention to the city of Charleston. The workers demanded union recognition, the end to racial discrimination in hiring and wages, and the reinstatement of the fired workers. SCLC was instrumental in mobilizing the black community by holding regular mass meetings and marches. Abernathy was arrested twice during protests, which generated significant publicity. Coretta Scott King visited him in jail during one of his stays and led a two-mile march from the Emmanuel African Methodist Episcopal Church to the Charleston County Hospital. Most important, SCLC helped organize an economic boycott of businesses in downtown Charlestown in which African Americans were asked to restrict their purchases to food and medicine. Union officials estimated that the boycott cost downtown businesses $15 million in revenue, which prompted business owners to pressure the hospital to negotiate with the union. As a result of the negotiations, workers won wage increases and a formal grievance procedure. In addition, all the fired workers were hired back without penalties. However, the workers did not receive union recognition. *Time* magazine noted that Abernathy and union officials were pleased not only by the settlement, but also because "the strike renewed the partnership between the labor and civil rights movements and represented a much needed victory for the advocates of activist nonviolence."[30]

The partial victory of the hospital workers' strike led SCLC to pursue additional coalitions with organized labor. Abernathy explained in his memoir, "I saw the immediate future as one in which we would intervene in behalf of poor people in their struggle for economic justice." Abernathy took a step in the organization's new direction by strengthening its relationship with the

UFWOC. The farmworkers were a natural choice for an alliance because they shared many things in common with the striking hospital workers; like the African American women who performed "unpleasant drudge work" in Charleston's hospitals, the farmworkers' economic exploitation was partly due to racial discrimination. Both the farmworkers and the hospital workers viewed their struggles as civil rights movements as well as labor movements and thus sought the support of civil rights organizations. Therefore, in the midst of the Charleston strike, Abernathy traveled to El Centro, California, in May to join the UFWOC for the last leg of its one-hundred-mile march from Coachella to Calexico. The farmworkers marched to the border immigration station in Calexico to "seek unity" with Mexican nationals used as strikebreakers by grape growers in the Coachella Valley. Chavez appreciated Abernathy's participation in the march and in thanking him wrote, "I was deeply moved by the actions you took in joining the farm workers' march in Coachella. The solidarity of black and brown brothers is essential to our common struggle for justice and dignity."[31]

Abernathy's vision for SCLC's future included Chavez's belief in the necessity of solidarity and cooperation between African Americans and Mexican Americans. On August 4, while addressing a meeting at the Revelation Baptist Church in Cincinnati, Ohio, Abernathy shared his Coachella march experience and informed the predominantly African American audience, "The same foot that is standing on the necks of the poor Black people is also standing on the necks of the poor red, brown and white." He then pointed to the UFWOC button on his lapel and declared, "There is one of the most important single things that you can do, and that is 'Boycott Grapes!'" The audience heeded Abernathy's call; less than a week later, a delegation from the Indianapolis SCLC marched to a local Kroger grocery store and joined a picket line in support of the grape boycott.[32]

*   *   *

Although SCLC's support for the farmworkers came later than that of other civil rights groups, the organization nonetheless contributed to the UFWOC's victory in obtaining union contracts with California grape growers in July 1970. Moreover, SCLC maintained its support for the union when, on the same day that Chavez declared victory in California's grape fields, he

Figure 9. Cesar Chavez and Ralph Abernathy during the UFWOC's march from Coachella to Calexico, California, May 1969. Courtesy of Walter P. Reuther Library, Wayne State University.

announced that the UFWOC would take action against the state's growers of iceberg lettuce. In 1967 the UFWOC began quietly organizing farmworkers in the Imperial Valley and surrounding areas. In 1968 the union farmworkers in these areas, who worked primarily in the lettuce and melon fields, wanted to strike from Imperial Valley to Salinas Valley. UFWOC leaders, however, recognized they could not orchestrate such a large-scale strike in the midst of the grape boycott. Instead, they urged the farmworkers to organize and pledged to begin strike activity when that boycott ended. Chavez recalled, "We had to tell them we could not handle two strikes at once, that they would have to wait until we finished the grapes. They agreed, but they extracted an agreement from me, too; I agreed that as soon as we started to win we could turn to their problems." True to his word, on June 4, 1970, two months after the first contracts were signed with grape growers, UFWOC melon pickers went on strike at Abbatti Produce, Inc., in the Imperial Valley, which signed a contract recognizing the union just two days later.[33]

With a victory in the melon fields and an increasing number of contracts with grape growers, the UFWOC felt confident enough to make a move on the lettuce growers of California. On July 23, 1970, Chavez sent telegrams to lettuce growers in the Imperial, Santa Maria, and Salinas Valleys notifying them that the UFWOC represented a majority of their workers and that therefore the union's leaders wished to meet with growers to negotiate a contract. Chavez warned the growers, "A prompt reply will avoid the bitter conflict experienced in the Delano grape strike." On receipt of the telegrams, the lettuce growers met and decided not to respond to Chavez's request and instead work with the Teamsters regarding representation for their workers. On July 28, thirty growers announced they had signed contracts with the Teamsters that covered 5,000 field workers in five counties, 75 percent of the farmworkers in the area. The workers discovered that the Teamsters represented them not through an election, but by reading about it in the newspaper. In signing the contracts, the Teamsters broke the jurisdictional agreement they had made with the UFWOC in July 1967 pledging that they would refrain from organizing field workers and in return the UFWOC would not organize cannery or shipping workers.[34]

The UFWOC's identification with the civil rights movement was an overwhelming factor in the growers' decision to work with the Teamsters. The owner of one Salinas farm declared, "The Teamsters are a trade union. Chavez's group is a civil rights movement." In many ways, he was correct. From the union's first strike of grapes in September 1965, Chavez had envisioned the UFWOC as a movement rather than simply a union. As such, Chavez looked to civil rights organizations for both inspiration and support. California's growers, however, were deeply suspicious of the civil rights movement, which it associated with communism. The Teamsters in the Central Valley therefore presented themselves as the responsible, conservative, and patriotic alternative to the UFWOC. During that first strike, the Teamsters printed a pamphlet that claimed, "A vote for the Teamsters was a vote 'against revolution, hatred of one race against another, the New Left, riots, beatniks, and destruction of the field crops that feed the nation.'" Despite the changes that had occurred in American social movements by 1970, the growers continued to distrust the UFWOC and viewed the Teamsters as a preferable alternative. The *Los Angeles Times* revealed that "some growers admitted the pacts with the Teamsters were designed to keep Chavez and the UFWOC out of agriculture because they regard the farm workers' union as too radical."[35]

Thus the union did not have the opportunity to celebrate when the remaining grape growers in Delano signed contracts with the UFWOC on July 29. Instead, the next day the farmworkers began marching through Salinas Valley to protest the action of the lettuce growers and Teamsters. Chavez explained, "The question was, do we really represent the workers and, if we do, how do we manifest it? I had to get people involved in a large way and demonstrate it—but it had to be something that builds up, not just a rally." The UFWOC leaders therefore decided to organize a four-pronged march— "from Greenfield in the south, Gilroy in the north, Aptos in the west, and Hollister in the east"—that would converge on the city of Salinas for a massive rally. At the concluding rally on August 2, over 3,000 workers voted to go on strike or boycott if the union leadership deemed it necessary. But Chavez was not ready to organize a strike; not only had the union leadership not decided on an appropriate grower to target, but they also knew that the union did not have enough funds to pay striking workers.[36]

Throughout August 1970, Chavez requested elections for union representation in order to avoid a strike, but was ignored by growers. When growers began firing farmworkers for refusing to sign with the Teamsters, strikes were called at many area ranches, but the UFWOC still resisted authorizing a full-fledged strike because they needed time to train and prepare workers for a strike. Furthermore, the UFWOC could use the expectation of a strike as a negotiating tool with the growers. It also appeared that the UFWOC could avoid a strike when it began negotiating a new jurisdictional agreement with the Teamsters. The willingness of the Teamsters to enter into negotiations was apparently due to pressure from the national leadership, who were furious with the Western Conference for breaking the 1967 pact. In direct opposition to the actions of the Teamster leaders in California, the executive assistant to acting Teamsters President Frank Fitzsimmons stated that "the policy of our union is to get out of the jurisdiction of the field workers and leave it to UFWOC." On August 12 the Teamsters and the UFWOC signed

Figure 10: Farm workers harvesting lettuce. Courtesy of Walter P. Reuther Library, Wayne State University.

an agreement in which the Teamsters promised to withdraw from the lettuce fields and not attempt to organize field workers. However, the growers refused to release the Teamsters from their contracts and to negotiate with the UFWOC. In response, seven thousand farmworkers went on strike in the Salinas and Santa Maria Valleys, making it "the largest strike of farm workers in U.S. history."[37]

The large scale of the strike severely affected the growers. The loss of so many field workers resulted in a two-thirds reduction in production that amounted to a revenue loss of $300,000 per day. Because of the serious fiscal consequences of the strike, lettuce and vegetable grower InterHarvest, Inc., held elections for union representation six days after the strike began, which the UFWOC won. InterHarvest therefore recognized the UFWOC and negotiated a contract that covered 1,500–2,000 field workers. A company spokesman acknowledged that the harvest would have been lost without the UFWOC because "the Teamsters had our contract but UFWOC has our workers." Eight days later, on September 4, FreshPict Foods agreed to recognize and negotiate with the UFWOC after the union won elections at its ranches.[38]

Despite this irrefutable evidence that workers in the lettuce fields wanted the UFWOC to represent them, many growers continued their attempts to halt the union's organizing activities. The growers pursued the matter in the courts, arguing that the strike was a jurisdictional dispute between unions from which employers were protected by California law, despite the truce between the UFWOC and the Teamsters. Even though the Superior Court in Santa Maria ruled against the growers on the grounds that there was no evidence the Teamsters represented the field workers, Salinas Superior Court Judge Anthony Brazil outlawed strike activity, including picketing, by the UFWOC on September 16, 1970. The bad timing of the ruling, falling on Mexican Independence Day, only stirred up the farmworkers' pride and spurred the UFWOC into launching an international boycott of nonunion iceberg lettuce grown in California and Arizona. Then on October 6, 1970, after lettuce grower Bud Antle, Inc., went to court using the same argument that the strike and boycott were the result of a jurisdictional conflict between unions, Monterey Superior Court Judge Gordon Campbell ordered the UFWOC to stop the boycott of Antle iceberg lettuce. The union responded by appealing on the basis of free speech, continued the strike and boycott, and stepped up the boycott.[39]

In aim and organization, the boycott of iceberg lettuce closely resembled the California grape boycott. The teams of UFWOC organizers and volunteers who coordinated the nationwide grape boycott also organized the lettuce boycott, which was to be concentrated in sixty-four cities across the country. But although SCLC was slow to respond to the grape boycott, it immediately supported the lettuce boycott. Operation Breadbasket was particularly involved in the boycott. On November 14, 1970, Chavez traveled to Chicago to draw attention to and enlist support for the boycott. That day he addressed Operation Breadbasket's weekly meeting, which was broadcast on radio station WVON. In his address, Chavez declared that the "poor must fight together" and called on Operation Breadbasket to support the union's picket lines at National Tea Company grocery stores, which sold California iceberg lettuce. As was the case during the grape boycott, Operation Breadbasket had a common foe with the UFWOC; the organization had already been protesting for National Tea to hire African American employees at the management level. Following Chavez's address, Jesse Jackson affirmed that Operation Breadbasket would support the lettuce boycott and declared that the organization "will march until National Tea is no more." Chavez appreciated Operation Breadbasket's support and sought to maintain a close relationship between the organizations. Shortly after his trip to Chicago, Chavez wrote to Jackson that he wanted to meet with him to "begin to put together some ideas on how we can help one another more directly and concretely."[40]

The support activities of Operation Breadbasket and SCLC increased when on December 4, 1970, Judge Campbell ordered that Chavez be arrested for contempt of court for failing to cease boycott activities that he had ruled on in October. On his arrest, Abernathy sent Chavez a telegram: "The SCLC wants you to know that we support you fully in your efforts to better the lives of poor working Americans." Chavez's imprisonment in the Monterey County jail elevated the lettuce boycott to the status of a cause célèbre, and Chavez was visited in jail by politicians, religious leaders, and celebrities. One of the visitors who received the most media attention was Coretta Scott King, who had become a SCLC board member. Scott King flew to Salinas on December 19, 1970, with SCLC executive vice president Andrew Young. Their jailhouse meeting with Chavez revealed the shared philosophies of their movements; Scott King later reported that she and Chavez spoke about "'non-violence—the best method of bringing about social change' through the glass partition of the jail's visiting room." Chavez later reflected on her visit, "She didn't tell me, but I could see that this reminded her of her husband being in jail. Unlike a lot of the farm worker women who came and cried, she looked at being in jail as part of the struggle."[41]

After meeting with Chavez in the jail visiting room, Scott King and Young conducted a brief press conference, during which they both stressed the connections between African Americans and Mexican Americans. Scott King also encouraged African Americans to boycott lettuce and explained, "When we come together and we know each other and we know what our common problems are, we realize that basically we have the same problems and that whenever there's progress for one, that means progress for all." Scott King elaborated on this sentiment later than evening when she addressed an audience of almost one thousand farmworkers and their supporters, including an estimated two to three hundred African Americans. As UFWOC vice president Dolores Huerta translated her speech into Spanish, Scott King proclaimed,

> I feel so close to you because nowhere in this country are people so fearlessly upholding their rights in a spirit of militant non-violence. Our brotherhood is not only grounded in our common exploitation, not only in our victimization of race, but it is based on our use of the same social weapon: non-violence, organization, militant mass action and soul force.

Scott King's speech demonstrates that she and SCLC had come to recognize the similarities between the farmworkers' fight for union representation and the civil rights movement's pursuit of equality, and therefore were determined to sustain their alliance with the UFWOC. As she proclaimed, "I know we will win our common fight because we are more united and have more mutual respect than ever in our history and because in mass ranks, we are moving forward."[42]

Scott King stressed both at the press conference and in her speech that she championed the farmworkers because of the similarities between the UFWOC and the civil rights movement. However, she was also motivated to support the farmworkers due to her rural background and personal experience with agricultural labor. At the conclusion of her speech, she revealed, "I do not have to read books or stimulate my imagination to understand how grueling it is to work in a sun-baked field all day." Scott King was born and raised in rural Alabama, where her family owned a small farm. As a child, she worked in the fields alongside her parents and siblings. Beginning when she was ten years old and throughout her teen years Scott King worked on local cotton farms to earn money. Although she was able to escape farm labor when she attended Antioch College in Ohio through a combination of scholarship and work-study, the severity of rural poverty followed her and money was a constant concern. For example, when she won a scholarship to the New England Conservatory of Music that only covered her tuition, she worked as a maid to pay for her room and board. But since the arrangement did not include dinner, she occasionally subsisted on graham crackers and peanut butter or went without eating.[43]

In contrast, Martin Luther King, Jr., was reared in urban Atlanta and had little knowledge of the problems confronting rural agricultural laborers. Although his paternal grandparents had been sharecroppers and his father worked in the fields as a child, King's only experience with agricultural labor was through a Morehouse College summer program at a tobacco farm in Connecticut. Under King's leadership, SCLC conducted most of its programs in urban areas. Moreover, after the Watts rebellion in 1965, King pushed the organization to focus on distinctly urban issues such as housing and employment. The urban focus of SCLC meant that the organization was not well versed in the structures of rural poverty. In the late 1950s King acknowledged the severity of rural poverty, but admitted that "he had been campaigning in cities and knew very little about it." Like Scott King, however, Ralph Abernathy was raised on a farm in rural Alabama, which informed his outlook and activism. He reflected in his autobiography, "My father always said that land would be the means by which we would rise in the world. He was convinced that the solution to the race problem was economic." Under Abernathy's leadership, SCLC's continued concern for the rural poor in the wake of the Poor People's Campaign facilitated its relationship with the UFWOC.[44]

Scott King's rural background and experience with poverty helped her to personally relate to the farmworkers of the UFWOC. It took no great intellectual leap or powers of imagination for her to recognize that the plight of Mexican American farmworkers mirrored those of rural African Americans. However, her support of the UFWOC was also part of a calculated effort to celebrate her husband's legacy. Within days of his assassination in April 1968, she began the process of establishing the King Center (later renamed the Martin Luther King, Jr. Center for Nonviolent Social Change). In her efforts to gain support for the Center and convince people of its necessity, Scott King struggled to keep King's memory in the public's consciousness. One way she did so was to connect King to contemporary issues and protests. For example, during her speech to the farmworkers in Salinas, she quoted King and declared, "You are carrying on, with other millions at the bottom, the work my husband began." Supporting the UFWOC therefore enabled Scott King not only to sustain King's legacy, but to expand it to causes in which he had not been involved.[45]

The support of Scott King, SCLC, and other prominent individuals, as well as the publicity it received, contributed to the California Supreme Court's decision to order Chavez's release from jail on December 23. Judge Campbell had no objections because of "the thought of what Chavez's supporters might do if their leader was still in jail on Christmas day." Just three weeks after his release, Chavez demonstrated his appreciation to Scott King and SCLC by appearing at a rally with Abernathy at Madison Square Garden in New York City to commemorate what would have been King's forty-second birthday. SCLC was determined to maintain its relationship with Chavez and the UFWOC. Reflecting the evolution of many in SCLC and their increasing openness to multiracial coalitions, SCLC national program director Hosea Williams explained in a letter to Chavez, "We have reached the point where we are prepared to think not solely about the people we have traditionally concentrated on helping, but about *all* the poor and repressed peoples of this country." The SCLC leadership hoped this expanded focus would help it to remain relevant in the face of significantly decreased funding, a fractured staff, and charges that it was doing little to benefit African Americans.[46]

SCLC also had to contend with the fact that by 1969 many Americans er-roneously believed the civil rights movement was over, which had prompted many on the left to move on to other causes, most notably the antiwar move-ment. Furthermore, conservative politicians such as Richard Nixon, Ronald Reagan, and George Wallace engaged in race baiting to inflame working- and middle-class white opposition to calls for civil rights and economic equality, especially those supported by Great Society programs. These changes also led to decreased support for the UFWOC. *El Malcriado* lamented in early 1970, "Affluent America seems to have turned its back on us and forgotten us, while taking for granted the food that we grow and harvest for this na-tion and much of the rest of the world." Furthermore, the weakened economy caused increased labor militancy, leading workers to protest for higher wages and improved working conditions in greater numbers and thus compet-ing with the farmworkers for the public's attention. For instance, there were 5,600 work stoppages in the United States in 1970 alone, including strikes in the railroad, electric, and automobile industries. A sustained relationship with SCLC would therefore benefit the UFWOC by guaranteeing a body of supporters for the union's activities.[47]

Loyal supporters were also essential to the UFWOC because it became increasingly difficult to maintain the support of the American public due to the complexity and unpredictability of the lettuce boycott. In March 1971 there appeared to be a breakthrough in the lettuce fields when the Teamsters and the UFWOC signed a revised three-year jurisdictional agreement that stipulated that the Teamsters would withdraw from the contracts they had made with the lettuce growers regarding representation of field workers. Af-ter the signing of the agreement on March 26 and with a resolution with the growers seemingly in sight, Chavez consented to order a moratorium on the boycotting of lettuce. The UFWOC position also appeared secure when the California Supreme Court ruled in April that Judge Campbell's injunction, which had led to Chavez's imprisonment, violated the First Amendment. Furthermore, the court ruled the injunction invalid on the basis of evidence that the growers had invited the involvement of the Teamsters, which dis-proved the growers' claim to be victims of a jurisdictional dispute between unions and thus deserved protection under California law.[48]

At first, the developments of March and April made it appear as if the let-tuce strike and boycott would soon end. On April 23, Mel Finerman Co., Inc., the largest independent lettuce grower in the United States, signed a two-year contract with the UFWOC that covered 5,000 workers. Soon thereafter, other growers agreed to meet with the union to discuss potential contracts. It was soon apparent to the UFWOC, however, that the growers did not enter into these negotiations in good faith. Following the Finerman contract, one grower remarked to a *Los Angeles Times* reporter that the other growers "are not going to knuckle under no matter what Chavez does." As promised, the lettuce growers rejected every offer by the UFWOC, even after the union offered "to give up certain clauses important to their interests." Negotiations stalled throughout the lettuce harvest. When the harvest ended in November, the growers broke off negotiations, leading the union to resume the boycott on November 11, 1971.[49]

Due to the machinations of the lettuce growers, 1971 was virtually a wasted year for the UFWOC. By putting faith in the growers and imposing a moratorium on the lettuce boycott, the farmworkers were not able to keep their cause in the national spotlight. Examination of national news coverage reveals a substantial decrease in reporting on the farmworkers during the period of negotiation with the growers. Furthermore, by not calling for a boycott of iceberg lettuce, the union's allies were not called upon to assist, as there was not much that their supporters could do to influence the UFWOC's negotiations with the growers. The resumption of the lettuce boycott in November did regain national attention for the farmworkers, but it also invigorated the union's adversaries. In February 1972, the AFL-CIO granted the UFWOC a charter, making it a full-fledged union. The union subsequently changed its name to the United Farm Workers, AFL-CIO (UFW). This change prompted the Republican-controlled National Labor Relations Board to file a petition in March with the Fresno Federal District Court requesting that the UFW be prohibited from conducting boycotts. Although agricultural workers were not covered by the National Labor Relations Act, the general counsel for the NLRB argued that because the AFL-CIO had granted the UFW its charter, the union was covered by extension. The actions of the NLRB thus ended the lettuce boycott after only four months.[50]

In response to the NLRB actions, the UFW decided to target the Republican Party because they believed the board's actions were politically motivated. Jacques Levy explained, "Facing national elections in 1972, the Nixon administration had turned to the Teamsters for its core of power within labor and had dispensed favors to many, including major segments of agribusiness." Because the general counsel and other members of the NLRB were Nixon appointees, the attack on the UFW appeared to be calculated to appeal to Nixon's backers. The union and its defenders therefore launched an extensive letter-writing campaign to Republican Party Chairman Senator Robert Dole and conducted pickets in front of Republican headquarters in 150 cities. Senator Edward Kennedy also called for an investigation of the NLRB and the Congressional Black Caucus threatened legal action.[51]

Scott King continued to support the UFW in its battle with the NLRB. The assistance she provided to the union was an extension of her work with the King Center, which had begun to conduct research and programs on using nonviolent protest to combat racial discrimination. After traveling with Young to the UFW headquarters at La Paz in February 1972 to meet with Chavez and other members of the union staff, Scott King offered the union the free services of Harry Wachtel, who was the legal counsel and vice president of the King Center and had provided legal services to King and SCLC. She also offered free use of the King Center's mailing lists and direct mailing operation. She explained, "Black churches, community groups across the country and hundreds of local unions who have shown their willingness to make contributions to progress can all be reached."[52]

The firestorm of protests led the NLRB to drop its case against the UFW in May 1972, enabling the lettuce boycott to resume. But just days later, the UFW experienced another setback when the Arizona legislature passed H.B. 2134, also known as the Farm Bureau Bill, that prohibited farmworker boycotts and was sponsored by lettuce growers. In response, Chavez began a twenty-four-day fast on May 9, the day the bill was signed by Governor Jack Williams. The UFW also decided to target Williams and make an example of him for signing the bill. Chavez explained, "We wanted to make the governor who signed that bill pay for it. We also didn't want to keep fighting similar bills in other states. So we thought if we recalled this governor, got him voted out of office, the others would get a little religion." SCLC promptly expressed support for the UFW's actions in Arizona. Officers of SCLC and Operation Breadbasket wrote letters endorsing Chavez's fast and signed petitions pledging to boycott lettuce. Ralph Abernathy sent a pledge card to the UFW vowing to join the boycott.[53]

Scott King also continued her support for the farmworkers in this phase of their struggle. On the nineteenth day of Chavez's fast, she visited him in Phoenix, Arizona. Throughout her visit with Chavez and the farmworkers, Scott King likened the oppression of Mexican Americans to that of African Americans and again connected her late husband's work to the farmworkers' fight for economic justice. She participated in a Roman Catholic mass at the Santa Rita Community Center, during which she read from King's book,

Strength to Love. In the course of her twenty-five-minute speech, she praised Chavez as "one of the truly nonviolent leaders in the tradition of my late husband." At the conclusion of her speech, the audience of over four hundred people sang the civil rights movement anthem "We Shall Overcome" in English and Spanish. Following the mass, Scott King gave a press conference in which she called on African Americans to boycott lettuce and participate in the effort to recall Governor Williams. She pledged she would "take the message back to the black community and try to communicate with the black community here in Phoenix so it understands the issues involved and how the two struggles of the black people and the farm workers are related." Scott King's visit was incredibly meaningful to the farmworkers. Lucia Vazquez, whose father volunteered with the UFW, recalled, "Her presence validated on some level the work we were doing. Even though many priests, sisters, and ministers were involved consistently, this minister's wife had brought us a blessing."[54]

Chavez was forced to break his fast on June 4 because of the toll it was taking on his health. Although he did not end the fast because of a clear victory for the farmworkers, it was announced at the mass ending the fast that over one million people had pledged to boycott lettuce. The congratulatory telegram from Abernathy summed up the effect of the fast: "Your call to sacrifice for justice and to alleviate the suffering of the farm workers has been an inspiration to all who strive for human rights." The UFW also did not succeed in recalling Governor Williams. Although 176,000 voters signed petitions calling for the governor's recall (far more than the minimum required to force a recall election), state election officials and the state attorney general prevented the recall election from being scheduled by invalidating 60,000 signatures; by the time that the UFW successfully proved in federal court that the signatures were valid, it was too close to the date of the general election to conduct a special recall election. However, the UFW was satisfied with the results of the Arizona campaign because it led farmworkers there to realize their political power. In the process of collecting recall signatures, the UFW registered 100,000 new voters among Mexican Americans, African Americans, Navajos, and working-class whites. These newly empowered voters promptly elected numerous Mexican Americans and Navajos to the state legislature, county offices, city councils, and school boards. Two years later, this bloc of voters provided the crucial margin of victory that led to the election of the first Latino governor of Arizona and gained the Democrats a majority in the state senate. UFW organizer Jim Drake explained, "We never lost sight

of the fact that we did not want a new governor, but that we wanted to organize the people and in the process send a clear message to all politicians that
they had to be responsive to the people, to the workers."[55]

One month after Chavez ended his fast, California growers followed
Arizona's example and attempted to diminish the power of the farmworkers
through legislation. In July 1972 the California produce growers and their
political allies sponsored the Agricultural Labor Relations Initiative, known
as Proposition 22, in an attempt to destroy the UFW by curtailing workers'
rights to organize and bargain collectively. Under Proposition 22, secondary
boycotts, such as the ones the UFW conducted against grocery stores during the grape boycott, would be illegal, as would "publicity directed against
any trademark, trade name of generic (species) nature of agricultural product." James L. Vizzard, a Jesuit priest who served as the UFW legislative liai-
son, noted that under this proposition, "For anyone to say 'Boycott lettuce'
would be a crime, punishable by fine and imprisonment, even if the statement were made outside California." Growers could be granted injunctions
automatically when a strike or boycott, real or threatened, was made against
their agricultural products. Finally, restrictions were to be placed on who
could participate in elections for union representation to workers who were
employed by one grower for 100 days a year. The measure also disqualified
farmworkers who had voted on another farm or ranch in the area during the
same year. If implemented, these provisions would have likely eliminated up
to 75 percent of Mexican American farmworkers from participation in union
elections.[56]

The growers used every tactic at their disposal to pass Proposition 22,
both legal and illegal. Just days before the election, sixteen paid petition cir-
culators were arrested and charged with fraud for forging signatures on petitions on behalf of Proposition 22. Growers and their supporters spent an
estimated $700,000 in their effort to gain support for the proposition, while
the UFW spent only $150,000 "mostly on food, transportation, and lodging
for hundreds of farm workers who traveled around the state making personal
contacts with the voters." The money and political influence of the growers
extended to agencies within the California state government. In the days after the fraud arrests, it was revealed that "the State Agriculture Department's
official statement in support of Proposition 22 actually was written by a public relations firm hired to promote the controversial initiative."[57]

Scott King was actively involved in the campaign against Proposition
22. Shortly before the election, she spoke at a rally in Los Angeles alongside

Figure 11. Coretta Scott King speaks at a rally against Proposition 22 held at Lincoln Park, Los Angeles, California, October 27, 1972. Courtesy of Walter P. Reuther Library, Wayne State University.

Chavez and Senator Edward Kennedy. As she had done at previous rallies, Scott King "praised Chavez as the leading present-day proponent of the nonviolent philosophy advocated by her late husband." However, Scott King's objections to Proposition 22 stemmed not only from her desire to perpetuate King's legacy, but also from her own views on economic justice. She decried the provisions of the proposition, most notably the prohibition of secondary boycotts. She asserted that, "the right to economic boycotts was 'as fundamental as the right to organize yourselves.'" Scott King had long been interested in the power of economic boycotts, especially those conducted by Operation Breadbasket. As the King Center grew, Scott King decided that it should perpetuate the economic boycott as an instrument of "militant nonviolence." She explained, "We want to institutionalize the boycott technique, teach people how to use it and create a network of groups to help support boycotts." Chavez's nonviolent use of the boycott during the grape and lettuce strikes epitomized her vision of the tactic's potential.[58]

Although Scott King's support of the farmworkers originated as a way to highlight King's legacy, it evolved to reflect her development as an activist in her own right. Moreover, supporting the UFW's highly publicized battles with growers and the Teamsters enabled her establish a visible role for herself. From her youth, Scott King had been committed to social justice and was especially active in peace organizations. However, her husband prevented her from engaging in most types of public activism because, as she explained in her memoir, "Martin was a very strong person, and in many ways had very traditional ideas about women." King therefore expected Scott King to perform the duties of a devoted housewife and mother and not to be a public figure. In fact, he did not allow her to speak in public for the first five years of their marriage. Scott King's desire for a more visible role in the movement, and King's adamant refusal, led to considerable marital tension, but she largely acquiesced to his wishes. King's assassination, however, allowed her to claim the public role she had coveted, prompting one journalist to compare Scott King's life without her late husband to "letting a songbird out of the cage." Scott King's commitment to the UFW, which contributed to the solid defeat of Proposition 22, indicates the degree to which she had come into her own as an activist.[59]

*   *   *

The SCLC participation in the UFW boycotts of grapes and lettuce, and campaign against Proposition 22, demonstrates the organization's significant evolution. During King's presidency, SCLC was uninterested in forming an alliance with the UFW. The farmworkers viewed *la causa* as comparable to the civil rights movement, but the UFW was still a union. Despite King's empathy for the poor and commitment to economic justice, he was largely distrustful of unions and ambivalent toward labor organizing. Moreover, the UFW was affiliated with the AFL-CIO—whose leadership both supported U.S. involvement in Vietnam and did little to end discrimination in its ranks—and was in conflict with the Teamsters, an ally of SCLC. Due to SCLC's lack of familiarity with Mexican Americans, the struggle of farmworkers in rural California also appeared to be unrelated to the issues confronted by African Americans in the urban North and South. To King, then, an alliance between SCLC and the UFW made little sense because it would be based on neither self-interest nor common goals. Only when King expanded his vision to include multiracial coalitions in the planning of the Poor People's Campaign did he consider establishing a relationship with Chavez and the farmworkers.

For Abernathy and Scott King, however, a coalition with the UFW was highly desirable. In the aftermath of the Poor People's Campaign, both recognized that African Americans and Mexican Americans were simultaneously the victims of racial discrimination and economic exploitation and therefore believed that an alliance between SCLC and UFW would be mutually beneficial. Abernathy and Scott King's rural backgrounds contributed to their empathy for the farmworkers; self-interest also motivated them. Abernathy was forced to guide SCLC as it struggled with a loss of supporters in an increasingly conservative and hostile climate, and therefore sought to gain new allies and improve its relationships with organized labor. Supporting the UFW enabled Scott King to sustain King's legacy while establishing herself as an activist.

Although Chavez was frequently likened to King due to their shared use of nonviolent resistance in the fight for racial equality, an alliance between the UFW and SCLC during King's presidency was untenable. It took the leadership of Abernathy and Scott King to engineer a relationship with the UFW that contributed to the union's victories in the boycotts against grapes and lettuce and the fight against Proposition 22.

CHAPTER 5

A Natural Alliance of Poor People

THE small plane careened over the fields, buffeted by the strong winds of California's Central Valley. Black Panther Party leaders Bobby Seale and Elbert "Big Man" Howard were taking the harrowing hour and a half flight, which seemed much longer to its passengers, to UFW headquarters at La Paz to meet with Cesar Chavez in March 1973. On landing, Seale and Howard were driven to the union's fenced-in compound and taken to the dining hall, where members were preparing dinner, and told to wait for Chavez. The aptly named "Big Man" recalled being awestruck at the sight of the small-statured Chavez: "When I saw him it [came] home to me how he could be such a charismatic leader. . . . He's the chosen one, I guess you might say." Chavez invited Seale and Howard to eat dinner with the assembled union members. After a communal grace, Chavez and Seale sat next to each other and had a private conversation. Richard Ybarra, Chavez's bodyguard and son-in-law, recalled that the two men got along "like very good friends. . . . It was a natural bonding." By the end of the meal, Chavez agreed to endorse Seale's candidacy for mayor of Oakland. Having obtained what they came for, later that evening Seale and Howard "left on that treacherous ride back on that little bitty plane."[1]

By the time that Seale announced his candidacy in May 1972, the alliance between the UFW and the BPP was five years old and had been beneficial for both. The farmworkers received much needed assistance from the Panthers on picket lines during the California grape boycott. The BPP also frequently published news on the farmworkers in the *Black Panther* newspaper. In turn, the union supported and spoke out in defense of the Party when it was subjected to both persecution in the courts and physical assault by law enforcement. But in 1972 the alliance that had formed during the California grape boycott had come to a turning point. During the previous five years of their relationship, both organizations had evolved in response to a variety of forces: the changing nature of their struggles, the internal dynamics of their own organizations, the vicissitudes of American society, and the increasing ruthlessness of their enemies. Independently and for different reasons, by the 1970s both organizations turned to electoral politics in order to achieve racial and economic equality. Their ability to once again find common cause strengthened their already advantageous alliance. Seale's mayoral campaign represented the culmination of this relationship and reinforced the importance of individual leadership and class solidarity in multiracial coalition building.

*   *   *

Although the Panthers had participated in the UFW grape boycott, they were not initially involved in the union's struggles with growers of iceberg lettuce, even after Chavez was imprisoned, mainly because the actions of law enforcement and COINTELPRO were causing serious, expensive, and time-consuming legal problems for the Party. Throughout 1969, Panthers across the country were being arrested regularly on charges ranging from disorderly conduct to murder as part of FBI and police attempts to "neutralize" the Party. In August 1969 Party leaders Seale and Ericka Huggins were arrested and charged with the kidnapping and murder of Alex Rackley, a Panther in New Haven, Connecticut, suspected of being an undercover agent. The persecution of the Panthers had much in common with that of the UFW. Judge Gordon Campbell, who ordered Chavez's arrest for refusing to end the union's boycott of iceberg lettuce, was the judge originally assigned to preside over the case of the "Soledad Brothers" (John Clutchette, Fleeta Drumgo, and BPP member George Jackson), who were accused of murdering a guard at Soledad State Prison and were supported by the Party. After Campbell stepped down from the case due to charges of racial bias, he was replaced by Judge Anthony Brazil, who later prohibited the UFW from picketing and conducting all other strike activity. Despite these connections, Panther leaders were unable to rally members to Chavez's defense during his imprisonment because their primary attention, fundraising, and mobilizing were focused on the Seale and Huggins trial, which lasted over six months (it took almost four months to select the twelve-member jury from 1,500 potential jurors). On May 25, 1971, the charges against Seale and Huggins were dropped after almost two years in jail.[2]

In the period immediately following the release of Seale and Huggins, the Panthers were still unable to provide significant support to Chavez and the UFW. Following the release of Party co-founder and Minister of Defense Huey P. Newton from prison in 1969, ideological differences developed between Newton and Minister of Information Eldridge Cleaver over the future direction of the Party. In light of the years of battles with law enforcement agencies, which led to the deaths, beatings, and imprisonment of scores of Panthers, Newton believed that the Party needed to shift from a revolutionary to a more reformist agenda. Newton therefore decided that the Party would prioritize its community service programs—which Seale had developed while Newton had been in prison—over armed self-defense and confrontation with police forces. Newton explained in his 1973 memoir, *Revolutionary Suicide*, that the programs, which were referred to as survival programs "pending revolution," "were designed to help the people survive until their consciousness is raised, which is only the first step in the revolution to produce a new America." The survival programs, which included free busing to prisons, escorts for seniors, home maintenance, grocery and shoe giveaways, and the Free Breakfast for Children Program, were enormously successful and had endeared the Panthers to Oakland's black community. Cleaver, on the other hand, believed that black liberation could only be achieved through armed struggle. He explained in a 1971 essay, "We have one and only one path open to us: to arm and organize ourselves into a powerful, deadly, invincible block inside the United States so that the United States cannot do anything of which we do not approve. There is no other path open to us."[3]

The disagreements between Newton and Cleaver, accelerated by a FBI campaign to create distrust and suspicion between the two leaders through the use of forged letters, escalated until February 26, 1971 when the conflict came to a head during a morning television news show in San Francisco, with Cleaver participating by telephone from exile in Algeria. During the live broadcast, the two argued and Cleaver criticized the leadership of the Party. Shortly thereafter, Newton expelled Cleaver from the BPP. This insurmountable rift between the two, known as "The Split," divided the Panthers into Newton and Cleaver factions. The Split, combined with the relentless attacks on Panthers by law enforcement, resulted in a substantial decrease in Party activity. Given the internal turmoil, it became virtually impossible for the Panthers in northern California to assist the farmworkers in their protests.[4]

By the early months of 1972, however, Newton and Seale had regained control of the BPP, at least in California, and set about implementing the group's new emphasis on its survival programs. The BPP had always intended the survival programs as "a means of organizing . . . the black community," but by 1972 the most popular program, the free breakfasts for children, had been adopted by churches, parent-teacher associations, and local governments across the country. This demonstrated to the Party that their programs could be used to organize people on a much larger scale and could also be successfully incorporated into existing social and political structures. The Panthers also realized that if they used the survival programs to gain political power, they would provide a model for poor communities nationwide. Panther Bill Jennings explained, "Our concept was we can't change the world, we can't change every state, but if we can use Oakland as an example of how to go about garnering political power then people everywhere could see it, just like the breakfast program."[5]

The BPP's turn to political power reflected larger shifts in black activism. Beginning in the late 1960s, a disparate array of black activists began to embrace electoral politics as a way to both remedy longstanding patterns of institutional racism and enact longstanding change through legislation and public policy. Reflecting the ideology of the Lowndes County Freedom Organization, black activists increasingly viewed voting as insufficient in the pursuit of racial equality if it meant that politicians who did not represent the interests of the black community were repeatedly elected. African Americans therefore pursued political power through office holding, especially on the local level; serving on city councils, boards of education, and police commissions enabled African Americans to implement programs that were often more important to local communities than sweeping civil rights legislation on the national level. Furthermore, political power exercised on the local level reflected Black Power's emphasis on community control, in which the members of the community would have greater power and decision making regarding the institutions in their community.[6]

The shift toward political representation led to several important developments in black politics, such as the election of Carl Stokes as mayor of Cleveland, Ohio in 1967 (the first African American mayor of a major city), the election of Richard Hatcher as mayor of Gary, Indiana that same year, the founding of the Congressional Black Caucus in 1971, the presidential campaign of Shirley Chisholm in 1972, and the National Black Political Convention in March 1972, in which BPP leaders participated. Inspired by these accomplishments and convinced that electoral politics was the best way to bring change to the black community, the Party's Central Committee decided in May 1972 that Seale would run for mayor of Oakland the following year; it was later decided that Panther Elaine Brown would run for Oakland City Council. While this seemed to some like an about-face in BPP strategy, Seale explained, "We're going to use the existing institution to serve the people. See, we're part of the system. You cannot get out of the system. . . . The very system that sends the cops down to beat our heads causes us to be hungry. I mean, how you're gonna stop it unless you take control of the system and then from there transform it." The election of Stokes also inspired the BPP because Panthers in Cleveland registered significant numbers of African Americans who voted for Stokes. The Central Committee believed that if their members could help deliver a victory to Stokes in Cleveland, then they should be able to replicate those results in Oakland. In order to harness the power of the entire BPP for Seale's campaign, Newton ordered all other Party chapters to close and summoned their members and resources to Oakland.[7]

This was not the first time that Panthers had run for office. In 1968 leaders of the BPP were candidates for political offices on the ballot of the Peace and Freedom Party (PFP), an independent political party formed by white radicals in California in 1967 to oppose the war in Vietnam. Seale and Kathleen Cleaver ran for the California State Assembly, Newton ran for U.S. Congress, and Eldridge Cleaver was the PFP candidate for president. In an effort to demonstrate its support for the black freedom struggle, the PFP had formed an alliance with the BPP in December 1967. The BPP, on the other hand, entered into this alliance to gain publicity and support for Newton, who had been arrested for shooting a police officer two months earlier. As such, the Party viewed the campaigns as opportunities for raising funds and awareness of Newton's case, as well as to mobilize for community control of the police. The BPP, however, did not expect to win the elections. After receiving a small percentage of votes, Seale continued to view the importance of the election in terms of its success in mobilizing people. He later wrote in *Seize the Time*, "One thing we found out for sure, was how many thousands of voters really support the Party. A person would have to support the Black Panther Party and know something about our basic ideas to vote for a member of our Party who was on the ballot." In 1972, however, symbolic victories were not enough

for the BPP; they intended to win. To both test the waters of municipal reform and demonstrate their sincerity, ten Panthers ran for and were elected
to antipoverty agencies in Berkeley and Oakland in the spring of 1972.[8]

Participation in electoral politics allowed the BPP to demonstrate its
continued commitment to interracial alliances, which was the product of
the racial and ethnic diversity of its base in Oakland. The BPP had emphasized multiracial cooperation in the belief that the working-class struggle
against capitalist exploitation superseded racial differences, a reflection of its
adoption of socialism. In February 1970 the BPP released a statement in the
Guardian that declared,

> The Black Panther party stands for revolutionary solidarity with
> all people fighting against the forces of imperialism, capitalism,
> racism and fascism. . . . We will not fight capitalism with black
> capitalism; we will not fight racism with black racism. Rather we
> will take our stand against these evils with a solidarity derived
> from a proletarian internationalism born of socialist idealism.

This statement reflected the Party's philosophy of revolutionary intercommunalism, which Newton developed while in prison and presented at the
Revolutionary People's Constitutional Convention in September 1970.
According to revolutionary intercommunalism, nationalist attempts to seize
power were meaningless in light of the forces of globalization. Due to the
global reach of capitalism, oppression and exploitation surpassed national
borders. Revolutionary intercommunalism therefore included a call for cooperation among oppressed communities worldwide in opposition to capitalism, imperialism, and racism. Although this philosophy put the BPP at
odds with black nationalists, it contributed to the BPP's ability to form a
number of interracial coalitions that provided valuable experience—and supporters—necessary to win a political campaign.[9]

The applicability of the BPP's philosophy of revolutionary intercommunalism and earlier interracial alliances to electoral politics was demonstrated
in the 1972 campaign against California Proposition 22, which growers sponsored just two months after Seale launched his campaign. Because Seale and
Brown's electoral bids overlapped with the UFW's campaign against Proposition 22, the BPP leadership once again allied the Party with the farmworkers.
For example, the September 23, 1972 issue of the *Black Panther* newspaper
devoted several pages to the farmworkers' plight and urged its readers to vote

Figure 12. Cover of September 23, 1972 issue of the *Black Panther*. © 2012 Emory Douglas/Artists Rights Society (ARS), New York.

against Proposition 22; the front page featured a striking graphic designed by Panther artist Emory Douglas of a head of iceberg lettuce with the UFW eagle superimposed over it under the words "Boycott Lettuce." In their support of the UFW, the *Black Panther* newspaper editorialized, "We, Black people, join with the Spanish-speaking people in common struggle against a common oppression. We know, far too well, the plight of the landless and the dispossessed." The Party's renewed support for the farmworkers was thus a product of the Panthers' firm belief in class-based, interracial solidarity and cooperation. Despite the ideological changes within the Party, the remaining leaders still understood that UFW members and the vast majority of black workers were victimized by the same capitalist institutions and structures.[10]

As the November 1972 election approached, the Black Panther Party increased its assistance to the UFW in its fight against Proposition 22. In order to publicize the issues surrounding the measure, farmworkers dispersed to cities all over California and went door to door to explain their plight to voters. Because the Panthers had been essential to the UFW's boycott of Safeway grocery stores, Chavez recognized that their assistance would be critical to reaching African American voters in Oakland. At his request, BPP members campaigned against Proposition 22 in the black community and helped get voters to the polls. The Panthers also arranged for UFW members campaigning in Oakland to stay at Mills College, a local women's college. On November 5, 1972 Chavez visited the BPP Central Headquarters. That evening, Panthers Elaine Brown and Ericka Huggins spoke to the farmworkers who were working the precincts in Oakland. Brown voiced the spirit of camaraderie and solidarity that the Panthers felt with the UFW and the need for interracial cooperation: "We must begin to work more with each other, because without each other, there will be no overcoming, there will be no power to the people, there will be no winning our own cause. This is our case, together. Proposition 22 is a part of our struggle." Huggins agreed with Brown's sentiments: "I think that having everybody here, at a time like this, is very, very beautiful. It says a lot about the progress that oppressed people can continue to make."[11]

Due to the strong campaigning by the farmworkers and support from the BPP and their other allies in organized labor, the church, and the left, Proposition 22 was soundly defeated by 58 percent of the vote. However, the victory over Proposition 22 did not end the alliance between UFW and BPP. Rather, each group learned lessons from the campaign that strengthened their relationship. The *Black Panther* poetically declared, "The failure of Proposition 22 clearly shows that we, farmworkers and all of us, have planted the seeds that can begin to yield the most beautiful harvest of all—freedom and liberation." When the Party included the fight against Proposition 22 in its own venture into electoral politics, the UFW and the BPP explicitly united their causes, broadened their political bases, and increased their power. In defeating Proposition 22, both groups had decisive evidence that their alliance could produce tangible—and significant—results. But the corrupt methods of the opposition also taught them that their opponents were strong, influential, and committed. In fact, immediately after the election the growers made it clear they intended to continue their campaign to destroy the UFW and "promised to try again not only in California, but across the country." Therefore, it was imperative that the UFW and BPP maintain their alliance in the face of their common foes. Building on the momentum from the battle against Proposition 22, the UFW and BPP continued to work together during Seale's mayoral campaign.[12]

*   *   *

From the beginning of Seale's campaign, he and the BPP set out to demonstrate that his platform was not solely concerned with African American issues and that he was intent on addressing the concerns of Mexican Americans as well. This demonstrated both the BPP's historic commitment to multiracial solidarity and its political savvy. The Party was well aware that African Americans and Mexican Americans were the fastest growing groups in Oakland in 1972, and thus had the power to determine the outcome of elections if they registered and voted. According to the 1970 census, Oakland's population was 34.5 percent African American and 7.6 percent Hispanic. Seale's campaign correctly recognized that if the two groups worked together, they would form a significant voting bloc in the city. The Party also understood that productive coalitions would be essential to its success in governing Oakland once in office. As "Big Man" Howard explained, "We probably got into a coalition of political power that could really make some significant changes along those levels. Not necessarily radical changes, but positive changes because we, the Party, couldn't run the city all on its own. We would have to work with that broad cross-section." Therefore, Seale's campaign, headed by Panther Bill Jennings, implemented a series of actions designed to appeal to Oakland's Mexican American community.[13]

Seale and the BPP made a concerted effort to strengthen their ties to Oakland's Mexican American community in meaningful ways. Because the vast majority of Mexican Americans in Oakland spoke Spanish in the home and were born either in Mexico or in the United States to Mexican-born parents, Seale's campaign committee printed campaign fliers in both English and Spanish. The BPP candidates held meetings in Mexican American churches and community centers in Oakland where Mexican Americans presented their needs and concerns. At the behest of activists in the city's Latino community, Seale called for Oakland to become the first city in California to provide ballots and electoral information in Spanish. In an open letter to the mayor and city council, he pointed out that failure to do so was not only "insulting" to Spanish speakers, but "injurious to good government." Seale also appealed to the current of nationalist sentiment in the Mexican American community by pointing out that Mexicans were the first settlers in California and that, therefore, "the Spanish language is, in a very real sense, the native language of California." Indeed, the BPP readily understood the importance of learning Spanish and thus offered Spanish language classes in its Oakland Community School, the Party's acclaimed elementary school.[14]

Two weeks after Seale sent the open letter, he and Chicano community organizers Mary Thomas and Antonio Rodarte presented the issue in front of the Oakland City Council, resulting in the council's endorsement of their proposition. While the proposal was being further evaluated by the council's Civic Action Committee, the BPP urged the black community to support the use of bilingual ballots. In doing so, the Party educated the African American and Mexican American communities on the connections between their struggles and reinforced the importance of multiracial unity. An article in the *Black Panther* declared,

> The Black Panther Party calls on the Black community to support the Chicano community's drive to make Spanish, a language spoken on California soil long before English, and the language from which many of Oakland's street and place names have been drawn, into the second language to be included on election ballots. We believe that the English-only ballot is discriminatory towards Spanish-speaking people, just at the poll tax and grandfather clause in the Jim Crow South were discriminatory towards Black people.

By supporting the call for bilingual ballots and election materials during the 1973 election, the BPP predated by two years the NAACP's support for the Mexican American Legal Defense and Education Fund's (MALDEF) successful bid to add language provisions in 1975 to the extension of the 1965 Voting Rights Act.[15]

Seale's call for bilingual ballots and election materials was only one aspect of his platform that appealed to Oakland's Mexican American community. In fact, nearly every part of Seale's political program contained an element of particular interest to Mexican Americans. In the area of employment, Seale planned to force the Port of Oakland to hire "Black and Spanish speaking people proportionate to their unemployed status in the city." Seale also called for the increased hiring of Mexican Americans in police departments, fire departments, and other public agencies. In the area of education, Seale's platform called for the hiring of Spanish-speaking teachers and teachers assistants and the implementation of bilingual education. Of particular interest to the UFW, Seale called for the opening of childcare centers for migrant workers, in addition to expanded preschools.[16]

At the same time that the BPP reached out to Oakland's Mexican American community, it sought to strengthen its relationship with the UFW. The *Black Panther* newspaper continued to publish updates on the union's struggles and called for support from the African American community, but in January 1973 the Party leadership began to pursue a more direct relationship with the UFW's leaders, especially Cesar Chavez. Many Panthers not only admired him, but Party leaders also reasoned that if Chavez endorsed Seale's campaign, it would attract more Mexican American voters to their campaign. Howard explained, "I saw him as a powerful force out there and if we could get him to endorse the running and see that we were being all-inclusive in the community to deal with the ills of everybody then that would be very important." Chavez's endorsement was indeed vital in rallying Mexican American voters to Seale's side. According to Richard Ybarra, Chavez was important to the BPP because "he validated their existence and their goals and told other people it was ok to support them if they might have been somewhat unpopular in the broader community." Ever since the Panthers marched on the California State Capital in Sacramento in May 1967 in protest of the Mulford Act, they had been portrayed in the media as violent and dangerous. The highly publicized arrests and deaths of Party members contributed to their negative image among much of the public. Just as the survival programs had salvaged the Panthers' image among the conservative elements of the African American community, Chavez's endorsement significantly improved their reputation in the Mexican American community.[17]

Chavez was also interested in strengthening the relationship between the UFW and the BPP. The Party had been indispensable in the UFW battle against Proposition 22, and he wanted to sustain the alliance. In early January 1973 Chavez and Seale began calling and corresponding with each other in an attempt to arrange a personal meeting. That March, Seale and Howard traveled to the UFW headquarters in La Paz to meet with Chavez and seek his endorsement, breaking Seale's earlier pledge that he would not actively seek endorsements. After dinner with Chavez and farmworkers in the union hall, Chavez agreed to support Seale's campaign, largely because of the Party's previous support for the UFW. Eliseo Medina recalled that the decision to endorse Seale was an easy one: "I think that we, all of us, felt such an affinity for the Panthers and for everybody connected with that that it was just natural."[18]

Chavez had become accustomed to giving endorsements to political candidates, which he viewed as instrumental to obtaining legislation favorable to farmworkers. Furthermore, by voicing their support for farmworkers, political candidates—and the constant media attention that they received—could provide a powerful platform for the UFW and its endeavors. Chavez's endorsement was also valuable to politicians who wanted to appeal to Latino voters; Chavez had become adept at mobilizing the Latino vote through the Viva Kennedy campaign and his work with the CSO and was therefore viewed as indispensable in reaching that demographic. However, he only endorsed those who he believed to be sincerely supportive of farmworkers. For example, in 1968 Chavez endorsed Senator Robert Kennedy's presidential campaign and agreed to serve as a delegate for him at the Democratic National Convention. Although the AFL-CIO supported President Lyndon Johnson, Chavez endorsed Kennedy because of his support of the farmworkers beginning with his participation in the Senate Subcommittee Hearings on Migratory Labor in 1966. Upon endorsing Kennedy, the union organized a voter registration drive and phone bank and distributed leaflets. Chavez also spoke in support of Kennedy at universities and churches. As a result of their hard work, the UFW was credited with obtaining the Mexican American vote for Kennedy in California. Due to this accomplishment, Senator Eugene McCarthy sought Chavez's endorsement following Kennedy's assassination. Chavez did not grant it, however, because not only was McCarthy ignorant of the farmworkers' issues, but he appeared to Chavez and other UFW leaders to be indifferent to and "uncomfortable with poor people."[19]

Mayors and mayoral candidates of cities with significant Latino populations, which had been growing steadily since the passage of the Immigration and Nationality Act in 1965, also prized Chavez's endorsement. Likewise, allies in municipal governments were important to the UFW. As Chavez explained to Jaques Levy, "We have to participate in the governing of towns and school boards. We have to make our influence felt everywhere and anywhere." The need to cultivate allies and power on the local level was especially important in California, which had elected Republican Ronald Reagan, who was notoriously hostile to the UFW, as governor in 1966. Chavez understood that sympathetic city governments were essential to the success of major boycotts. For example, mayors could prohibit city agencies from purchasing boycotted products. Accordingly, during the grape boycott Chavez met with the mayors of several major cities to secure their support. This included recently elected African American mayors, with whom he felt an affinity based on the shared experience of racial discrimination. In 1968 Chavez met with Cleveland mayor Carl Stokes and came away deeply impressed. In 1969 the UFW endorsed Los Angeles city councilman Tom Bradley in his campaign for mayor of that city. The union's newspaper noted, "As a Black man, Bradley is familiar with the problems that minority groups, especially Chicanos and Blacks have with L.A.'s notorious cops and with the city bureaucracy." However, the most important factor in the UFW's endorsement of Bradley was his longtime support of the farmworkers and the potential of having such a strong ally in the mayor's office. *El Malcriado* explained that a Bradley victory over incumbent Samuel Yorty was in the best interest of the UFW: "The present administration, with its anti-labor, anti-Chicano, anti-Black attitude, has created a reactionary atmosphere in the city, and contributed towards making L.A. the largest consumer of scab grapes in the country. A new mayor, more sympathetic to the poor people, might help to change that atmosphere." The endorsement of Chavez and the union was then used by the Bradley campaign to garner support from the Latino community.[20]

Chavez's endorsement of Seale was thus in keeping with his pattern of supporting farmworkers' political allies. Chavez and the UFW announced their endorsement of Seale's campaign in a press release on March 29, 1973: "We laud Bobby Seale's approach to gaining political power for his people and all poor people in the city of Oakland. . . . We support their efforts and urge all registered voters of Oakland to support them on April 17." From that moment, Seale's mayoral campaign was explicitly tied to the struggles of the

UFW. For example, the BPP held voter registration rallies where free bags of groceries were distributed to the community. The bags of groceries included UFW literature and buttons, which were worn by African Americans in Oakland. A few days after the UFW's endorsement of Seale, it was announced that two days before the election, Chavez would deliver a sermon at St. Louis Bertrand Church, a Spanish-speaking Catholic parish in Oakland, on behalf of Seale's campaign, followed by a reception to raise funds for the UFW.[21]

Unfortunately, the mayoral election came at a critical juncture in UFW history. On the day Chavez was scheduled to speak in Oakland, he was forced to cancel because the leaders of the Western Conference of Teamsters announced that they had signed contracts with grape growers in the Coachella Valley who were previously under contract with the UFW. In a telegram to Seale, Chavez reinforced the unity between the BPP and the UFW by stating, "We are present in spirit, for we are part of the same struggle for justice and dignity which these candidates represent."[22]

The Teamsters had been attempting to undermine the UFW's contracts with California's grape growers since January of that year. With little evidence, the Teamsters began to publicly claim that they represented the majority of the field workers. They succeeded in instilling so much doubt in the minds of the growers that the UFW contract renewal negotiations stalled through March, until all of the growers withdrew by early April to reevaluate their options. Although the growers had consistently been opposed to union representation for its workers, they welcomed the return of the Teamsters, who were considered to be preferable to the UFW. The growers' resentment of the UFW stemmed in part from racial prejudice. *New York Times* reporter Steven V. Roberts noted, "The white growers never felt comfortable with the farm workers union, which is largely Mexican-American, and many of them continued to believe that Mr. Chavez was a wild-eyed radical whose ultimate aim was to expropriate their land." Even the growers who respected Chavez and the UFW were dissatisfied with the union's administration of its contracts, especially regarding the operation of the hiring hall and the handling of grievances. But the basis of their dissatisfaction was also rooted in their commitment to maintaining the hierarchy between the growers and the workers. Ronald B. Taylor observed, "The shifting of power away from the grower and placing it in the hands of the workers, through the ranch committees and hiring halls, was traumatic." The grape growers' dissatisfaction and resentment enabled the Teamsters to easily take over the UFW contracts.[23]

On April 15, the expiration date of the contracts, the Western Conference of Teamsters announced that the union had signed contracts with 85 percent of the grape growers in the Coachella Valley. The Teamsters also claimed to be the union of choice of the field workers, as evidenced by petitions that "carried signatures in favor of the teamsters from 4,000 of the 5,000 workers seasonally employed." Chavez vigorously denied these claims, asserting that only 1,800 field workers were employed in the region at that time, "with only about 1,000 more during the peak harvest season." Furthermore, Chavez cited the poll taken by clergy and labor leaders on April 10 to determine the worker's preferences for organization, which revealed that out of 953 workers, 795 wanted to be represented by the UFW, 80 preferred the Teamsters, and 78 did not want any union representation. One thousand farmworkers attended a UFW rally on April 13 in Coachella where they voted to strike any grower who signed a contract with the Teamsters. In the wake of the Teamsters' announcement, the UFW immediately followed through not only by striking the offending growers, but by declaring a renewed boycott of table grapes.[24]

The UFW declaration of a new strike and boycott served to intensify the alliance between the union and BPP. Seale's campaign still held its planned rally on April 15 at St. Louis Bertrand Church, despite the fact that Chavez was not to appear. An administrative assistant for the union read Chavez's telegram to the audience. Elaine Brown forcefully expressed support for the UFW's efforts by reading a telegram she and Seale had sent to Chavez in response:

> Though you could not be here with us today, we wish to express to you, Cesar Chavez, to the entire membership of the United Farmworkers Organizing Committee, and to the countless men, women and children whose lives are currently and callously being parleyed for profits by deceitful growers and opposition unions, our complete and open solidarity and support with your efforts to secure the basic human rights for the farmworkers of this country.

Seale then gave a stirring speech in which he described his personal reasons for supporting the UFW. The farmworkers' battle hit close to home for Seale, whose father supplemented his carpentry income as a farm labor contractor. When Seale was fourteen years old, his father bought a surplus Army bus to transport farmworkers to the fields surrounding the Bay Area. Seale, his brother John, his sister Betty, and other black youths often picked fruit along with the other farmworkers and "got to know a lot of young Mexican American people who were also in the fields trying to make a living." The elder Seale charged the growers one dollar per head that he brought to the fields, and he charged the farmworkers one dollar each for the bus ride. Seale was disturbed by his father's practices and when the crop was not good, he and his brother, sister, and mother would insist that the elder Seale only charge the workers fifty cents for the ride. Seale revealed to the audience that night, "I know what [the farmworkers] are talking about, I know what they mean when they demand their rights. I just couldn't charge a mother who was trying to ride the bus out to the farm . . . who made only three or four dollars a day. I couldn't charge her a dollar . . . I wouldn't do it."[25]

Seale's childhood experiences with Mexican Americans reinforce the importance of close knowledge and personal relationships in cross-racial coalition building. Because Seale's sense of injustice had been aroused at a young age by the exploitation of farmworkers, he was sympathetic to the UFW cause and the farmworkers' plight. Long before his leadership of the BPP, Seale came to see that the trials and tribulations of exploited workers crossed racial lines. The UFW did not introduce him to the plight of farmworkers, and mere political expediency was not the reason for Seale's support. Rather, the memories of his early experience with Mexican American farmworkers stayed with him and influenced his leadership within the Party and his political career. His knowledge and leadership were therefore instrumental in establishing the alliance between the UFW and the BPP.

The affection Seale felt for the UFW was mutual. On Election Day, April 17, the UFW was subjected to violent attacks by Teamsters. The UFW informed the BPP that "a squad of about 50 Teamster goons, armed with baseball bats and chains, arrived to try to intimidate our members who are striking in the Coachella Valley." However, Seale and the Party were not far from the minds of Chavez and the UFW. When it was revealed that Seale had obtained enough votes to qualify for a run-off election against incumbent Mayor John Reading, the embattled UFW leadership took the time to send a letter of congratulations and a donation to Seale's campaign. The union once again united its cause with Seale's campaign: "We face a long, difficult struggle, but we are confident. In the end we will be thankful for the strength that will come to us through struggle. Good luck on the run-off election. Our best wishes are with you for government which will give power to the people."[26]

Panther leaders were moved by the UFW's show of support for Seale during such a tumultuous time for the union. Huey Newton sent a telegram to Chavez thanking him and offering assistance to the union: "We know that your union is fighting for its very life, and we offer any support needed in any way we can be of help." Chavez thanked Newton the following week for his offer, but he did not take him up on it. Chavez knew that to involve the Panthers might escalate the level of violence from the Teamsters. Without explicitly turning him down, Chavez wrote to Newton, "I think that this struggle will show the American public that our non-violence is more persuasive than Teamster goonism."[27]

Seale and Party leaders understood and respected the UFW's commitment to nonviolence and continued to support the farmworkers with methods they had used in the past, such as reporting on all of the union's developments in lengthy and detailed articles in the *Black Panther*. These articles, while comprehensive, were far from unbiased and heaped praise on the farmworkers, referring to the grape boycott as a "struggle for justice and human dignity." At the same time, the BPP never criticized the UFW for maintaining their commitment to nonviolence in the face of violent attacks by the Teamsters. The *Black Panther* editorialized,

> There is no question as to whether the United Farm Workers will
> defeat the Teamsters in this latest round, for one fact remains
> clear: the desire of people to live in dignity cannot be crushed. The
> Farm Workers Union represents that hope for dignity, while the
> Teamsters Union, grown fat from corruption, remains the arm of
> the agricultural growers.[28]

The UFW was in dire need of the Party's support, in any form, as the violence between farmworkers and Teamsters increased. In early May, the UFW filed a lawsuit seeking more than $32 million in damages from eight Coachella growers, who along with hired goons had "entered into a conspiracy and systemized campaign of terrorism, intimidation, threats, assault, battery and collusion designed to forcefully prevent the farm union (UFW) from exercising its constitutional rights of free speech and expression." Realizing that the UFW needed to rally its supporters after making such a bold move, Chavez met with Seale on May 9, a few days after the lawsuit was filed. During a speaking tour of Bay Area colleges where Chavez was explaining the new grape boycott, he and Seale met at Merritt College in Oakland. The two leaders talked privately and then moved to a conference room where they provided details about Seale's campaign and the UFW's boycott to a large audience of supporters and the press. A reporter for the *Black Panther* noted, "Though using different tactics to serve their people, both understood the undeniable bond of their struggles." Chavez pledged to send UFW members to Oakland to campaign for Seale in the days leading up to the runoff election. Although Chavez and the UFW had previously endorsed several Democratic candidates across the country, this was one of the few times when Chavez went beyond issuing a press release and sent UFW members to assist. When Seale asked how he and the Party could aid the UFW boycott, Chavez replied, "The most important thing you can do now is to channel all of your forces into the campaign and win the elections for all of us."[29]

Even though the UFW rural base was far from Oakland, Chavez and the farmworkers understood the importance of Seale's election for the union. If Seale was mayor of Oakland, one of the farmworkers' strongest allies could use his position to publicize the UFW cause and to order city agencies to participate in the boycott. Moreover, Seale's leadership would undermine the historically antilabor stance of the Oakland city government. Beginning in the 1930s, the Oakland Police Department had assisted in breaking strikes and had frequently been accused of brutality directed at labor organizers. By the 1940s, the staunch antilabor position of the city government had rendered workers and their unions virtually powerless. Chavez was well aware of these dynamics because his first paid position with the CSO was to organize a chapter and voter registration campaign in Oakland. Moreover, Oakland's city government was heavily influenced by California's powerful agribusiness corporations. For example, throughout the 1960s a vice president of Safeway consistently sat on the Oakland School Board. And during the first six years of his tenure as mayor of Oakland, Republican incumbent John H. Reading was also president of Ingram's Food Products Co., which produced packaged foods. Therefore, Seale's election would simultaneously strengthen the position of the UFW in Oakland and weaken the hold of the union's enemies in agribusiness on city officials.[30]

Following the press conference, Chavez and Seale filmed a television endorsement for the campaign and met with students from Malcolm X Elementary School in Berkeley. Pictures taken of Chavez and Seale with the students were immediately used in a bilingual campaign flier that was distributed within Oakland's Spanish-speaking community. The flier proclaimed Chavez's endorsement of Seale's campaign, listed several other prominent Latinos who had endorsed Seale, and noted how Seale's platform met "the needs of Oakland's Raza community" by advocating for bilingual election materials, bilingual education, and increased Latino representation in city government. But perhaps

Figure 13. Cesar Chavez, Bobby Seale, and Richard Ybarra greet students from Malcolm X Elementary School following a press conference at Merritt College, Oakland, California, May 9, 1973. Courtesy of Walter P. Reuther Library, Wayne State University.

more significant was Chavez's act of walking the Spanish-speaking precincts of Oakland, personally going door-to-door asking the people to vote for Seale, which he did later that day. Richard Ybarra recalled, "I remember when we were walking precincts for Bobby, [Chavez] felt very good walking, very comfortable, and very proud." This simple act not only demonstrated the level of Chavez's personal commitment to Seale and his campaign, but may have influenced others to join him in supporting the Panther candidate.[31]

*   *   *

Although Seale lost the run-off by a narrow margin, he did not abandon the cause of the UFW with the end of the election. Rather, Seale channeled much of his surplus time and energy into supporting the farmworkers. The BPP followed suit, reporting on boycott developments in each issue of the *Black Panther*. Beginning with the June 9, 1973 edition, each issue of the paper included a clip-and-send form for readers to send monetary donations directly to the UFW. The Panthers were closely involved in the UFW's renewed battle with Safeway grocery stores. On June 6, 1973, the union called on Safeway to sell only UFW grapes and lettuce, but the store chain's executives refused. As a result, the UFW began picketing at 150 Safeway stores. However, a week later Safeway won an injunction that limited UFW pickets to "one per store entrance or parking lot entrance and seven per parking lot." As during the earlier grape boycott, the Panthers rallied to the side of the union when it once again went up against the Party's old nemesis, reinforcing the importance of common interests (and enemies) in their alliance.[32]

Panther leaders did not let Safeway's injunction against the UFW prevent them from helping the farmworkers. Instead, the BPP launched its own boycott of Safeway. On July 6, Elaine Brown and Seale held a press conference in front of the store on 27th and West Streets in West Oakland that the Party had succeeded in shutting down four and a half years earlier for supporting neither the UFW grape boycott nor the Free Breakfast for Children Program. This time, Brown announced that the Party would organize a massive boycott of all six Safeway stores in Oakland if non-UFW grapes and lettuce were not removed from the shelves. Prior to the press conference, Brown and Seale hand-delivered letters to the managers of the six stores, presenting them with the ultimatum. The letters declared,

> Your failure to accede to this demand will leave us no choice but to mobilize the full force of our Party, the 2,000 and more individuals who diligently participated in our recent campaign . . . and the entire Black, Mexican-American and justice-seeking community of this city in a boycott of Safeway Stores in Oakland on a scale unprecedented in California.

At the press conference, Seale stressed the Party's longtime support of the UFW and explained that the boycott would begin immediately on Safeway's refusal of their demand.[33]

Seale and the BPP continued to support the UFW in the aftermath of their failed campaigns for political office because they continued to appreciate the common racial discrimination and economic exploitation experienced by

African Americans and Mexican Americans. Furthermore, they recognized the
potential of sustaining a coalition between these groups in achieving political
and social change in Oakland. At a banquet held on June 21 in honor of Seale
and Brown's campaign workers, supporters, and donors, it was announced
that the Community Committee to Elect Bobby Seale and Elaine Brown had
been reborn as the New Democratic Organizing Committee (NDOC). Seale
explained at the banquet that the purpose of the NDOC was to run progressive
candidates for Oakland city offices who would implement the platform that he
and Brown had advocated. Like Seale and Brown's campaign, the NDOC was
multiracial both in its make-up and its focus. The *Black Panther* editorialized,

> Through it, Oakland's Black, Brown and poor White communities
> will join hands and hearts with honest, committed and dedicated
> citizens of Oakland from all strata and walks of life, to win elective
> power for those who represent the best interest of all the people;
> the best that exists within the truly democratic ideals of this land.

At the NDOC launch banquet, it was clear that the UFW was part of the organization's focus. During a speech thanking their supporters, Brown introduced a representative from the UFW, who received a standing ovation from
the audience, and explained "how the Mexican-American struggle was a part
of the over-all struggle for human dignity."[34]

With the formation of the NDOC, Seale and Brown were able to harness the power of their campaigns and combine it with that of the BPP in
order to assist the UFW from a larger base. Seale and Brown exploited this
enhanced power source when, as promised, the Party launched a boycott of
all Oakland Safeway stores on July 20, 1973 after the store managers refused
to remove non-UFW grapes and lettuce from their shelves. In a dramatic
show of unity, members of the BPP, NDOC, and UFW marched together at
the press conference at the West Oakland Safeway. Brown articulated that
unity to the press when, in explaining their support of the UFW, she stated,
"It's a natural alliance of poor people and people that understand that everyone has a right to live." The Mexican American community in Oakland
appreciated that the BPP upheld its commitment to multiracial solidarity
after Seale and Brown's campaigns had ended, and in turn maintained its
support of the Panthers. Mary Thomas, a Mexican American activist who
had worked with Seale on the creation of Spanish-language election materials, declared with regard to Panthers' boycott of Safeway, "I think they're

Figure 14. Members of the Black Panther Party, New Democratic Organizing Committee, and UFW picket a Safeway grocery store in West Oakland, California, July 20, 1973. Courtesy of It's About Time: Black Panther Legacy & Alumni, http://www.itsabouttimebpp.com.

doing great. . . . They get on the job and stay with it. It's not just a one shot deal, or one day or one hour. They'll stay with it until they shut down the damn place."[35]

During the boycott of Oakland's Safeway stores, the BPP also took up the cause of the UFW when it targeted E&J Gallo Wineries. The massive Gallo Wineries, which produced a quarter of all wine grapes in California, had been under contract with the UFW since 1967. The UFW-Gallo contract, which had been amicably renewed in April 1970, had been positive for both the union and the winery. Under the contract, wages had increased and working conditions had improved at the same time that Gallo's daily production capacity doubled. But when the contract negotiations began in April 1973, it was clear that unlike in 1970 the renewal of the UFW-Gallo contract would not go smoothly. During the negotiation period, Gallo supervisors prevented UFW organizers from speaking to workers in the field, which the organizers had been allowed to do in the past. Gallo's UFW stewards were gradually fired for such infractions as taking sick leave or "using strong language." When the negotiations stalled in June, Gallo notified its workers and the UFW, "The Teamsters have sent us notice that they represent the majority of our workers. We are scheduling a meeting with them immediately." The

UFW had vowed in April to strike any grower who turned to the Teamsters, so on June 27 the union went on strike at all Gallo ranches. On July 9 Gallo had a single negotiation meeting with the Teamsters, during which a four-year contract was signed. The next day, the UFW launched a major boycott of all Gallo wines.[36]

The Panthers immediately voiced their support for the UFW's latest protest. Seale and Brown spoke in support of the Gallo boycott at a rally at Sproul Plaza at the University of California, Berkeley, just days after the strike began. During his speech Seale again dismissed racial differences and emphasized solidarity with the UFW as exploited workers who were fighting their common foe, the forces of corporate capitalism. Seale received "a thunderous ovation" when he proclaimed,

> We have to relate humanistically when people decide to get themselves together in order to stop being exploited; in order to stop the slave labor, the cheap labor. When people say they want decent wages, when they say [they] want certain fringe benefits, certain health benefits, it is their constitutional right to protest exploitation. I ask you to unite with us and strike against these capitalists and support the UFW.

On August 4, 1973 Seale again spoke in support of the boycott at a rally in Richmond, California that the UFW had organized, along with a march through the city, in order to demonstrate broad public support of the farmworkers.[37]

But the public's support of the UFW had little bearing on the grape growers, who were emboldened by Gallo's actions. Soon after Gallo signed with the Teamsters, Franzia Wines followed suit. But the final blow came on August 16 when twenty-five grape growers who had previously been under UFW contract signed contracts with the Teamsters. The UFW had been in talks with national Teamster officials regarding union jurisdiction, but while the meetings were taking place, Teamster officials in California signed the twenty-five contracts. The *Black Panther* reported, "UFW officials generally concede that it is unlikely that negotiations will resume in the near future."[38]

In response to the growers' Machiavellian maneuvers with the Teamsters, the UFW attempted to increase the attention paid to the nationwide boycott of California grapes, which had begun in April. However, Chavez called off the accompanying strike four months after it began in response to the deaths of two farmworkers: Nagi Daiffullah was beaten to death by a sheriff's deputy on August 14, and Juan de la Cruz was shot and killed by strikebreakers two days later. Not wanting to incur further violence, Chavez promptly called off the strike.[39]

In October 1973, however, the UFW resumed its call for the boycott of Gallo wines. Chavez had waited for the end of Gallo's harvest season and for approval from the AFL-CIO, whose Distillery and Wine Workers Union could have been hurt by a boycott. Although the boycott continued, the fear of violence against UFW members prevented Chavez from calling for another strike. Chavez explained the move in a fundraising letter: "Rather than see more of our people slain, we moved our picketlines from the fields to the cities, taking our cause once again before the American people." The BPP maintained its support for the UFW and its newspaper continued to report on these developments and to call for solidarity with the UFW. Also in the fall of 1973, however, one of Chavez's political positions served to weaken the UFW's relationship with the BPP for the first time. Chavez began to speak out in defense of Israel and in November released a statement proclaiming, "We appeal to our government to provide Israel with material aide to those in need and moral influence to bring both sides to the bargaining table in the hope of achieving peace." This did not sit well with the BPP, which had been pro-Palestine from its founding. David Du Bois, editor-in-chief of the *Black Panther*, advised Huey Newton to issue a statement criticizing Chavez's position, "which at the same time states the Party's continuing support for the struggle of the Farm Workers themselves."[40]

* * *

Chavez's position on Israel, combined with the cancellation of the grape strike and the two-month suspension of the Gallo boycott, coincided with a precipitous decline in coverage of the UFW in the *Black Panther*, though the Party still officially supported the farmworkers. But the most significant blow to the relationship between the UFW and the BPP was Seale's resignation from the Party. After losing the campaign for mayor of Oakland, Seale needed to chart a new course for himself. This was compounded by the turmoil plaguing the Party that resulted from Newton's erratic leadership. For the duration of Seale's campaign, power in the BPP had been concentrated in Newton's hands. During this time, Seale claimed that he "did not know the extent of Newton's substance abuse, extortion of local crime organizations, misappropriation of Party funds, and violence against fellow Party comrades and members of the community." Seale finally left the Party in July 1974 after a major disagreement with Newton. Therefore, Seale's electoral defeat meant not only that the UFW would be deprived of a supporter in the highest rank of city government, but it also lost one of its earliest and strongest allies who had taken the lead in maintaining the alliance between the UFW and the BPP.[41]

Seale's loss in the Oakland mayoral election precipitated an overall decline in BPP membership and activity in California. Following Seale's departure, many Panthers defected from the BPP due to disappointment in the election, questions over the Party's future, and increasing disarray within the organization. The latest losses in membership had a significant impact on the Party's already decreasing numbers. According to some estimates, membership had decreased from five thousand in 1969 to fewer than five hundred in 1972. The serious drop in membership was assisted, directly and indirectly, by actions taken by FBI agent provocateurs who had infiltrated the organization and helped to orchestrate the violent conflicts and the subsequent imprisonments of scores of Panthers. These FBI agents ensured that discord and suspicion reigned among the remaining members, which resulted in a series of expulsions and purges that dramatically decreased Party membership.[42]

The decrease in the BPP's numbers also had a detrimental effect on the UFW. When the Central Committee decided that Seale should run for mayor, it passed a resolution calling on Panther chapters in other cities to close and for members to relocate to Oakland to assist with the political campaign. Rather than go to California to work on Seale's campaign, many Panthers simply left the Party. But more importantly, by closing the chapters outside of Oakland, the BPP eliminated its nationwide network. This meant that the BPP was no longer a national organization, which deprived the UFW of Party support in the major cities across the country. The UFW had always depended on its supporters in other cities to provide housing, walk picket lines, and attend rallies during the boycott campaigns. Without allies across the country, such as the BPP chapters, it would be virtually impossible for the UFW to successfully conduct a massive grape boycott. Although Chavez had decided to continue the grape boycott in the aftermath of the deaths of

Daiffullah and de la Cruz and continued to receive support from organized labor and religious groups, it was more difficult for the UFW to organize a nationwide boycott without the assistance it received from Panther chapters during the earlier grape boycott.[43]

Just as Mike Miller's departure from SNCC hastened the end of the alliance between it and the UFW, Seale's exit emphasized the importance of individual leadership in maintaining coalitions. Following Seale's departure, the *Black Panther* continued to report sporadically on the progress of the UFW. But less than one month after Seale left, Newton fled to Cuba to escape new criminal charges against him. The defection of both founders signaled the beginning of the end of the BPP. Even though Elaine Brown took the helm as the Party's leader, the BPP had less than two hundred members and restricted its organizing to community service programs in Oakland. This coincided precisely with the UFW's loss of power; by 1974, after having lost all but a few of their original contracts to the Teamsters, the union faced dwindling membership, depleted financial resources, and a struggle for its very survival. The coalition between the UFW and the BPP that had blossomed during Seale's campaign was productive while it lasted, but was not sufficient to guarantee the survival of both organizations. However, this was not due to conflicts between the groups, or a failure to adequately assist each other. Because both groups were embroiled in battles for their very existence, the alliance could not save them.[44]

However, the UFW-BPP coalition should not be viewed as a failure. Both organizations used the relationship to educate their constituencies on the importance of crossing racial lines to establish class-based solidarity. Richard Ybarra reflected on his experience in the UFW: "I learned about diversity by working there because it was all about people, not about color. . . . It was never about race or color differences. It was always about similarities." Their mutual struggles against Safeway brought the UFW and BPP together, but they continued to support each other as each organization moved into electoral politics because they recognized their similar interests and the potential in combining forces. By uniting around their common interests, each organization benefited from the alliance. The defeat of Proposition 22 and Seale's impressive showing in the 1973 mayoral election demonstrated the effectiveness of the partnership between the UFW and the BPP and the political potential for future coalitions between Mexican Americans and African Americans. Members of the UFW and BPP to this day fondly remember the alliance based on their common identity as workers who shared values, mutual respect, and dedication to the pursuit of political power and racial and economic equality. In 2005, Panther Bill Jennings declared, "Every time I'm at an event and somebody says, 'I'm a farm worker from back in the day,' I make it a point to shake their hand and tell them, 'We supported you guys and it was our same struggle.'"[45]

Conclusion

THE black freedom struggle's support of the UFW demonstrates the potential benefits of coalitions. Alone, the farmworkers of California's Central Valley were virtually powerless against the forces of agribusiness. But by linking *la causa* with the dynamic movements for social change of the 1960s and early 1970s, the UFW was able to attract allies beyond the farmworker community of California. Only with the support of these allies was the UFW able to publicize its fight for social and economic justice and bring nationwide pressure on the growers, resulting in the first union contracts for agricultural workers. However, these relationships also reveal the challenges inherent in coalition building, including identification of common goals, establishment of mutual trust and respect, and achievement of beneficial outcomes for both sides. Forming and maintaining coalitions was therefore a difficult process, more so when the parties involved had to cross racial lines to come together. Nevertheless, the organizations of the black freedom struggle considered here were able to rise to these challenges and form productive alliances with the UFW.

These coalitions demonstrate that multiracial coalitions are multidimensional. A sense of solidarity and common purpose are essential building blocks in the formation of a coalition, but are not sufficient to sustain it. Race, class, and geographic location were all influential factors. Compatible ideologies and organizational praxis, as well as individual leadership, were also instrumental. Accordingly, coalitions can best be understood at the multiple points of intersection and overlap of those variables.[1]

The multiple forms that alliances could take illustrate the differences among the organizations of the black freedom struggle. While their shared pursuit of black equality united them, they varied in their ideologies, organizational praxis, and priorities. Organizations were also shaped by their differing leadership and constituencies, as well as external forces. These differences manifested in both their efforts on behalf of African Americans and their approaches toward cross-racial coalitions. The relationships reveal the diversity of social movement culture within the black freedom struggle that translated into variations of coalition politics.

Race served to both unite and divide the black freedom struggle and the UFW. The recognition that African Americans and Mexican Americans suffered from similar patterns of racial discrimination facilitated and strengthened coalitions. SNCC and the BPP in particular felt kinship with the Mexican American farmworkers based on solidarity as oppressed peoples of color. With the advent of black separatism within SNCC, however, the potential for cross-racial understanding and coalition building with Mexican Americans was lost. At the same moment that Mexican Americans embraced a "brown," Chicano identity, nationalist elements in SNCC labeled them as white, which precluded the possibility for racial solidarity as peoples of color. Furthermore, white organizers—who had made the coalition between the civil rights organization and the UFW truly multiracial—departed from SNCC in the wake of its ideological shift. Although the BPP was one of the foremost representatives of Black Power, its program did not advocate racial separatism. Rather, Huey Newton's philosophy of revolutionary intercommunalism, which was shaped by the multiracial character of the BPP's base in Oakland, facilitated its cross-racial coalitions with the UFW and others. The divergent SNCC and BPP philosophies led not only to differing relationships with the UFW, but also to animosity between them. In 1969 Eldridge Cleaver wrote in a letter to Stokely Carmichael, who objected to the BPP's multiracial alliances, "You should know that suffering is color-blind, that the victims of Imperialism, Racism, Colonialism, and Neo-colonialism come in all colors, and that they need a unity based on revolutionary principles rather than skin color."[2]

For most, the racial divide was too wide to cross without assistance. Geographic location aided the formation of alliances across race. The unique racial and ethnic diversity of the American West often prompted the formation of multiracial coalitions. The lack of clearly defined patterns of racial segregation in the West exposed minorities to the discrimination, economic exploitation, unequal education, and police brutality that they all experienced. For example, Bobby Seale's awareness that "brown American people are suffering from the same thing black American people are" prompted him to call for "Power to the People, *all* the people, white, black, green, red, brown, yellow." Multiracial alliances therefore became an integral component of the BPP's ideology and praxis. In other cases, activists in the West pioneered the coalitions between the UFW and organizations that were based in the South and Northeast. For instance, SNCC field secretaries who were originally from California persuaded the rest of the organization to support the farmworkers before the union became nationally known. Similarly, the NAACP chapters in the West fought to convince the national office, which was based in New York, to support the UFW. Conversely, a lack of exposure to the unique patterns of race and racial discrimination in the West inhibited the potential for coalitions with the UFW. SCLC had few affiliates in the West and thus operated within the confines of the black/white paradigm of the biracial South. The New York-based Urban League became supportive of the UFW, but only after the California grape boycott spread to that city.[3]

Geographic location was also important in understanding the rural character of the farmworkers' struggle. SNCC conducted much of its organizing in rural areas and had thus experienced the challenges of fighting for social justice in that setting. The NAACP, NUL, and SCLC were all based in urban areas and largely focused on urban forms of discrimination. It was therefore more difficult for the UFW to interest these organizations in their movement. However, when Ralph Abernathy took the helm of SCLC and Coretta Scott King began to advocate for the UFW, their rural backgrounds facilitated the organization's support of the farmworkers. Similarly, although the BPP organized in urban areas, the rural backgrounds of its members and their families prompted recognition and solidarity with the UFW.

Class also played a decisive role in the UFW's multiracial coalitions. Due to their lived experiences, both the BPP and SNCC had a profound understanding of the connections between racial discrimination and economic exploitation, which caused them to readily acknowledge the similarities between African Americans and Mexican Americans. Furthermore, the BPP's socialist ethos enabled it to relate to the farmworkers as members of the working class. According to the BPP, the forces of capitalism maintained their power by separating people of differing races and ethnicities, and therefore class solidarity across racial lines was necessary to achieve liberation. SNCC staff members and volunteers readily understood the importance of economic justice through its work with impoverished African Americans in the rural Deep South. SNCC members also rejected the trappings of the middle class, which further enhanced their ability to connect with agricultural workers. However, when the organization embraced black separatism, it prioritized racial solidarity over the class struggle and thus dramatically weakened its coalition with the UFW.[4]

Class was also an important factor in the UFW's relationships with those who were decidedly middle class. The national leadership of the NAACP did not embrace the UFW's cause and instead were committed to obtaining the support of the business community, including elements of agribusiness that exploited farmworkers. When the national NAACP did support the UFW, which was done at the urging of the association's chapters in the West, it did so through middle-class tactics such as letter writing. Similarly, despite public expressions of support for the farmworkers, the NUL was limited by its ties to agribusiness.

The interplay of race, class, and geography determined the trajectories of the coalitions. Furthermore, compatible ideologies and organizational praxis helped to ensure that likeminded groups could work together. But even with all of the necessary ingredients in place, individuals were needed to serve as catalysts. Bridge leaders had to recognize the potential in forming a coalition and convince their colleagues of its merits. Forming a coalition across race is therefore an act of will. Individuals must be willing to not only recognize commonalities, but must also be willing to act on them. They must prioritize commonalities over differences and put common interest over self-interest.

*   *   *

The importance of the coalitions between the UFW and these civil rights/ Black Power organizations must not be underestimated. Although some did not last long, they were still crucial at important moments. Some civil rights activists were deeply involved in the coordination of the UFW boycotts, but most participated in smaller ways. These activities, which ranged from joining picket lines to writing letters to boycotting a product, demonstrated the variations and utility of nonviolent protest. Chavez explained,

> The whole essence of nonviolent action is getting a lot of people
> involved, vast numbers doing little things. It's difficult to get
> people involved in a picket line, because it takes their time. But
> any time a person can be persuaded not to eat a grape—and we

persuaded millions not to eat grapes—that's involvement, that's
the most direct action, and it's set up in such a way that everybody
can participate.

The black freedom struggle's participation in the UFW boycotts contributed
to the union's victories over agribusiness. Furthermore, civil rights activists'
involvement—in addition to that of student groups, organized labor, religious orders, housewives, and celebrities—demonstrated to the growers that
the farmworkers had widespread support. By publicizing the farmworkers'
struggles in their own publications and speeches, they also helped to obtain
additional supporters for the UFW. Thus, the actions of SNCC, SCLC, the
NAACP, the NUL, and the BPP, even if they were short-term, contributed to
the UFW's success.[5]

Coalitions with the UFW were also important for civil rights organizations. Working with and supporting Mexican American farmworkers
demonstrated the applicability of their philosophies and strategies to other
oppressed peoples and at the same time proved the relevance of the black
freedom struggle to Mexican Americans. Participating in multiracial coalitions also expanded these organizations' ideas about racial identity, economic justice, and discrimination. Furthermore, forming coalitions with the
UFW provided more concrete benefits for some organizations. For example,
the BPP's alliance with the UFW gave the Party legitimacy among conservative elements of the Mexican American community during Bobby Seale's
mayoral campaign. Supporting Chavez and the farmworkers enabled Coretta
Scott King to step out of her late husband's shadow and gave Ralph Abernathy the opportunity to expand SCLC's mission. Civil rights activists also
learned from the UFW. Marshall Ganz and Dickie Flowers of SNCC adopted
the union's use of house meetings. Some also learned from the union's mis-
takes. María Varela had been invited to work for the UFW, but she decided
to organize for land reform in New Mexico instead. She explained, "I didn't
want to spend the rest of my years helping improve working conditions while
the land stayed concentrated in the hands of the wealthy. . . . I began to feel
that owning land was a key requirement for defeating poverty, taking control
of community, and reclaiming culture."[6]

The coalitions between the black freedom struggle and the UFW have im-
plications beyond the organizations involved. By illustrating these relationships, this book demonstrates the interconnectedness of the 1960s to 1970s
social movements. The participants of each movement had a more expansive

understanding of themselves and their role in the world than scholars currently acknowledge. Rather than operating independently and in isolation, the movements of the era continuously participated in dynamic exchanges of ideas and resources. Most activists viewed strategic alliances as necessary to achieve social change in the face of overwhelming discrimination and repression. Activists therefore considered themselves part of *the* Movement, rather than *a* movement. The coalitions between the black freedom struggle and the UFW thus expand our understanding of social movement politics by demonstrating both the challenges and potential inherent in overcoming differences and surmounting racial divides in order to achieve "freedom for other men."

NOTES

Introduction

1. Eleanor Ohman, "Strikers to March on Sacramento," *Sun-Reporter*, March 19, 1966, 4.

2. A note on terminology: "Mexican American" is the term used to describe Americans of Mexican descent; "Mexican" is used for ethnic Mexicans who retained Mexican citizenship. The term "Latino/a" refers to all people of Latin American descent including, but not limited to, Mexicans or Mexican Americans. The term "Hispanic" is used strictly in the context of the U.S. Census because of the word's origins in federal bureaucracy. "Chicano/a" refers to those who identified with the Chicano Movement, particularly its emphasis on racial pride and active resistance to discrimination. Although many consider the struggles of the UFW to be foundational to the Chicano Movement, Chavez considered the union separate from the movement. Chicana/o is therefore not used to describe the union or its members.

3. During the period under consideration, the NFWA changed its name twice—first to the United Farm Workers Organizing Committee (UFWOC) and later to the United Farm Workers (UFW), as it is currently known. The UFW is therefore referred to by its proper name as time progresses in the book; Meyer and Whittier, "Social Movement Spillover," 277.

4. At the conclusion of a collection that provides a variety of perspectives on relations between African Americans and Mexican Americans, ranging from animosity to fraternity, historian Matthew Whitaker curiously argues, "Although the Chicano movement was inspired by the black freedom struggle, these two movements never formed an alliance," and places the blame squarely on Chicanos. Whitaker, "A New Day in Babylon," 267. For other examples of scholarship that argue that African Americans and Mexican Americans were most often in conflict, see Behnken, *Fighting Their Own Battles*; Foley, *Quest for Equality*; Ogbar, "Brown Power to Brown People," 258–59; Mantler, "Black, Brown and Poor: Martin Luther King, Jr., the Poor People's Campaign and Its Legacies"; Ferreira, "All Power to the People."

5. For more on the NAACP, see Berg, *"The Ticket to Freedom"*; Sullivan, *Lift Every Voice*; and Verney and Sartain, eds., *Long Is the Way and Hard*. Scholarship on the NUL is sparse and only covers the first half of its history. See Moore, Jr., *A Search for Equality*; T. Reed, *No Alms But Opportunity*; and Weiss, *The National Urban League*. With the exception of the work of Thomas R. Peake, scholarship on SCLC revolves around the leadership of Martin Luther King, Jr. See Fairclough, *To Redeem the Soul of America*; and Garrow, *Bearing the Cross*; Peake, *Keeping the Dream Alive*. For scholarship on SNCC, see Carson, *In Struggle*; Hogan, *Many Minds, One Heart*; and Stoper, *The Student Nonviolent Coordinating Committee*. Scholarship on the BPP is in a period of proliferation. See, for example, Bloom and Martin, *Black Against Empire*; Cleaver and Katsiaficas, eds., *Liberation,*

Imagination, and the Black Panther Party; C. Jones, ed., *The Black Panther Party*; and Murch, *Living for the City*.

6. Kelley, *Race Rebels*, 4, 6–8; Pulido, *Black, Brown, Yellow, and Left*, 89.

7. J. Levy, *Cesar Chavez*, 201. For information on Mexican American labor organizing in the first half of the twentieth century, see Vargas, *Labor Rights Are Civil Rights*. Sociologist J. Craig Jenkins argues, "The fewer resources a group has, the more powerless it is and the more it needs an infusion of outside support." Jenkins, "The Transformation of a Constituency into a Social Movement Revisited," 280.

8. J. Levy, *Cesar Chavez*, 151; quoted in Mariscal, *Brown-Eyed Children of the Sun*, 162–63.

9. Much of the recent scholarship that addresses multiracial coalition building in the West focuses on California. See Bernstein, *Bridges of Reform*; Brilliant, *The Color of America Has Changed*; Kurashige, *The Shifting Grounds of Race*; and Pulido, *Black, Brown, Yellow, and Left*. Reflecting the population of the South during the 1950s and 1960s, nearly all scholarship on movements in the region focuses on race relations between blacks and whites. The notable exception is scholarship on Texas, which has a sizeable Latino population and is alternately defined as both southern and western. For recent works on activism in Texas, see Behnken, *Fighting Their Own Battles*; and Krochmal, "Labor, Civil Rights, and the Struggle for Democracy in Texas, 1935–1975." Despite the racial and ethnic diversity of the Northeast, scholarship on movements in the region are frequently confined to a black/white paradigm. See, for example, Theoharis and Woodard, eds., *Freedom North*; of the eleven essays in this collection, only one deals with the activism of Latinos. See also Sugrue, *Sweet Land of Liberty*.

10. Mariscal, *Brown-Eyed Children of the Sun*, 182, 190, 192–201.

11. Foley, "Partly Colored or Other White," 125, 135–36; Foley, *Quest for Equality*, 128, 131. For more on the evolution of Chicano identity, see I. M. García, *Chicanismo*.

12. For scholarship that examines relations between African Americans and Mexican Americans through the lens of race, see Behnken, *Fighting Their Own Battles*; Foley, *Quest for Equality*; and Vaca, *The Presumed Alliance*. I suggest that the negative assessment of black/Latino relations in these works is partly a product of the prioritization of race over other, equally important factors in interracial relations.

13. Omi and Winant, *Racial Formation in the United States from the 1960s to the 1990s*, 24; Camfield, "Re-Orienting Class Analysis," 424; Jenkins and Leicht, "Class Analysis and Social Movements," 371; Kelley, *Race Rebels*, 5, 29, 37.

14. Nelson, *Huelga!*, 75. Much recent scholarship addresses the intersection of civil rights and economic justice. See, for example, Arnesen, ed., *The Black Worker*; T. F. Jackson, *From Civil Rights to Human Rights*; and Mantler, *Power to the Poor*.

15. Moore, *To Place Our Deeds*, 21, 33; Alvarez and Widener, "Brown-Eyed Soul," 214; Brilliant, *The Color of America Has Changed*, 6; U.S. Bureau of the Census, *U.S. Census of Population: 1960, Subject Report: Persons of Spanish Surname*; *U.S. Census of Population: 1970, Subject Report: Persons of Spanish Surname*.

16. The scholarship on the complicated relationship between organized labor and African Americans is extensive. For example, see Arnesen, *The Black Worker*; Cherny; Issel, and Taylor, eds. *American Labor and the Cold War*; Foner, *Organized Labor and the Black Worker, 1619–1981*; and Goldberg and Griffey, eds., *Black Power at Work*.

17. Dobbie, "Evolving Strategies of Labor-Community Coalition Building," 114–15. Brian Mayer refers to such leaders as "bridge brokers." He explains, "An individual acts as a bridge broker when he or she can effectively communicate to multiple parties that are differentiated by some structural or identity-based divide that would ordinarily reduce the likelihood of communication and therefore collaboration." Mayer, "Cross-Movement Coalition Formation," 226; Robnett, "African-American Women in the Civil Rights Movement, 1954–1965," 1661–93.

18. Bernstein, *Bridges of Reform*, 8; Ohman, "Strikers to March on Sacramento."

Chapter 1. This Is How a Movement Begins

1. Elizabeth Sutherland Martínez, interview by author, San Francisco, October 30, 2000; Martínez, Notes on the Delano to Sacramento March, March 17–April 10, 1966, reel 21, Student Nonviolent Coordinating Committee Papers, 1959–1972 (Sanford, N.C.: Microfilming Corp. of America, 1982) (hereafter SNCC Papers). Martínez and María Varela were the only Latino/a members of SNCC.

2. Hogan, *Many Minds, One Heart*, 160.

3. Martínez, Notes on the Delano to Sacramento March.

4. Raines, *My Soul Is Rested*, 76, 101. For more on the consumer power of African Americans, see Greenberg, *"Or Does It Explode?"*; and Cohen, *A Consumer's Republic.*

5. Carson, *In Struggle*, 31; Raines, *My Soul Is Rested*, 242, 256.

6. According to the 1970 U.S. Census, approximately 49 percent of farm laborers or foremen in California were Latino. U.S. Bureau of the Census, "Table 179: Occupation of Employed Persons by Education, Race, and Sex: 1970," *1970 Census of Population, vol. 1: Characteristics of the Population, Part 6: California—section 2*; Kushner, *Long Road to Delano*, 17–19; "Far from Being Undesirables," in Rosales, ed., *Testimonio*, 87; McWilliams, *Factories in the Field*, 124–25; Arnesen, "The Quicksands of Economic Insecurity," 47; Reisler, "Always the Laborer, Never the Citizen," 233–35, 249; Gordon, "Poison in the Fields," 56–58.

7. "Mexican Unions Emerge in the United States," in Rosales, ed., *Testimonio*, 241–42; "Unionism in the Agricultural Fields," in Rosales, ed., *Testimonio*, 243–45; J. Levy, *Cesar Chavez*, 151–53; McWilliams, *Factories in the Field*, 152–64; R. B. Taylor, *Chavez and the Farm Workers*, 48, 52–55; Foner, *Organized Labor and the Black Worker*, 146–47, 192–93; Mike Miller to SNCC staff, December 21, 1964, box 48, Social Action Vertical File, State Historical Society of Wisconsin, Madison (hereafter Social Action Vertical File).

8. Hogan, *Many Minds, One Heart*, 198; Mike Miller to SNCC National Staff, October 23, 1964, reel 1, Charles M. Sherrod Papers, State Historical Society of Wisconsin, Madison (hereafter Sherrod Papers); Carson, *In Struggle*, 134–36.

9. Mike Miller, interview by author, San Francisco, February 19, 2004; Geoff Mann, "Class Consciousness and Common Property"; Mike Miller, telephone interview by author, December 20, 2003; "SLATE Newsletter," SLATE Archives Digital Collection.

10. Miller interview, February 19, 2004.

11. Miller interview, December 20, 2003.

12. Terry Cannon, e-mail message to author, September 8, 2004; Cannon, telephone interview by author, December 11, 2003; Miller, *A Community Organizer's Tale*, xvii.

13. Sellers, *The River of No Return*, 117; Payne, *I've Got the Light of Freedom*, 236–56; Mike Miller, "San Francisco: What Is an Organizer?" *The Movement*, June 1965, 1.

14. J. Levy, *Cesar Chavez*, 161 (quote), 95; Bernstein, *Bridges of Reform*, 139–40.

15. J. Levy, *Cesar Chavez*, 158, 100; Payne, *I've Got the Light of Freedom*, 255–56.

16. J. Levy, *Cesar Chavez*, 110, 101, 136; Payne, *I've Got the Light of Freedom*, 26; Varela, "Time to Get Ready," 559. SNCC's freedom schools were based on the Citizenship Education Program developed in the mid-1950s by Septima Clark, Director of Education of the Highlander Folk School. See Charron, *Freedom's Teacher*; and Hall and Walker, "I Train the People to Do Their Own Talking."

17. "Prospective Project with Migrant Workers," box 1, folder 5, National Farm Workers Association Collection, Archives of Labor and Urban Affairs, Wayne State University, Detroit, (NFWA Collection); Mike Miller to SNCC National Staff, October 23, 1964.

18. Miller interview, February 19, 2004; Miller interview, December 20, 2003; Coleman Blease to Dolores Huerta, January 20, 1965, box 1, folder 3, NFWA Collection.

19. Behnken, "The Movement in the Mirror," 60; Foley, *Quest for Equality*, 94–139.

20. The housing supplied by growers for their workers—at exorbitant rents—ranged from shacks and tents to old boxcars, was generally unsanitary, and frequently lacked heat, running

water, and adequate insulation. "Viva! Tulare County Rent Strike, March," *The Movement*, August 1965; R. B. Taylor, *Chavez and the Farm Workers*, 108; Flier, "Why We Are Picketing," July 1965, box 12, folder 9, NFWA Collection; A. V. Krebs, "La Causa: The Word Was Made Flesh," Farmworker Movement Documentation Project, accessed May 30, 2010; Farm Workers Association, "March Rules," July 16, 1965, box 12, folder 9, NFWA Collection; "Student Nonviolent Coordinating Committee Statement of Purpose," in Grant, ed., *Black Protest*, 289–90.

21. Cannon interview; "Viva! Tulare County Rent Strike, March"; "Tennessee Freedom Labor Union: Poorest County Organizes," *The Movement*, August 1965, 1.

22. Cannon interview; George Ballis, interview by author, Oakland, Calif., November 19, 2003.

23. Hardy Frye, interview by author, Berkeley, Calif., November 18, 2003; Hardy Frye, "Narrative," April 2003, Veterans of the Civil Rights Movement, accessed June 20, 2009; Kwame Ture (Stokely Carmichael) and Charles V. Hamilton criticized Tuskegee's black elite for deferring to the white power structure: "These black people built fine homes and went about their business at the college or the hospital without challenging the control of the sixteen percent white population." Ture and Hamilton, *Black Power*, 127; Wendy Goepel Brooks, "The Story of Wendy Goepel Brooks, Cesar Chavez and La Huelga," December 2003, Farmworker Movement Documentation Project, accessed May 19, 2009; Terry Cannon to Cesar Chavez, September 8, 1965, box 13, folder 22, NFWA Collection.

24. "Rent Strike," *El Malcriado*, September 9, 1966, 12; "Tulare Camps Rebuilt," *El Malcriado*, December 14, 1968, 7; J. Levy, *Cesar Chavez*, 181; Gilbert Padilla, interview by author, Berkeley, Calif., May 18, 2004.

25. J. Levy, *Cesar Chavez*, 182–83; Bernstein, *Bridges of Reform*, 142, 146.

26. J. Levy, *Cesar Chavez*, 93, 189, 196; Brooks, "The Story of Wendy Goepel Brooks, Cesar Chavez and La Huelga."

27. Meier and Rudwick, *CORE*, 4; Dunne, *Delano*, 24; Wendy Goepel Brooks, telephone interview by author, September 13, 2004; Miller interview, February 19, 2004; Stoper, *The Student Nonviolent Coordinating Committee*, 69, 72.

28. Marshall Ganz, telephone interview by author, May 4, 2004; Ganz, *Why David Sometimes Wins*, viii; J. Levy, *Cesar Chavez*, 199; Terence Cannon to Cesar Chavez, September 22, 1965, box 13, folder 22, NFWA Collection; It was not unusual that Ganz spent a weekend chauffeuring Chavez. Dunne noted, "[Chavez] is constantly on the move, and virtually the only way to spend any time with him is to volunteer to be his chauffeur. He seems to transact most of his business in Delano from the back of a car." Dunne, *Delano*, 57.

29. Carson, *In Struggle*, 20–21; J. Levy, *Cesar Chavez*, 191, 252–53; Matthiessen, *Sal si Puedes*, 155; The term "Okies" refers to people from Oklahoma, Arkansas, Texas, and Missouri who migrated to California to escape the Dust Bowl of the 1930s. See Gregory, *American Exodus*; Bernstein, *Bridges of Reform*, 142, 144.

30. Eliseo Medina, telephone interview by author, August 12, 2004; Brooks interview; Brooks, "The Story of Wendy Goepel Brooks, Cesar Chavez and La Huelga"; Memo, "Dateline: Delano," October 1, 1965, box 12, folder 5, NFWA Collection.

31. The concern over the volunteers from the civil rights movement is a matter of some confusion. Chavez cryptically told Jacques Levy, "At the beginning I was warned not to take volunteers, but I was never afraid of the students. People warned me, 'Look what happened to the Civil Rights Movement.' 'Well,' I said, 'sure that could happen to us, and if it does, we'll find out why.'" The specific misgivings about the volunteers were not explained in the version of the interview published in J. Levy, *Cesar Chavez*, 197; Dunne, *Delano*, 117–18, 60.

32. Dittmer, *Local People*, 23, 341; For more on unions and anticommunism during the Cold War, see Cherney, Issel, and Taylor, eds., *American Labor and the Cold War*; Dunne, *Delano*, 119; R. B. Taylor, *Chavez and the Farm Workers*, 37, 159–60; Bernstein, *Bridges of Reform*, 145–51.

33. Flier, "Tulare County—California's Selma," July 1965, box 12, folder 9, NFWA Collection; "Editorial: Igual que los Negritos," *El Malcriado*, July 1965, 2, translated and reprinted as "The Voice

of the Farm Workers Same as the Negroes," *The Movement*, August 1965, 1; "Editorial: Enough People with One Idea," *El Malcriado*, September 1965, 2.

34. Cannon interview.

35. Muriel Tillinghast to Cesar Chavez, September 25, 1965, box 13, folder 22, NFWA Collection; Polletta, *Freedom Is an Endless Meeting*, 118; Miller interview, February 19, 2004.

36. "Strike in the Grapes," *The Movement*, October 1965, 1; "Interview with Cesar Chavez of FWA," *The Movement*, October 1965, 5; Terence Cannon, "Guerilla Warfare in the Grapes," *The Movement*, October 1965, 4; "Harassment by Growers, Police," *The Movement*, October 1965, 5.

37. María Varela, telephone interview by author, November 11, 2000; Dunne, *Delano*, 24; "SNCC Radios Go to CORE, Delano Strike," *The Movement*, October 1965; Joe Schulman to Richard Haley, November 5, 1965, box 1, folder 5, NFWA Collection; Joe Schulman to Cesar Chavez, box 2, folder 2, United Farm Workers Organizing Committee Collection, Archives of Labor and Urban Affairs, Wayne State University, Detroit (hereafter UFWOC Collection).

38. Mike Miller to Cyn [Cynthia Washington], November 10, 1965, reel 9, SNCC Papers; Cynthia Washington to Mike [Miller], November 20, 1965, reel 9, SNCC Papers.

39. Student Nonviolent Coordinating Committee, Tentative Agenda, Third Staff Meeting for 1965, November 24–28, 1965, reel 3, SNCC Papers; Miller interview, February 19, 2004; Ganz interview, May 4, 2004; Marshall Ganz, telephone interview by author, November 25, 2003.

40. Ganz interview, May 4, 2004; Dunne, *Delano*, 17, 108; J. Levy, *Cesar Chavez*, 198, 123–24.

41. Ganz interview, May 4, 2004; Larry Rubin, "A Walk in Holly Springs: 1964," Veterans of the Civil Rights Movement; J. Levy, *Cesar Chavez*, 247–48.

42. Miller interview, February 19, 2004; J. Levy, *Cesar Chavez*, 201; Mike Miller to Wayne C. Hartmire, December 5, 1965, reel 9, SNCC Papers; Fred Ross, Sr., "History of the Farm Worker Movement," October 1974, box 13, folder 1, Fred Ross Papers, Department of Special Collections, Stanford University Libraries, Stanford University, Stanford, Calif. (hereafter Ross Papers); Ganz, "Five Smooth Stones," 323–24.

43. "Schenley (Roma Wine) Offices in SF Picketed," *The Movement*, November 1965; "Farm Labor Pickets in S.F.," *San Francisco Chronicle*, October 13, 1965.

44. Minutes, Report on Delano Farm Workers Strike given by Wendy Goepel, New York SNCC office, December 6, 1965, reel 21, SNCC Papers; George Wiley and Elizabeth Sutherland, "Boycott Schenley!" December 24, 1965, reel 21, SNCC Papers; "National Delano Boycott Report," *The Movement*, January 1966, 3.

45. "News Notes, California," *Student Voice*, December 20, 1965, 3; Cyn [Cynthia Washington] to Friends of SNCC, reel 59, SNCC Papers.

46. Ganz, "Five Smooth Stones," 333–34; Dunne, *Delano*, 131; J. Levy, *Cesar Chavez*, 206–7; Terence Cannon to Members of the Press and Media, reel 21, SNCC Papers; Terence Cannon, Press Release, "Striking Farm Workers Begin 300 Mile March," March 16, 1966, reel 21, SNCC Papers.

47. "The History of the Pilgrimage," *El Malcriado*, April 10, 1966; "List of Honor," *El Malcriado*, April 10, 1966; "Perigrinacion Route," box 10, folder 21, Social Protest Collection, Bancroft Library, University of California, Berkeley (hereafter Social Protest Collection); "The Route of the March," *El Malcriado*, April 10, 1966; "Farm Workers Begin 300 Mile Pilgrimage," *El Malcriado*, March 17, 1966; "The Plan of Delano," reel 47, SNCC Papers. The march was not without conflict. For one thing, only men were allowed to march. Chavez admitted, "Of course, none of the women liked it, but they stayed" (J. Levy, *Cesar Chavez*, 207). Other farmworkers, particularly those who were not Catholic, resented that a banner of the Virgin of Guadalupe led the march. Obdulia "Abby" Flores Rivera, "Remembering the Huelga," Farmworker Movement Documentation Project, accessed December 2, 2011.

48. Cannon interview; Cesar Chavez to Marin Friends of SNCC, April 16, 1966, box 14, folder 6, NFWA Collection; Mike Miller to Karen Whitman, April 13, 1966, reel 33, SNCC Papers.

49. R. B. Taylor, *Chavez and the Farm Workers*, 175; J. Levy, *Cesar Chavez*, 215–17; Cannon interview.

50. Lorna Marple, Report of the Political Action Chairman to Portland Branch NAACP, March 20, 1966, box 19, Records of the National Association for the Advancement of Colored People, West Coast Region, Bancroft Library, University of California, Berkeley (hereafter West Coast NAACP Records); Harry C. Ward to Roy Wilkins, March 22, 1966, box 19, West Coast NAACP Records; Roy Wilkins to Harry C. Ward, April 12, 1966, part 28A, reel 18, Papers of the NAACP, Bethesda, Md.: University Publications of America, 2001 (hereafter NAACP Papers).

51. Jonas, *Freedom's Sword*, 364; In January 1966, in the midst of the boycott, Schenley donated $10,000 to the Interracial Council for Business Opportunity in Los Angeles. The following month the company donated $2,000 to an African American scholarship fund. Many African American leaders refused to cross the NFWA picket line to attend the luncheon in Los Angeles where the check was to be presented. "Kickoff," *Denver Blade*, January 6–12, 1966; "The Downfall of Schenley in Los Angeles," *El Malcriado*, February 28, 1966; Peter Bart, "Focus is Shifted in Grape Strike," *New York Times*, February 20, 1966, 64; J. Levy, *Cesar Chavez*, 217; Robert O. Powell to Roy Wilkins, April 21, 1966, part 28A, reel 17, NAACP Papers; Roy Wilkins, Statement, part 28A, reel 17, NAACP Papers.

52. Jackie Robinson to Martin Luther King, Jr., March 15, 1966, box 20, folder 24, Martin Luther King, Jr. Papers, Martin Luther King, Jr., Center for Nonviolent Social Change, Inc., Atlanta, (hereafter MLK Papers); J. Levy, *Cesar Chavez*, 217; Jackie Robinson was aggressive in defending Schenley. Without revealing his relationship to the company, Robinson criticized the Schenley boycott—and SNCC's role in it—in his *Chicago Defender* column, "Jackie Robinson Says." With the dramatic headline, "Hurting Friend Helps Enemy," he lauded Schenley for its financial contributions to the black community and for sponsoring a television special starring Lena Horne. He also questioned the legitimacy of the boycott and suggested that civil rights organizations were misguided in supporting the farmworkers. Jackie Robinson, "Hurting Friend Helps Enemy," *Chicago Defender*, January 8, 1966, 11.

53. It should be noted that the national headquarters of the NAACP was more committed than the local branches to establishing connections in the business community. See Chapter 3; Stoper, *The Student Nonviolent Coordinating Committee*, 60, 32–37; Carson, *In Struggle*, 71.

54. J. Levy, *Cesar Chavez*, 163; "The Farm Workers' Movement: A People's Fight Against Corporate Exploitation, 1972," Farmworker Movement Documentation Project, accessed June 13, 2010.

55. Zinn, *SNCC*, 5.

56. Frye interview.

Chapter 2. To Wage Our Own War of Liberation

1. J. Levy, *Cesar Chavez*, 100; Miller, *A Community Organizer's Tale*, 10–18; Dunne, *Delano*, 171.

2. Racial theorists Michael Omi and Howard Winant have argued that the concept of race is "an unstable and 'decentered' complex of social meanings constantly being transformed by political struggle." This theory is useful in considering the evolution of SNCC's ideology regarding race, which was the product of the organization's experiences during their fight for racial equality. Omi and Winant, *Racial Formation in the United States*, 55.

3. Payne, *I've Got the Light of Freedom*, 368; Carson, *In Struggle*, 97–100, 133.

4. Chronology, box 23, folder 26, United Farm Workers: Office of the President Collection, Part 2, Cesar Chavez Papers, 1947–1990, Archives of Labor and Urban Affairs, Wayne State University, Detroit (hereafter Chavez Collection, Part 2); "History of the Delano Grape Strike and the DiGiorgio 'Elections,'" box 33, folder 10, Chavez Collection, Part 2; "The DiGiorgio Struggle, *The Movement*, June 1966, 5; "The National Farm Workers Association Asks You: Please Don't Buy Tree-Sweet Fruit Juices, S & W Fine Foods," *The Movement*, June 1966, 5.

5. "United Farm Workers: Chronological History," box 9, folder 11, Ross Papers; "The DiGiorgio Struggle," *The Movement*, June 1966: 5; "Field Workers Boycott Di Giorgio Rigged Election," *The*

Movement, July 1966, 1; For more on the reasons behind the Teamsters' attempt to represent the farmworkers, see Dunne, *Delano*, 141–42.

6. Dunne, *Delano*, 123; "Field Workers Boycott DiGiorgio Rigged Election," *The Movement,* July 1966, 1; Chronology, Chavez Collection, Part 2; Flier, "The Student Summer Project of the National Farm Workers Association, June 19 Through August 1966," box 7, folder 18, UFWOC Collection; Ganz, "Five Smooth Stones," 388; Ganz, *Why David Sometimes Wins*, 185.

7. Flier, "Urgent Lack of Food Right Now: United Labor 'Food for Delano' Committee," box 7, folder 18, UFWOC Collection; "Film Benefit for Delano Strikers," *Sun-Reporter,* September 24, 1966; Cesar Chavez to College of Marin Friends of SNCC, October 26, 1966, box 14, folder 13, NFWA Collection; "Behind the August 30 Di Giorgio Election," *The Movement*, August 1966, 6, 8.

8. Dunne, *Delano*, 155; "After the Pilgrimage—A Burst of Organizing," *The Movement*, June 1966, 8; "NFWA and AFL-CIO Merge: A Movement Analysis," *The Movement*, September 1966, 8.

9. Salmond, *Southern Struggles*; P. B. Levy, *The New Left and Labor in the 1960s*, 9, 18, 15, 27; P. B. Levy, "The New Left and Labor," 391; Carmichael, with Thelwell, *Ready for Revolution*, 423.

10. P. B. Levy, "The New Left and Labor," 313; Ransby, *Ella Baker and the Black Freedom Movement*, 263; Sellers, *River of No Return*, 42; For more on anticommunism in organized labor, see Schrecker, "Labor and the Cold War: The Legacy of McCarthyism"; and Storch, "The United Packinghouse Workers of America, Civil Rights, and the Communist Party in Chicago"; P. B. Levy, *The New Left and Labor in the 1960s*, 52, 14; Forman, *The Making of Black Revolutionaries*, 220.

11. D'Emilio, *Lost Prophet*, 327–28; Anderson, *Bayard Rustin*, 242, 248; Jones, "The Unknown Origins of the March on Washington," 41–43; Forman, *The Making of Black Revolutionaries*, 331–33, 335; Garrow, *Bearing the Cross*, 273, 280; Not everyone in SNCC shared Forman's cynicism about the March on Washington. Field Secretary Bob Zellner, for one, was deeply moved by the participation of thousands of union members. P. B. Levy, "The New Left and Labor," 310, 315; T. F. Jackson, *From Civil Rights to Human Rights*, 178.

12. Carson, *In Struggle*, 123–28; Ture and Hamilton, *Black Power*, 96; For more on the MFDP action at the Democratic National Convention, see Forman, *The Making of Black Revolutionaries*, 386–96.

13. Miller, *A Community Organizer's Tale*, 61–62.

14. Nelson, *Huelga!*, 75; Dunne, *Delano*, 80–81, 109, 156, 158.

15. Chronology, Chavez Collection, Part 2; "Farm Workers Win DiGiorgio Elections," *El Malcriado,* September 9, 1966, 2–3; "United Farm Workers: Chronological History"; United Farm Workers Organizing Committee, "The Case Against Perelli-Minetti: An Appeal for Justice," January 19, 1967, box 9, folder 27, UFWOC Collection; Fred Ross, "History of the Farm Worker Movement," October 1974, box 13, folder 1, Ross Papers; Ganz, *Five Smooth Stones*, 415, 420; Matthiessen, *Sal si Puedes (Escape if You Can)*, 131; "Teamsters Bring in Scabs, Sign Contract," *The Movement*, October 1966, 7.

16. "Is Arvin Next?" *El Malcriado,* September 9, 1966, 3; J. Levy, *Cesar Chavez*, 247–49.

17. Terence Cannon, "Arvin Workers Win Right to DiGiorgio Election: Farm Workers, Labor Officials, SNCC Editor Arrested," *The Movement*, November 1966, 1, 10; Dick Meister, "Arrests of DiGiorgio Pickets Here," *San Francisco Chronicle*, October 21, 1966, 1, 18; J. Levy, *Cesar Chavez*, 250–51, 253; Brooks Penny, "Arvin Farm Workers Vote UFWOC," *The Movement*, December 1966, 4.

18. Ganz, *Five Smooth Stones,* 431, 441–42; "United Farm Workers: Chronological History."

19. Emily Stoper argued about the evolution of SNCC, "Class and race did serve as unifying factors in the early years and then . . . as barriers that helped to divide the organization." Stoper, *The Student Nonviolent Coordinating Committee*, 103.

20. Malcolm X, "Message to the Grassroots," October 10, 1963, *Teaching American History*; For an explanation of the different forms of black nationalism, see Van Deburg, *New Day in Babylon*, 129–91; Carson, *In Struggle*, 191–92.

21. Payne, *I've Got the Light of Freedom,* 368; H. K. Jeffries, *Bloody Lowndes,* 56; Carson, *In Struggle,* 191.

22. For more on the LCFO, see H. K. Jeffries, *Bloody Lowndes;* Ture and Hamilton, *Black Power,* 105.

23. H. K. Jeffries, *Bloody Lowndes,* 51–52, 60, 81–82; Carmichael and Thelwell, *Ready for Revolution,* 466; Hampton and Fayer, *Voices of Freedom,* 273; The staff of *El Malcriado* were inspired by the LCFO, which they viewed as an organization of black farmworkers. They also likened the LCFO to the union: "These brave people have been beaten and jailed many times, but they, like those who are fighting in Delano, know that their cause is just and will not give up until they win." "The Farm Workers of Alabama: Where in Order to Vote, One Pays with His Home, His Safety, and Sometimes His Life," *El Malcriado,* December 2, 1966, 28.

24. Forman, *The Making of Black Revolutionaries,* 476, 450.

25. Carson, *In Struggle,* 240; Miller, *A Community Organizer's Tale,* 174; Martínez interview.

26. Miller interview, December 20, 2003; Cannon interview; Responses to both black nationalism and the vote at the December staff meeting varied widely. For example, Howard Himmelbaum, the white SNCC field director in Arkansas, continued organizing for SNCC until December 1967. Historian Jennifer Jensen Wallach argues that "Himmelbaum found ways to embrace the ideology of Black Power, never seeing a conflict between it and his own involvement with SNCC. In fact, the infamous December 1966 expulsion meeting never affected Himmelbaum directly." Wallach, "Replicating History in a Bad Way?" 281–83.

27. Wallach, "Replicating History in a Bad Way?" 275; Miller interview, February 19, 2004; "To Our Readers," *The Movement,* December 1966, 2; Report on Student Nonviolent Coordinating Committee, San Francisco Office, December 18, 1967, reel 2, FBI File on the Student Nonviolent Coordinating Committee, 1964–1973 (Wilmington, Del.: Scholarly Resources, 1991) (hereafter FBI-SNCC File).

28. Ganz interview, May 4, 2004; Ganz interview, November 25, 2003.

29. Campbell Gibson and Kay Jung, "Table 4: South Region—Race and Hispanic Origin: 1790 to 1990," "Table 2: Northeast Region—Race and Hispanic Origin: 1790 to 1990," U.S. Bureau of the Census, Population Division, *Historical Census Statistics on Population Totals by Race, 1790 to 1990, and by Hispanic Origin, 1970 to 1990, for the United States, Regions, Divisions, and States,* Working Paper 56, September 2002; Campbell Gibson and Kay Jung, "Table 5: California—Race and Hispanic Origin for Selected Large Cities and Other Places: Earliest Census to 1990," in U.S. Census Bureau, Population Division, *Historical Census Statistics on Population Totals by Race, 1790 to 1990, and by Hispanic Origin, 1970 to 1990, For Large Cities and Other Urban Places in the United States,* Working Paper 76, February 2005. Mark Brilliant notes, "In the large swaths of the United States where the 'race problem' was synonymous with the 'Negro problem,' civil rights reformers concentrated their attention on that fight. . . . In California, however, the presence of multiple 'race problems,' each of which tended to attach itself to the state's different racial groups in different ways or degrees, militated against the making of a single civil rights movement." Brilliant, *The Color of America Has Changed,* 6.

30. Varela, "Time to Get Ready," 557–66; Martínez, "Neither Black nor White in a Black-White World," 533–34; Martínez, "Black, White and Tan," June 1967, reel 47, SNCC Papers; Martínez interview; Varela interview.

31. Varela, "Time to Get Ready," 568.

32. Martínez, "Black, White and Tan"; Varela interview.

33. Omi and Winant, *Racial Formation in the United States,* 82; Foley, "Partly Colored or Other White," 124–25, 129–32; Carrigan and Webb, "The Lynching of Persons of Mexican Origin or Descent in the United States, 1848 to 1928," 411–38. Mexican Americans' strategy of pursuing whiteness has been the subject of considerable discussion and debate, particularly in regards to how that strategy affected their relations with and attitudes toward African Americans. Shana Bernstein explains, "Some, like some Jews, sought to claim whiteness as a way to deflect discrimination and shunned cooperation with other minority groups. Such Mexican Americans distanced themselves,

for instance, from African Americans for fear of lowering their status by association. . . . But other times Mexican Americans' attempts to claim whiteness, like some Jews' attempts, reflected an assertive claim to equality with other Americans more than a desire to separate from other more 'tainted' groups." Bernstein, *Bridges of Reform*, 170.

34. As Omi and Winant argue, "The black movement redefined the meaning of racial identity, and consequently of race itself, in American society." Omi and Winant, *Racial Formation in the United States*, 99; I. M. García, *Chicanismo*, 6, 8, 12; Cesar Chavez had reservations about the nationalist aspects of the Chicano movement, but nonetheless articulated racial and cultural pride and sought alliances with other peoples of color. He explained, "When La Raza means or implies racism, we don't support it. But if it means our struggle, our dignity, or our cultural roots, then we're for it." J. Levy, *Cesar Chavez*, 123.

35. Carmichael, *Ready for Revolution*, 584; Carson, *In Struggle*, 265–67, 272, 274–75; Carmichael, *Stokely Speaks*, 102.

36. Carson, *In Struggle*, 273; Carmichael, *Stokely Speaks*, 105; Carmichael, *Ready for Revolution*, 588; Varela interview.

37. Carmichael, *Ready for Revolution*, 626; Carson, *In Struggle*, 277; Varela interview; Forman, *The Making of Black Revolutionaries*, 501; María Varela to James Forman, 1967, María Varela Papers, Private Collection (hereafter cited as Varela Papers).

38. H. K. Jeffries, *Bloody Lowndes*, 57; Ferreira, "All Power to the People," 18, 15; Historian Lorena Oropeza notes in her study of the Chicano movement's opposition to the war in Vietnam, "By drawing parallels between the American conquest of Mexico's northern territories in 1848 to the U.S. military effort in Southeast Asia, Chicano antiwar activism embraced and promoted the radical thesis that Chicanos and Vietnamese were together a 'Third World' people facing a common enemy." Oropeza, "Antiwar Aztlán," 213.

39. H. K. Jeffries, *Bloody Lowndes*, 55, 149; Carmichael, *Ready for Revolution*, 465; Ture and Hamilton, *Black Power*, 120; Griswold del Castillo and Garcia, *César Chávez*, 33; J. Levy, *Cesar Chavez*, 205, 288–89; Kushner, *Long Road to Delano*, 163–64.

40. Sellers, *The River of No Return*, 147; Stoper, *The Student Nonviolent Coordinating Committee*, 15; Forman, *The Making of Black Revolutionaries*, 442; Dittmer, *Local People*, 364; P. B. Levy, *The New Left and Labor in the 1960s*, 134–35; SCLC and CORE similarly verbally expressed support, but did not provide any resources to the MFLU. T. F. Jackson, *From Civil Rights to Human Rights*, 231; Such was civil rights organizations' abandonment of southern farmworkers that a group of African American farmers and sharecroppers in Mississippi wrote to the UFWOC to request the union's help in organizing. In a letter to *El Malcriado*, a representative of the Hinds County Farmers Association wrote, "Rural Negro farms and farm workers are worse off today than ten years ago because we are not organized, and unable to get backing from any powerful national organization." "The Slavery in Mississippi," *El Malcriado*, January 13, 1967, 4–5, 18.

41. Dunne, *Delano*, 170; U.S. Bureau of the Census, *U.S. Census of Population: 1960, Subject Report: Persons of Spanish Surname*; U.S. Bureau of the Census, *U.S. Census of Population: 1970, Subject Report: Persons of Spanish Surname*. The UFWOC's lack of interest in the upward mobility of its members caused John Gregory Dunne to become utterly disillusioned with *la causa* by the end of his study of the Delano grape strike. He argued, "In the narrowest sense, a union of farm workers can only lighten its members' burden of misery. . . . There is simply too little future in farm work" (Dunne, *Delano*, 196). Some Chicanos also became disenchanted with Chavez's mission. A character in a play by Chicano playwright Nepthalí de Leon critiqued, "Don't our people still do stoop labor? Only it's by contract now. Now they are really true slaves, for they have told the yankee farmers: 'We will sell our bodies and our souls to you, but only if you promise us you'll buy them.'" Quoted in Mariscal, *Brown-Eyed Children of the Sun*, 144.

42. Mantler, "Black, Brown, and Poor: Martin Luther King, Jr., the Poor People's Campaign and Its Legacies," 104–5; Forman, *The Making of Black Revolutionaries*, 503; Varela, "Time to Get

Ready," 569–70; María Varela to Ethel Minor, 1967, Varela Papers; Stoper, "The Student Nonviolent Coordinating Committee," 360; Varela interview; Some in SNCC were apparently reluctant to include Varela in the delegation, the rest of which was African American. However, she insisted on attending with SNCC. She pointed out in a letter to one of her SNCC colleagues, "It would be somewhat damaging to whatever alliances are pending, if there is question about my being part of that delegation." Letter from Mary Varela, Varela Papers.

43. Program, Convencion Nacional de la Alianza Federal de los Pueblos Libres, October 19–22, 1967, box 2, folder 22, Peter Nabakov Papers, University of New Mexico, Center for Southwest Research, Albuquerque (hereafter Nabakov Papers); Peter Nabakov, "During Albuquerque Convention Alianza Discovers New Mood of Militant Action," *New Mexican*, October 24, 1967, A3; Pete Herrera and V. B. Price, "Alianza Meet Climaxed by Bomb Scare," *Albuquerque Tribune*, October 23, 1967.

44. "Lawlessness in New Mexico (New Mexico Government Attacks and Frames-Up SNCC Ally)," January 16, 1968, Aframerican News Service, Varela Papers; Peter Nabokov, "Tijerina Off Today to Explain Alianza in California," *New Mexican*, February 14, 1968.

45. Cesar Chavez to Denise F. Reeves, February 15, 1967, box 4, folder 22, UFWOC Collection.

46. "Cesar Chavez: 'Nothing Has Changed,'" *The Movement*, April 1967, 6.

47. Stokely Carmichael to María Varela, January 24, 1968, Varela Papers; Larry Jackson, "SNCC Notes," *Inferno*, February 29, 1968, 13.

Chapter 3. Consumers Who Understand Hunger and Joblessness

1. Lopez, *The Chavista Daze*, 101–2; "National Delano Boycott Report," *The Movement*, January 1966, 3; Padilla interview; Bobby Seale, interview by author, Oakland, California, May 24, 2004.

2. Lopez, *The Chavista Daze*, 104–6; Countryman, *Up South*, 102–3.

3. Cesar Chavez to Giumarra Vineyard Corporation, June 26, 1967, box 42, folder 1, Chavez Collection, Part 2; Cesar Chavez to Joseph Giumarra, July 19, 1967, box 42, folder 1, Chavez Collection, Part 2; "Chronology."

4. Ross, "History of the Farm Worker Movement." Under the provisions of the Immigration and Nationality Act of 1965, employers may request permission from the U.S. Department of Labor to hire foreign nationals to perform temporary agricultural labor. However, they are not allowed to hire such workers if the employment vacancies are due to a strike or lockout. U.S. Department of Labor, Wage and Hour Division, "Fact Sheet #69: Requirements to Participate in the H–2B Program," accessed May 22, 2012; "Chronology."

5. Cesar Chavez to Sisters and Brothers, October 31, 1968, box 22, folder 11, United Farm Workers Administration Department Files, Archives of Labor and Urban Affairs, Wayne State University, Detroit (hereafter UFW Administration Files); "Chronology"; Ross, "History of the Farm Worker Movement"; R. B. Taylor, *Chavez and the Farm Workers*, 219.

6. "Mary Lou Watson, 1966–1968"; "Rudy Reyes, 1965–1980"; "Ed Chiera, 1966–1969"; "Mark Silverman, 1968–1970"; all Farmworker Movement Documentation Project, accessed April 4, 2012.

7. "National Delano Boycott Report," *The Movement*, January 1966, 3; Dolores Huerta to Boycotters, September 26, 1968, box 6, folder 7, United Farm Workers Boycott: New York Files, Archives of Labor and Urban Affairs, Wayne State University, Detroit (hereafter UFW New York Boycott Files); United Farm Workers Organizing Committee, AFL-CIO, "Your Grocer Promotes Poverty by Selling California Grapes," box 17, folder 23, UFW New York Boycott Files.

8. Reed, *No Alms But Opportunity*, 11–12; Moore, Jr., *A Search for Equality*, 52–55.

9. The Bracero Program was a cooperative agreement between the U.S. and Mexican governments in 1942–1964 to import Mexican agricultural workers into the United States to offset wartime labor shortages. Despite agreements that the braceros would be treated fairly, they were discriminated against, exploited, and used as strikebreakers. Growers also used braceros so that they

would not have to pay American workers higher wages. The scholarship on the Bracero Program is extensive. For more information, see the Bracero History Archive; Whitney Young, Jr., "To Be Equal . . . ," *Sun-Reporter*, July 10, 1965; Miriam Redstone to Joseph Giumarra, February 21, 1968, box 2, folder 33, UFW New York Boycott Files.

10. Dickerson, *Militant Mediator*, 207–9; Parris and Brooks, *Blacks in the City*, 333–34.

11. Reed, *No Alms But Opportunity*, 191; Dickerson, *Militant Mediator*, 208–9; Moore, *A Search for Equality*, 58; Weiss, *The National Urban League*, 293–94.

12. Weiss, *The National Urban League*, 214; Dickerson, *Militant Mediator*, 2, 219.

13. Berg, "*The Ticket to Freedom*," 10–13; Adam Fairclough, "Foreword," in Verney and Sartain, eds., *Long Is the Way and Hard*, ix; NAACP, *Annual Report for 1968* (New York: NAACP, 1969), 79, 81; Dittmer, *Local People*, 30.

14. Reed, "The Chicago NAACP," 176–78; W. P. Jones, "The Unknown Origins of the March on Washington," 35; Sociologist Martin N. Marger argues, "A common criticism of the NAACP during the 1960s was that it did not—indeed, could not concern itself fully with the interests of lower-class blacks. . . . The organization's legal and political successes during the 1950s and 1960s served mainly middle-class black interests, while leaving the more entrenched economic problems of lower-class blacks relatively untouched." Marger, "Social Movement Organizations and Response to Environmental Change," 22, 26.

15. According to Fairclough, "There was always a tension between the national office in New York and the local branches. . . . The branches often kicked back, defying or simply ignoring New York." Fairclough, "Foreword," xii; "Biographical Sketch of Leonard H. Carter," box 1, NAACP Collection, African American Museum and Library at Oakland, Oakland, Calif. (hereafter NAACP Collection); Leonard H. Carter to Region I Branches and Youth Chapters, June 6, 1966, part 28A, reel 17, NAACP Papers; "An Idea Who Time Has Come," *The Beanstalk: NAACP News* 14 (May 1966), part 29C, reel 1, NAACP Papers; "Calendar," *The Beanstalk: NAACP News* 14 (May 1966), part 29C, reel 1, NAACP Papers; "NAACP Resolution Urges Grower-Farm Labor Talks," *Salinas Californian*, June 16, 1966; "Around the Country," *NAACP Freedom Journal: Palo Alto-Stanford Branch* 14, 9 (September 1966), part 29C, reel 1, NAACP Papers.

16. Leonard, "'In the Interest of All Races,'" 315. Quintard Taylor notes that in wartime nightclubs, "Chicanos eagerly embraced black dances such as the jitterbug, and clothing styles like the zoot suit, while African American jazz and rhythm and blues musicians drew inspiration from pachuco dances and music." Q. Taylor, *In Search of the Racial Frontier*, 272. For more on the culture of African American and Mexican American youth during the 1940s, See Alvarez, *The Power of the Zoot*.

17. Leonard, "'In the Interest of All Races,'" 318, 320, 324, 326; Watson, "The NAACP in California," 188, 198. For more on the Zoot Suit Riots, see Pagán, *Murder at the Sleepy Lagoon*.

18. Q. Taylor, *In Search of the Racial Frontier*, 284–85, 292; Despite a large Mexican American population in Texas, the climate of racial discrimination prevented the formation of multiracial coalitions because, in such an atmosphere of Jim Crow, Mexican Americans often chose to distance themselves from African Americans. Neil Foley argues, "Despite its long border with Mexico, Texas was still very much a Southern state on the western border of the Deep South." Foley, *Quest for Equality*, 68; Brian D. Behnken, "Fighting Each Other's Battles: Mexican American/African American Cooperation During the Civil Rights Era in Texas," paper presented at annual conference of the Western History Association, Incline Village, Nevada, October 13–16, 2010. Franco also noted that African Americans were actually a minority of the membership of the Long Beach branch. "NAACP Interracial," *Portland Scanner*, June 29, 1978, 23.

19. Gibson and Jung, "Table D–4: Hispanic Origin (of Any Race), for the United States, Regions, Divisions, and States: 1940 and 1970 (Sample Data)," *Historical Census . . . for the United States, Regions, Divisions, and States*; Gibson and Jung, "Table 33: New York—Race and Hispanic Origin for Selected Large Cities and Other Places: Earliest Census to 1990," *Historical Census . . . for Large Cities and Other Urban Places in the United States*.

20. Berg, *"The Ticket to Freedom"*, 167–68, 172, 188; Ryan, "Leading from the Back," 50; Sewell, "The 'Not-Buying Power' of the Black Community," 137.

21. Berg, *"The Ticket to Freedom"*, 175; Sewell, "The 'Not-Buying Power' of the Black Community," 136–37; Biographical Sketch of Leonard H. Carter, box 1, NAACP Collection.

22. Berg, *"The Ticket to Freedom"*, 238; "National Association for the Advancement of Black People's Caucus of the NAACP Goals Endorsed by the Board—We Are Not Leaving the NAACP," *NAACP Freedom Journal: Palo Alto-Stanford Branch* 16, 8 (August 1968), part 29C, reel 1, NAACP Papers; NAACP 58th Annual Convention Resolutions, July 10–15, 1967, supplement to part 1, reel 15, NAACP Papers.

23. Dolores Huerta to Cesar [Chavez] and Jim [Drake], box 2, folder 2, UFWOC Collection; Herbert Hill to Branch President, February 13, 1968, part 28B, reel 10, NAACP Papers; Roscoe R. McDowell to Joseph Giumarra, February 26, 1968, box 2, folder 33, UFW New York Boycott Files; Charles W. Alexander to Don Joseph, March 6, 1968, box 2, folder 33, UFW New York Boycott Files.

24. Lee, *Mobilizing Public Opinion*, 97, 100, 140–41, 143. According to Martin N. Marger, "The largely middle-class composition of the NAACP's membership—and especially its leadership—helped account for the organization's extreme cautiousness." Marger, "Social Movement Organizations and Response to Environmental Change," 22. The Chicago Urban League forbade its members from participating in boycotts or pickets and thus did not assist the UFWOC. Gellman, "'The Stone Wall Behind,'" 115.

25. Cesar Chavez to Sisters and Brothers, October 31, 1968, box 22, folder 11, UFW Administration Files; Ross, "History of the Farm Worker Movement"; Dick Meister, "'La Huelga' Becomes 'La Causa,'" *New York Times*, November 17, 1968, SM52.

26. J. Levy, *Cesar Chavez*, 268; "Mary Quinn Kambic, 1969," Farmworker Movement Documentation Project, accessed April 29, 2012.

27. Reed, *No Alms But Opportunity*, 81; Weiss, *The National Urban League*, 204, 207, 211, 290–91; The AFL and CIO merged to form the AFL-CIO in 1955; Dickerson, *Militant Mediator*, 104, 146–48.

28. P. B. Levy, *The New Left and Labor in the 1960s*, 1–4. Decidedly more radical unions not affiliated with the AFL-CIO, such as the UE, and organizations of black trade unionists, also supported the UFWOC. For example, in Philadelphia the Negro Trade Union Leadership Council called for its members to support the grape boycott. UFWOC boycott organizers in Pittsburgh enjoyed a close relationship with the Black Construction Coalition, which fought to end discrimination in hiring in the construction industry. UFWOC organizers participated in the Coalition's protests against the construction of Three Rivers Stadium. Lawrence H. Geller, "Three Labor Organizations Vow to Support Supermarket Boycott," *Philadelphia Tribune*, January 6, 1968, 3, and "Mary Quinn Kambic, 1969"; Whitney Young, Jr., "To Be Equal . . . ," *Sun-Reporter*, December 14, 1968. Peter Levy argues, "By allying with the disadvantaged and unorganized and supporting racial equality, labor improved its general reputation and discredited the claim that it was merely a special interest group." P. B. Levy, "The New Left and Labor," 319.

29. "Valley Congressmen Oppose Civil Rights," *El Malcriado*, May 1, 1968; Marjorie Hunter, "House Panel Bars Quick Rights Vote Asked by Johnson," *New York Times*, March 20, 1968. In September 1967 Sisk strenuously objected to a complaint filed by the California Rural Legal Assistance and the West Coast NAACP with the U.S. Department of Labor regarding growers' use of braceros. Leonard H. Carter to NAACP Leadership, October 2, 1967, part 29C, reel 9, NAACP Papers.

30. Leonard H. Carter to Staff, July 18, 1968, box 6, West Coast NAACP Records; West Coast Region NAACP, Press release, July 25, 1968, box 67, folder 14, United Farm Workers: Office of the President Collection, Part 1, Cesar Chavez Papers, 1951–1971, Archives of Labor and Urban Affairs, Wayne State University, Detroit (hereafter Chavez Collection, Part 1).

31. Leonard H. Carter to All NAACP Branches and Youth Chapters of Region I, box 6, West Coast NAACP Records; Portland Branch-NAACP, Newsletter, December 1968, box 19, West Coast NAACP Records; Virna Canson, Annual Report, 1968, part 29A, reel 2, NAACP Papers.

32. West Coast Region NAACP, Press release.

33. Matthiessen, *Sal si Puedes*, 324.

34. Leonard H. Carter to Lucille Black, October 19, 1967, part 29C, reel 9, NAACP Papers; Leonard H. Carter to Roy Wilkins and Gloster Current, August 22, 1968, part 29C, reel 9, NAACP Papers; "Freedom News," *The Crisis*, June–July 1968, 209–10.

35. P. B. Levy, "The New Left and Labor," 318; Sullivan, *Lift Every Voice*, 203, 275–76; Fairclough, "Foreward," xi; Jonas, *Freedom's Sword*, 290–91; P. B. Levy, *The New Left and Labor in the 1960s*, 20.

36. "Freedom News," *The Crisis*, October 1968, 296. New York native Peter Matthiessen described the parallels between African American migrant farmworkers in New York and Mexican American farmworkers in California in his biography of Chavez. See Matthiessen, *Sal si Puedes*, 66–72; "THRESH," *The Crisis*, November 1968, 318–20; "BOYCOTTGRAPES," *El Malcriado*, September 1, 1968, 5.

37. Durant, Jr., and Louden, "The Black Middle Class in America," 253–63. Du Bois argued, "The Negro race, like all other races, is going to be saved by its exceptional men." See W. E. B. Du Bois, "The Talented Tenth," September 1903, Teaching American History, accessed May 4, 2010.

38. "Information on Safeway," box 12, folder 6, Ross Papers. At the onset of the grape boycott, the Department of Defense purchased 107 tons of grapes to be sent to feed the troops in Vietnam, six times the amount it had purchased the year prior to the boycott. Rep. Phillip Burton therefore charged the federal government as operating "the greatest anti-organized labor establishment in the country." Quoted in Matthiessen, *Sal si Puedes*, 282; Cesar Chavez to Robert A. Magowan, February 24, 1969, box 13, folder 2, Ross Papers.

39. Whitney Young, Jr. to Robert A. Magowan, May 16, 1969, Robert A. Magowan to Whitney Young, Jr., May 26, 1969, both box 1, folder 11, UFW Administration Files.

40. Whitney Young, Jr., "To Be Equal . . . ," *Sun-Reporter*, June 7, 1969; Dickerson, *Militant Mediator*, 209, 222.

41. "NAACP to Boycott Safeway Chain," *Western Messenger*, April–May 1969, 2; Program of NAACP Northwest Area Conference in Klamath Falls, Oregon, May 24–25, 1969, box 1, folder: Misc. Grapes, United Farm Workers: Klamath Falls Collection, Archives of Labor and Urban Affairs, Wayne State University, Detroit (hereafter UFW Klamath Falls Collection); Resolution of the NAACP Northwest Area Conference, May 25, 1969, box 1, folder: Misc. Grapes, UFW Klamath Falls Collection.

42. "Viva La Huelga!" Newsletter of the NAACP Local Branch—Tucson, Arizona, April 1969, part 29C, reel 1, NAACP Papers; "Boycott Grapes!," Newsletter of the NAACP Local Branch—Tucson, Arizona, May 1969, part 29C, reel 1, NAACP Papers; Gibson and Jung, "Table 3: Arizona—Race and Hispanic Origin for Selected Large Cities and Other Places: Earliest Census to 1990," *Historical Census . . . For Large Cities and Other Urban Places in the United States*.

43. "Grapes Are Fattening!" Newsletter of the NAACP Local Branch—Tucson, Arizona, July 1969, part 29C, reel 1, NAACP Papers; Dody Goldstein, "Letter to the Editor," *NAACP Freedom Journal—Palo Alto Stanford Branch* 17, 10–11 (October–November 1969), part 29C, reel 1, NAACP Papers.

44. NAACP, *Annual Report 1969* (New York: NAACP, 1970), 19; "Judge's Latin Slurs Bring Call for Removal," *Los Angeles Times*, October 2, 1969; "Calls Mexicans 'Animals,' Judge Resigns from His Seat," *Jet*, February 5, 1970, 4.

45. Montgomery County Branch—NAACP, "News-Flash: Boycotts," June 20, 1970, part 29B, reel 1, NAACP Papers; NAACP, 60th Annual Convention Resolutions, June 29–July 5, 1969, supplement to part 1, reel 9, NAACP Papers.

46. Special Meeting Minutes, December 23, 1969, box 7, folder 8, Chavez Collection, Part 1; "Mary Quinn Kambic, 1969"; Babson, *Working Detroit*, 178; NAACP, *Annual Report 1969*, 30.

47. Seale, *Seize the Time*, 71–72.

48. Hua Hsu, "Dave Hilliard: Former Black Panther Runs for Office"; Self, *American Babylon*, 218, 224–25.

49. Flier, "Rally to Support Striking Farmworkers," August 7, 1968, box 2, folder 28, Leon F. Litwack Collection of Berkeley, California, Protest Literature, Yale Collection of Western Americana, Beinecke Rare Book and Manuscript Library, Yale University, New Haven, Conn. (hereafter Litwack Collection); "Grape Boycott Grows," *Black Panther*, October 26, 1968; Dr. Huey P. Newton Foundation, *The Black Panther Party*, 49.

50. Murch, *Living for the City*, 6, 44–45.

51. Murch, *Living for the City*, 20–21; "Interview with the Chief of Staff David Hilliard," *Black Panther*, April 20, 1969. The organizations of the Revolutionary Union Movement combined to form the League of Revolutionary Black Workers. See Geschwender and Jeffries, "League of Revolutionary Black Workers," 135–62; Bill Jennings, e-mail message to author, June 29, 2012.

52. Bill Jennings, interview by author, Sacramento, California, August 5, 2005; "Grape Boycott Grows," *Black Panther*; Eldridge Cleaver, "Pronunciamento: Address given at the Berkeley Community Center," *Black Panther*, December 21, 1968; Bobby Seale, Lecture given at the Sargent Gallery, African-American Art and Cultural Complex, San Francisco, May 6, 2004. Although Panthers obeyed the ban, others in the radical community were not impressed by Cleaver's speech. In a letter to *Black Politics*, an underground periodical in Berkeley, California, a reader critiqued, "This is a bitter realization that this man lacks political knowledge. . . . Mr. Cleaver, who seems vaguely aware of the grape strike, has not kept himself informed of the fact that it is a boycott of table grapes. . . . As a strong supporter of the Black Panther Party from its inception, and as one who sees the only hope of the future in the Black struggle, I deplore evidences of ignorance and weakness among the leadership." Takeo Goto, "Letter to the Editor," *Black Politics* 2, 11–12 (January–February 1969), 60.

53. Van Peebles, Taylor, and Lewis, *Panther*, 100–101; "Philadelphia, PA, Breakfast," *The Black Panther*, July 19, 1969; "Information on Safeway"; Big Man, "Fascist Calif. Grape Growers Use Mass Media To Combat a Living Wage," *Black Panther*, July 26, 1969; Jennings interview.

54. Padilla interview; "Rudy Reyes, 1965–1980." A Puerto Rican militant in New York applauded the Panthers' ability to inspire fear and suggested they be used more aggressively to aid the boycott. He told Peter Matthiessen, "They don't argue man. They go up to the guy and say, 'Don't sell.' It's unfair, it's undemocratic, but it works. . . . If the Panthers bomb a store, so what? All you people have to do is say, 'They didn't bomb because of *grapes*, whitey! The Panthers are *your* problem'" (Matthiessen, *Sal si Puedes*, 309). Later, a *New York Times* reporter alleged that an alliance between the UFWOC and the New York BPP "was quietly dropped when several stores selling grapes were mysteriously fire-bombed." Steven V. Roberts, "Grape Boycott: Struggle Poses a Moral Issue," *New York Times*, November 12, 1969, 49.

55. Seale interview; "B.P.P. Delivers Ultimatum to Safeway," *Black Panther*, July 14, 1973, 3.

56. Padilla interview; Medina interview; "Farm Workers Meet Panthers," December 19, 1969, *La Vinia: Pittsburgh, Pa. Grape Boycott Committee News*, box 20, folder 27, Chavez Collection, Part 2.

57. "UFW Backs the Black Panther Party," *¡VENGA!*, January 1970, box 1, folder 1, UFW Klamath Falls Collection; Judith Blake, "Panthers' Progress," *Seattle Times*, October 24, 1986, E6. The Seattle BPP medical clinic, later renamed the Carolyn Downs Family Medical Clinic, is still in operation as of this writing. See Cara Solomon, "The Story of Seattle's Black Panther Party," *Seattle Times*, May 21, 2006; UFW, "Boycott News," March 9, 1970, box 4, folder 12, United Farm Workers Boycott: Washington State Files, Archives of Labor and Urban Affairs, Wayne State University, Detroit (hereafter UFW Washington State Files).

58. Les Jarvis to Cesar Chavez, June 10, 1970, Cesar Chavez to Les Jarvis, July 22, 1970, both box 59, folder 13, Chavez Collection, Part 1.

59. "United Farm Workers: Chronological History," box 9, folder 11, Ross Papers; Ross, "History of the Farm Worker Movement"; "Huelga Ends!" *El Malcriado*, August 1, 1970; Leonard H. Carter to Cesar Chavez, July 30, 1970, box 6, folder 35, UFW Administration Files.

60. Watson, "The NAACP in California, 1914–1950," 188.

Chapter 4. More Mutual Respect Than Ever in Our History

1. Matthiessen, *Sal si Puedes*, 177, 179; R. B. Taylor, *Chavez and the Farm Workers*, 220; J. Levy, *Cesar Chavez*, 272–73.

2. Martin Luther King, Jr., to Cesar Chavez , March 5, 1968, box 22, folder 11, UFW Administration Files; Gwen to Andrew Young, March 8, 1968, part 2, reel 6, Records of the Southern Christian Leadership Conference, 1954–1970 (Bethesda, Md.: University Publications of America, 1995) (hereafter SCLC Records).

3. National Advisory Committee on Farm Labor, "Information Letter," Number 31, September 1966, reel 21, SNCC Papers; Martin Waldron, "Farm Workers in Texas End Two-Month March," *New York Times*, September 5, 1966, 10; Martin Luther King, Jr., to Cesar Chavez, September 22, 1966, box 2, folder 1, NFWA Collection.

4. David R. Jones, "Mrs. Liuzzo's Body Is Returned To Detroit in Teamsters' Plane, *New York Times*, March 27, 1965, 10; "Teamsters to Help 5 Liuzzo Children," *New York Times*, March 27, 1965, 10; David R. Jones, "Michigan Honors Alabama Victim," *New York Times*, March 28, 1965, 58; Witwer, *Corruption and Reform in the Teamsters Union*, 176–79, 233–35; Branch, *At Canaan's Edge*, 565; Report of Special Agent b7C, "Stanley David Levison," November 8, 1966, Bureau file 100–393452, Federal Bureau of Investigation, Freedom of Information Act File on Stanley Levison, Part 12b, accessed December 14, 2010; "Dr. King to Meet Hoffa on Rights," *New York Times*, November 8, 1966, 23; Garrow, *Bearing the Cross*, 536.

5. "Chronology," Chavez Collection, Part 2; Ganz, *Why David Sometimes Wins*, 215; T. F. Jackson, *From Civil Rights to Human Rights*, 301. Faced with criticism for his relationship with Hoffa and the Teamsters, King followed his advisors' recommendation to spin it as being in the best interest of African Americans on the basis of their large numbers in the union. Ignoring the fact that the union had been expelled from the AFL-CIO for corruption, in 1967 King praised the Teamsters for their inclusion of African American workers in his book, *Where Do We Go from Here: Chaos or Community?* However, in doing so, King overlooked the fact that despite Hoffa's attempts to recruit African American workers, discriminatory practices in union locals persisted and African American members were generally barred from leadership positions. King, *Where Do We Go from Here*, 150; Witwer, *Corruption and Reform in the Teamsters Union*, 146–48, 225.

6. Matthiessen, *Sal si Puedes*, 177, 179; Taylor, *Chavez and the Farm Workers*, 220; J. Levy, *Cesar Chavez*, 272–73.

7. The scholarship on the debate between nonviolence and self-defense in the civil rights movement is extensive. See, for example, Tyson, *Radio Free Dixie*; Lipsitz, *A Life in the Struggle*; Wendt, *The Spirit and the Shotgun*; Strain, *Pure Fire*; Payne, *I've Got the Light of Freedom*, 204–6; and H. K. Jeffries, *Bloody Lowndes*, 104; Raines, *My Soul Is Rested*, 266.

8. Matthiessen, *Sal si Puedes*, 183; J. Levy, *Cesar Chavez*, 275.

9. Martin Luther King, Jr., to Cesar Chavez, March 5, 1968; Branch, *At Canaan's Edge*, 718; Dunne, *Delano*, 181–82; Gwen to Andrew Young, March 8, 1968.

10. Carson, introduction to T. Jackson, *Becoming King*, xix; C. T. Vivian, *Black Power and the American Myth*, 5; T. F. Jackson, *From Civil Rights to Human Rights*, 239; Garrow, *Bearing the Cross*, 439; Abernathy, *And The Walls Came Tumbling Down*, 362, 368; SCLC, Statement of Purpose: Washington, D.C. Poor People's Campaign, January 1968, reel 12, SCLC Records; Mantler, "Black, Brown and Poor: Martin Luther King, Jr., the Poor People's Campaign and Its Legacies," iv.

11. SCLC, "Black and White Together: American Indians, Poor Whites, Spanish-Americans Join Poor People's Washington Campaign," March 15, 1968, Birmingham Police Department Surveillance Files, 1947–1980, Birmingham Public and Jefferson County Free Library; Baldemar Velásquez, interview by author, San Francisco, September 22, 2000; Mantler, "Black, Brown, and Poor: Civil Rights and the Making of the Chicano Movement," 182–83; Branch, *At Canaan's Edge*, 715–16; Bert Corona, leader of the Mexican American Political Association (MAPA), also attended the

meeting in Atlanta and recalled that King "always exhibited a sensitivity to the needs of *mexicanos*." He believed that had King not been assassinated, a national coalition between Mexican Americans and African Americans might have been possible. M. T. García, *Memories of Chicano History*, 216.

12. U.S. Bureau of the Census, *U.S. Census of Population: 1960, Subject Reports, Nativity and Parentage*, Final Report PC(2)–1A; Gibson and Jung, *Historical Census . . . for the United States, Regions, Divisions, and States*, U.S. Bureau of the Census, Population Division, Working Paper 56, September 2002; Gene Guerrero, telephone interview by author, October 1, 2000.

13. Martin Luther King, Jr., to Cindy Walters, October 11, 1961, box 40, folder 2, Martin Luther King, Jr., Collection, Howard Gotlieb Archival Research Center, Boston University (hereafter MLK-BU Collection); Martin Luther King, Jr., "Martin Luther King, Jr.: The Playboy Interview," interviewed by Alex Haley, *Playboy*, January 1965.

14. Honey, "Martin Luther King, Jr., the Crisis of the Black Working Class, and the Memphis Sanitation Strike," 164; Young, *An Easy Burden*, 445; Cesar Chavez to Marcos Muñoz, April 3, 1968, box 5, folder 6, United Farm Workers Boycott: Boston Files, Archives of Labor and Urban Affairs, Wayne State University, Detroit (hereafter UFW Boston Boycott Files); Matthiessen, *Sal si Puedes*, 242–43. Scholar Stewart Burns claims that Chavez sent a delegation to represent the UFWOC in the Poor People's Campaign, but all evidence demonstrates that he refused to do so. Burns, *To the Mountaintop*, 430.

15. J. Levy, *Cesar Chavez*, 289; Cesar Chavez, interviewed by Jacques Levy, box 4, folder 163, Jacques E. Levy Research Collection on Cesar Chavez, Yale Collection of Western Americana, Beinecke Rare Book and Manuscript Library, Yale University, New Haven, Conn. (hereafter Levy Collection); Cesar Chavez to Coretta Scott King, April 6, 1968, box 69, folder 11, Chavez Collection, Part 1; Medina interview; "The Man They Killed," *El Malcriado*, April 15, 1968; "Frances Ryan, 1966–1968," Farmworker Movement Documentation Project, accessed May 4, 2012. Although saddened by King's death, Chavez did not attend his funeral, unlike Chicano leaders Reies López Tijerina and Corky Gonzales. Mantler, "Black, Brown, and Poor: Martin Luther King, Jr., the Poor People's Campaign and its Legacies," 182.

16. Cesar Chavez, interviewed by Jacques E. Levy, box 4, folder 163; box 2, folder 146; box 1, folder 138; and box 1, folder 136, all in Levy Collection. With Chavez's approval, Levy heavily edited the interviews before including them in the book. None of these criticisms appear in the published version; Mariscal, "Cesar and Martin, March '68," 157–58.

17. Mantler, "Black, Brown, and Poor: Martin Luther King, Jr., the Poor People's Campaign and its Legacies," 147–54. Scholar Jorge Mariscal argues that Chavez did not participate in the Poor People's Campaign because he was in poor health following his fast. However, historian Gordon Mantler demonstrates that Chavez traveled extensively on the East Coast during the Campaign in May 1968 and simply used his health as an excuse when he did not want to attend events. Mariscal, "Cesar and Martin, March '68," 170; Mantler, "Black, Brown, and Poor: Civil Rights and the Making of the Chicano Movement," 207; Cesar Chavez and Larry Itliong to Southern Christian Leadership Conference, April 29, 1968, Cesar Chavez to Southern Christian Leadership Conference, July 26, 1968, both box 69, folder 11, Chavez Collection, Part 1; "Grape Boycott Backed," *Chicago Defender*, November 14, 1968, 2.

18. For more on the Poor People's Campaign and its aftermath, see Mantler, "Black, Brown and Poor : Martin Luther King, Jr., the Poor People's Campaign and Its Legacies"; Fairclough, *To Redeem the Soul of America*, 386–89; Abernathy, *And the Walls Came Tumbling Down*, 494, 497; Garrow, *Bearing the Cross*, 562; Branch, *At Canaan's Edge*, 625–26, 739.

19. Honey, "Martin Luther King, Jr., the Crisis of the Black Working Class, and the Memphis Sanitation Strike," 163–64; King, *Stride Toward Freedom*, 199; T. F. Jackson, *From Civil Rights to Human Rights*, 76, 94–95; King, "*All Labor Has Dignity*", 42.

20. P. B. Levy, *The New Left and Labor in the 1960s*, 18; T. F. Jackson, *From Civil Rights to Human Rights*, 136, 212; Hooper and Hooper, "The Scripto Strike," 13, 15; C. S. King, *My Life with Martin Luther King, Jr.*, 18; King's attitude toward organized labor is in keeping with Robin D. G. Kelley's

argument that "even if religious ideology, spiritual values, and gospel music united Southern working people and offered a moral justification to fight the bosses, Southern black church leaders were, more often than not, hostile or indifferent to organized labor." Kelley, *Race Rebels*, 42.

21. Hooper and Hooper, "The Scripto Strike," 23–24.

22. Hooper and Hooper, "The Scripto Strike," 7–8, 27; T. F. Jackson, *From Civil Rights to Human Rights*, 230, 349–50; Honey, "Martin Luther King, Jr., the Crisis of the Black Working Class, and the Memphis Sanitation Strike," 159.

23. Peake, *Keeping the Dream Alive*, 263; Faith C. Christmas, "Abernathy Planning Economic Withdrawals," *Chicago Defender*, October 14, 1968, 3.

24. "Grape Boycott Backed"; Peake, *Keeping the Dream Alive*, 108–9; Wallace, "From the Fullness of the Earth," 16–20; Sewell, "The 'Not-Buying Power' of the Black Community," 135–51; Abernathy, *And the Walls Came Tumbling Down*, 408.

25. Medina interview; Eliseo Medina to Cesar [Chavez], December 23, 1968, box 4, folder 15, UFW New York Boycott Files; "Jewel Increases Negro Employment," *Chicago Daily Defender*, May 1, 1967, 5; "Nation: Black Pocketbook Power," *Time*, March 1, 1968.

26. Medina to Chavez, December 23, 1968.

27. Abernathy, *And the Walls Came Tumbling Down*, 408; Medina to Chavez; "No Grapes for Chicago," *El Malcriado*, February 15, 1969, 5.

28. Chavez to E. L. Barr, Jr., Good Friday [April 4], 1969, box 4, folder 12, UFW New York Boycott Files; Cesar Chavez, "Letter from Delano," *Christian Century* 86 (April 23, 1969): 539.

29. Abernathy, *And the Walls Came Tumbling Down*, 541–45; *I Am Somebody*, prod. Madeline Anderson, 30 minutes, Icarus Films, 1970, videocassette; Young, *An Easy Burden*, 497.

30. Young, *An Easy Burden*, 498; O. Vivian, *Coretta*, 33–37, 106–8; *I Am Somebody*; "Labor: Settlement in Charleston," *Time*, July 4, 1969. In contrast to the claims of *Time* of a labor/civil rights alliance, historians Leon Fink and Brian Greenberg note that black trade unionists in Charleston and the majority white South Carolina AFL-CIO distanced themselves from the strike because they resented attempts to turn it into a civil rights struggle, as evidenced by the participation of SCLC. They also argue, "Each side claimed victory, but the fact is that within a year of the strike the union movement among Charleston hospital workers had withered." Fink and Greenberg, *Upheaval in the Quiet Zone*, 130, 140.

31. Abernathy, *And the Walls Come Tumbling Down*, 545, 576; Fink and Greenberg, *Upheaval in the Quiet Zone*, 138; "Abernathy Joins 100-Mile Trek," *Chicago Daily Defender*, May 20, 1969, 1; "Chronology"; Cesar Chavez to Ralph Abernathy, September 17, 1969, box 69, folder 11, Chavez Collection, Part 1.

32. "Rev. Ralph D. Abernathy Endorses [sic] Boycott in a Special Ohio Meeting in Cincy," *Los Quatro Piquetes: United Farm Workers Grape Boycott Newsletter for Western Ohio Area* 4, box 20, folder 28, Chavez Collection, Part 2; "SCLC Joins the Boycott," *Newsletter of the Indiana Committee to Aid Farm Labor*, August 21, 1969, box 20, folder 27, Chavez Collection, Part 2.

33. R. B. Taylor, *Chavez and the Farm Workers*, 252; "United Farm Workers: Chronological History."

34. Eric C. Brazil, "Salinas Valley Field Workers: Recognition Sought by Chavez's Union," *Salinas Californian*, July 25, 1970; "United Farm Workers: Chronological History"; Eric C. Brazil, "Chavez Furious: 30 Growers Sign Teamster Contract," *Salinas Californian*, July 28, 1970; National Farm Worker Ministry, "Chronology of Lettuce Struggle," March 1973, box 3, folder 4, Marc R. Grossman Collection, Archives of Labor and Urban Affairs, Wayne State University, Detroit (hereafter Grossman Collection); Cesar Chavez, "Press Statement," July 28, 1970, box 1, folder 6, Chavez Collection, Part 2. For more on the jurisdictional agreement between the UFWOC and the Teamsters, see R. B. Taylor, *Chavez and the Farm Workers*, 207–8, and J. Levy, *Cesar Chavez*, 257–61.

35. Brazil, "Chavez Furious"; Dunne, *Delano*, 119, 158; Harry Bernstein, "Chavez Calls for Boycott of Lettuce Lacking Union Label," *Los Angeles Times*, September 18, 1970, 3.

36. J. Levy, *Cesar Chavez*, 329–31; "Chavez Backers Start March to Salinas Rally," *Salinas Californian*, July 31, 1970.

37. J. Levy, *Cesar Chavez*, 335; National Farm Worker Ministry, "Brief History of United Farm Workers," November 1973, box 12, folder 18, Ross Papers; Inter-Faith Committee, "Salinas Strike & Lettuce Boycott—Farm Workers Non-Violent Struggle Continues," January 1971, box 3, folder 4, Grossman Collection; "Summary of August 12, 1970 Jurisdictional Agreement," August 12, 1970, box 5, folder 15, Grossman Collection; Harry Bernstein, "5,000–7,000 Strike in Largest Farm Walkout in U.S. History," *Los Angeles Times*, August 25, 1970, 1.

38. National Farm Worker Ministry, "Chronology of Lettuce Struggle"; Bernstein, "5,000–7,000 Strike."

39. R. B. Taylor, *Chavez and the Farm Workers*, 260, 263; "United Farm Workers: Chronological History"; "Chavez Calls Lettuce Boycott," *New York Times*, September 18, 1970, 11; Bernstein, "Chavez Calls for Boycott of Lettuce Lacking Union Label."

40. Bernstein, "Chavez Calls for Boycott of Lettuce Lacking Union Label"; R. B. Taylor, *Chavez and the Farm Workers*, 260; FBI, "National Farm Workers Association (NFWA)," November 17, 1970, reel 1, FBI File on Cesar Chavez and United Farm Workers (Wilmington, Del.: Scholarly Resources, 1995) (hereafter FBI-UFW File); Cesar Chavez to Jesse Jackson, November 17, 1970, box 5, folder 38, UFW Administration Files.

41. "United Farm Workers: Chronological History"; Ralph Abernathy to Cesar Chavez, December 8, 1970, box 3, folder 4, Chavez Collection, Part 2; "Seeks Aid for Chavez," *Chicago Daily Defender*, December 22, 1970, 12; J. Levy, *Cesar Chavez*, 430–31.

42. "Mrs. King Visiting Chavez," *Salinas Californian*, December 19, 1970, 1; Eric C. Brazil, "Mrs. King Predicts Chavez Victory," *Salinas Californian*, December 21, 1970; "Coretta Scott King at Rally," AV 212, Tape 5, Levy Collection; "Coretta King Visits with Cesar Chavez in Jail, Asks Blacks to Boycott Lettuce!" December 19, 1970, box 21, folder 458, Levy Collection.

43. "Coretta King Visits with Cesar Chavez in Jail, Asks Blacks to Boycott Lettuce!"; Crawford, "Coretta Scott King and the Struggle for Civil and Human Rights, 107–8; O. Vivian, *Coretta*, 33–37; C. S. King, *My Life with Martin Luther King, Jr.*, 48–49.

44. T. F. Jackson, *From Civil Rights to Human Rights*, 26–27, 36, 105, 239; Garrow, *Bearing the Cross*, 439; Abernathy, *And the Walls Came Tumbling Down*, 5; Peake, *Keeping the Dream Alive*, 269.

45. Howard Pousner, "Coretta King Married the Man and His Vision," *Atlanta Constitution*, January 16, 1986, sec. A; "Coretta King Visits with Cesar Chavez in Jail, Asks Blacks to Boycott Lettuce!" Similarly, Scott King told the striking hospital workers in Charleston, "If my husband were alive today he would be right here with you," quoted in Fink and Greenberg, *Upheaval in the Quiet Zone*, 144.

46. R. B. Taylor, *Chavez and the Farm Workers*, 261; "Abernathy Plans 3 Protest Rallies," *New York Times*, January 15, 1971, 40; Hosea Williams to Cesar Chavez, March 12, 1971, box 5, folder 38, UFW Administration Files; Williams's letter to Chavez demonstrates that his opinion of forming multiracial alliances had changed dramatically, as he had been vocally opposed to the inclusion of other minority groups in the Poor People's Campaign just three years earlier. Branch, *At Canaan's Edge*, 716; Fairclough, *To Redeem the Soul of America*, 396.

47. Peake, *Keeping the Dream Alive*, 254; Honey, *Going Down Jericho Road*, 180; "Editorial, The 1970s: The Challenge for America's Farm Workers," *El Malcriado* 8, 18–19 (January 1–31, 1970), 2; P. B. Levy, *The New Left and Labor in the 1960s*, 166.

48. "United Farm Workers: Chronological History"; Wallace Turner, "Chavez-Teamsters Pact Ends Lettuce Labor Rift," *New York Times*, March 27, 1971, 1; National Farm Worker Ministry, "Chronology of Lettuce Struggle"; R. B. Taylor, *Chavez and the Farm Workers*, 261–62.

49. John Kendall, "Chavez Signs Nation's Largest Independent Lettuce Producer," *Los Angeles Times*, April 24, 1971, B9; National Farm Worker Ministry, "Brief History of United Farm Workers"; National Farm Worker Ministry, "Chronology of Lettuce Struggle."

50. A search of the online archive of the *New York Times* reveals only one article published on the UFWOC during the negotiation period; "United Farm Workers: Chronological History"; R.

B. Taylor, *Chavez and the Farm Workers*, 289; Steven V. Roberts, "Conservative Groups Mount Campaign Against Chavez Union," *New York Times*, March 26, 1972, 48; Bella Stumbo, "The Anglo Army Behind Cesar Chavez," *Los Angeles Times*, April 6, 1972; "New Boycott of Lettuce Announced by Chavez," *New York Times*, May 3, 1972, 32.

51. J. Levy, *Cesar Chavez*, 441, 470–72.

52. In 1971 Chavez moved the UFW headquarters from Delano fifty miles south to an abandoned tuberculosis sanatorium, which the union dubbed La Paz. Ferris and Sandoval, *The Fight in the Fields*, 174–75; Cesar Chavez to Coretta Scott King, February 4, 1972, box 4, folder 48, United Farm Workers Work Department Papers, Archives of Labor and Urban Affairs, Wayne State University, Detroit (hereafter UFW Work Department Papers); Coretta Scott King to Cesar Chavez, February 10, 1972, April 27, 1972, both box 4, folder 48, UFW Work Department Papers.

53. National Farm Worker Ministry, "Chronology of Lettuce Struggle"; "Steelworkers to Back Bid to Oust Arizona Governor," *New York Times*, June 8, 1972, 42; Ed Meagher, "Union Presses Recall Campaign in Arizona," *Los Angeles Times,* October 23, 1972, A19; J. Levy, *Cesar Chavez*, 464; John L. Scott to Cesar Chavez, May 17, 1962, box 16, folder 5, UFW Administration Department Files; Lettuce Boycott Petition, May 23, 1972, United Farm Workers Boycott: Michigan Files, Box 2, Folder 35, Archives of Labor and Urban Affairs, Wayne State University, Detroit (hereafter UFW Michigan Boycott Files); Ralph Abernathy, "No Lettuce" Pledge to Support Farmworkers, box 16, folder 2, UFW Administration Department Files.

54. Athia Hardt, "Blacks Urged to Support Chavez," *Arizona Republic*, May 30, 1972; "Lucia Vazquez, 1968–1981," Farmworker Movement Documentation Project, accessed December 2, 2010.

55. Ralph Abernathy to Cesar Chavez, June 5, 1972, box 16, folder 11, UFW Administration Department Files; "United Farm Workers: Chronological History"; J. Levy, *Cesar Chavez*, 466–68; R. B. Taylor, *Chavez and the Farm Workers*, 280–81; Raul Castro, a Democrat, was born in Mexico and served as governor of Arizona until 1977 when he was appointed by President Jimmy Carter as ambassador to Argentina.

56. "United Farm Workers: Chronological History"; James L. Vizzard, S.J., "The Measure Would Restrict the Union to the Point That It Would Be Killed," *Los Angeles Times*, August 31, 1972, C7.

57. LeRoy Chatfield, "Proposition 22," Farmworker Movement Documentation Project; William Karr, "5 Charged with Fraud on Prop. 22 Petitions," *Los Angeles Times*, November 3, 1972, A3; Harry Bernstein, "State's Growers Say They'll Keep Trying to Curb Chavez," *Los Angeles Times*, November 9, 1972, A3; Harry Bernstein, "Prop. 22 Firm Wrote State Official's Report," *Los Angeles Times*, November 4, 1972, OC1.

58. Frank del Olmo, "Kennedy Urges Defeat of Farm Labor Initiative," *Los Angeles Times*, October 28, 1972, A13; C. S. King, *My Life with Martin Luther King, Jr.*, 289–90; Henry P. Leifermann, "'Profession: Concert Singer, Freedom Movement Lecturer,'" *New York Times*, November 26, 1972.

59. C. S. King, *My Life with Martin Luther King, Jr.*, 208; Leifermann, "'Profession: Concert Singer, Freedom Movement Lecturer'"; Garrow, *Bearing the Cross*, 617. King's patriarchal attitude, which led to the marginalization of women in SCLC, is well documented. See Ling, "Gender and Generation," 101–29; and Robnett, "African-American Women in the Civil Rights Movement."

Chapter 5. A Natural Alliance of Poor People

1. Elbert Howard, interview by author, Berkeley, California, November 19, 2005; Richard Ybarra, interview by author, by telephone, October 12, 2004.

2. Aptheker, *The Morning Breaks*, 9–10; Lesley Oelsner, "Charges Dropped in the Seale Case; 'Publicity Cited,'" *New York Times*, May 26, 1971.

3. Newton, *Revolutionary Suicide*, 322; Alkebulan, *Survival Pending Revolution*, 80–81; E. Cleaver, "Towards a People's Army," in *Target Zero*, 223.

4. Thomas A. Johnson, "Panthers Fear Growing Intraparty Strife," *New York Times*, April 10, 1971, 24; O. A. Johnson, "Explaining the Demise of the Black Panther Party," 399–403; K. Cleaver,

"Back to Africa," 236, 238; Earl Caldwell, "The Panthers: Dead or Regrouping," *New York Times*, March 1, 1971, 1, 16.

5. Abron, "'Serving the People,'" 178; Jennings interview.

6. Murch, *Living for the City*, 192, 194; Political scientist Cedric Johnson argues that the turn toward electoral politics ultimately diminished black radicalism and direct action. C. Johnson, *Revolutionaries to Race Leaders*, xxiii.

7. Murch, *Living for the City*, 195–96; "The Black Scholar Interviews: Bobby Seale," *Black Scholar*, September 1972, 7; Jennings interview.

8. J. Wilson, "Invisible Cages," 192; Phoebe Graubard, "In Defense of a Coalition Between the Peace & Freedom Movement and the Black Panther Party for Self-Defense," box 1, folder 3, Litwack Collection; Murch, *Living for the City*, 156, 158, 203; *The Black Panther*, November 2, 1968; Seale, *Seize the Time*, 209–10, 240; Alkebulan, *Survival Pending Revolution*, 118.

9. "The Black Panther Party Stands for Revolutionary Solidarity," in *The Black Panthers Speak*, ed. Foner, 220; Murch, *Living for the City*, 193; F. Hayes and Kiene, "'All Power to the People,'" 167, 171.

10. "United Farm Workers: Chronological History"; Vizzard, "The Measure Would Restrict the Union to the Point That It Would Be Killed"; Bernstein, "State's Growers Say They'll Keep Trying to Curb Chavez"; Karr, "5 Charged with Fraud on Prop. 22 Petitions"; Bernstein, "Prop. 22 Firm Wrote State Official's Report"; "Boycott Lettuce," *The Black Panther*, September 23, 1972, 2.

11. Jessie de la Cruz, interviewed by Anamaría de la Cruz, Fresno, California, November 29–30, 1973, Farmworker Movement Documentation Project; Roberto de la Cruz, interviewed by Anamaría de la Cruz, Farmworker Movement Documentation Project; "Farmworkers Plant the Seeds of Freedom," *The Black Panther*, November 16, 1972, 6, 14.

12. Daniel, "Cesar Chavez and the Unionization of California Farm Workers," 374; Bernstein, "State's Growers Say They'll Keep Trying to Curb Chavez."

13. "The Black Scholar Interviews: Bobby Seale"; Earl Caldwell, "Seale Campaign Gains in Oakland," *New York Times*, April 8, 1971, 38; Gibson and Jung, "Table 5. California—Race and Hispanic Origin for Selected Large Cities and Other Places: Earliest Census to 1990," *Historical Census . . . For Large Cities and Other Urban Places in the United States*.

14. U.S. Bureau of the Census, *U.S. Census of Population: 1970, Subject Report: Persons of Spanish Surname*, 1973; Flier, "Conozcan a los Candidatos," February 23, 1973, box 18, folder 18, Social Protest Collection; Community Committee to Elect Bobby Seale and Elaine Brown to City Offices of Oakland, "Bobby Seale Calls upon Oakland City Council to Become the First City in California to Provide Bilingual (English/Spanish) Ballots for Local Elections," March 7, 1973, series 2, box 45, folder 19, Dr. Huey P. Newton Foundation, Inc. Collection, Department of Special Collections, Stanford University Libraries, Stanford University, Stanford, Calif. (hereafter Newton Collection); "Bilingual Ballots for Oakland," *The Black Panther*, March 17, 1973, 5, 13; Spencer, "Inside the Panther Revolution," 312.

15. "Bilingual Ballot Endorsed," *Black Panther*, March 31, 1973, 5, 14; Vilma Martinez, telephone interview by author, October 9, 2000; The 1975 extension of the Voting Rights Act banned the use of English literacy tests and mandated that translated voting materials be provided in areas with a significant population of non-English speakers. "About Language Minority Voting Rights," U.S. Department of Justice, Civil Rights Division. The NAACP initially objected to the expansion of the Voting Rights Act, but later reversed course at the urging of MALDEF.

16. "Vote for the People's Plan," *The Black Panther*, April 14, 1973, A, B, C; Flier, "People Have a Right to a Job, With or Without a Skill," April 17, 1973, box 18, folder 18, Social Protest Collection.

17. Howard interview; Ybarra interview. The Mulford Act prohibited carrying loaded firearms in public. California assemblyman Don Mulford wrote the bill to curtail the BPP's armed patrols of the police. Murch, *Living for the City*, 148, 171.

18. Bobby Seale and Elaine Brown to Cesar Chavez, February 13, 1973, box 6, folder 7, UFW

Work Department Papers; Bobby Seale to Cesar Chavez, March 7, 1973, box 6, folder 7, UFW Work Department Papers; Howard interview; Ybarra interview; Medina interview.

19. Matthew Jarvis, e-mail message to author, May 31, 2011; J. Levy, *Cesar Chavez*, 288–90; Matthiessen, *Sal si Puedes*, 243–44.

20. J. Levy, *Cesar Chavez*, 151, 537; Eric Boehme, e-mail message to author, May 29, 2011; Matthiessen, *Sal si Puedes*, 280; "UFWOC Backs Bradley for Mayor of L.A.," *El Malcriado*, March 15–31, 1969, 6; Flier, "La Raza Con Bradley Para Mayor," box 5, folder 5, UFWOC Collection; Although Bradley lost the election in 1969, he was later elected in 1973 and served as Mayor of Los Angeles until 1993.

21. Community Committee to Elect Bobby Seale and Elaine Brown to City Offices of Oakland, Press Release, March 29, 1973, series 2, box 45, folder 19, Newton Collection; Murch, *Living for the City*, 201; Community Committee to Elect Bobby Seale and Elaine Brown to City Offices of Oakland, Press Release, April 5, 1973, series 2, box 45, folder 19; Newton Collection, "Cesar Chavez Due in Oakland for Campaign," *The Black Panther*, April 14, 1973, 8; Howard interview; Jennings interview.

22. Cesar Chavez to Bobby Seale, April 14, 1973, box 6, folder 7, UFW Work Department Papers.

23. R. B. Taylor, *Chavez and the Farm Workers*, 273, 292–93; Steven V. Roberts, "Chavez and Union Fight for Lives," *New York Times*, April 29, 1973, 17.

24. "Teamsters Gain California Farms," *New York Times*, April 16, 1973, 40; R. B. Taylor, *Chavez and the Farm Workers*, 293, 297; Roberts, "Chavez and Union Fight for Lives."

25. "Cesar Chavez, Bobby and Elaine Exchange Messages of Solidarity," *The Black Panther*, April 21, 1973, 7, 14; Seale interview; Seale, *A Lonely Rage*, 46.

26. José Gomez to Bobby Seale, April 18, 1973, box 6, folder 7, UFW Work Department Papers.

27. Huey Newton to Cesar Chavez, April 22, 1973, box 6, folder 7, UFW Work Department Papers; Cesar Chavez to Huey Newton, May 2, 1973, series 2, box 46, folder 7, Newton Collection.

28. "Chavez Calls for Grape Boycott," *The Black Panther*, April 28, 1973, 6, 14.

29. "Farm Workers File $32 Million Conspiracy Terrorism Suit," *The Black Panther*, May 5, 1973, 6; "Bobby Seale Meets Cesar Chavez," *The Black Panther*, May 12, 1973, 5.

30. Rhomberg, *No There There*, 110; J. Levy, *Cesar Chavez*, 112–14; E. C. Hayes, *Power, Structure, and Urban Policy*, 7, 17, and 35; "John Reading, 85; as Mayor, Expanded the Oakland Airport," *Los Angeles Times*, February 14, 2003.

31. "Bobby Seale Meets Cesar Chavez," *The Black Panther*, May 12, 1973, 5; Flier, "Why Should the Spanish Speaking Community Vote for Bobby Seale for Mayor of Oakland?/¿Porque debe votar la raza por Bobby Seale para alcalde de Oakland?" May 1973, series 2, box 46, folder 5, Newton Collection; Ybarra interview.

32. "Aid the Farmworkers," *The Black Panther*, June 9, 1973, 16; "Safeway Aid Asked in Coachella Strike," *Los Angeles Times*, June 7, 1973, A3; Myrna Oliver, "Court Says Chavez Union Must Limit Safeway Picketing," *Los Angeles Times*, June 15, 1973, D1.

33. "B. P. P. Delivers Ultimatum to Safeway," *The Black Panther*, July 14, 1973, 3.

34. "New Oakland Democratic Organizing Committee Launched," *The Black Panther*, June 30, 1973, A-B; "Editorial: New Democracy," *The Black Panther*, June 30, 1973, 2.

35. "Boycott Safeway," *The Black Panther*, July 28, 1973; "Safeway Boycott: A Conspiracy of the Poor?" *The Black Panther*, August 4, 1973, A, B; KPIX Eyewitness News, the CBS affiliate in the San Francisco Bay Area, reported on Elaine Brown's press conference and the picket line at Safeway. For video footage, see "Panthers Boycott Safeway in Solidarity with United Farm Workers," San Francisco Bay Area Television Archive, https://diva.sfsu.edu/collections/sfbatv/bundles/208085.

36. "Chronology, Gallo-UFWA-Teamsters, February 1–July 10 1973," box 3, folder 4, Grossman Collection; "Gallo Chronology," box 13, folder 2, Ross Papers; R. B. Taylor, *Chavez and the Farm Workers*, 305 .

37. Flier, "Elaine Brown," July 1973, Social Protest Collection; "Boycott Safeway," *The Black Pan-

ther, July 28, 1973; Flier, "Support Farm Workers: Mass Support Rally and March Through Richmond," August 4, 1973, box 10, folder 25, Social Protest Collection.

38. "Brief History—UFWA in Wine Industry—Schenley to Gallo," box 30, folder 3, Chavez Collection Papers, Part 2; "Chavez: Farmworkers 'Stabbed in the Back,'" *The Black Panther,* August 18, 1973, 4.

39. "Farm Workers March in Memory of Slain Brothers," *The Black Panther,* September 15, 1973, 5, 16; National Farm Worker Ministry, "Brief History of United Farm Workers," box 12, folder 18, Ross Papers; R. B. Taylor, *Chavez and the Farm Workers,* 313.

40. National Farm Worker Ministry, "Brief History of United Farm Workers," November 1973, box 3, folder 4, Grossman Collection; Frank del Olmo, "Gallo Winery May Face Boycott by Farm Union," *Los Angeles Times,* September 24, 1973, A1; Cesar Chavez to friend, December 1973, box 2, folder 11, Grossman Collection; Cesar Chavez, "Statement on Israel," November 1973, series 2, box 54, folder 13, Newton Collection; David Du Bois to Huey Newton, December 23, 1973, series 2, box 54, folder 13, Newton Collection. None of Chavez's biographers have mentioned his position on Israel, which may have stemmed from George Meany and the AFL-CIO's longstanding support of the nation. A month before Chavez issued his statement on Israel, the AFL-CIO passed a resolution at its tenth constitutional convention calling for the U.S. government to supply arms to Israel and for member unions to support Israel. At the same convention, the AFL-CIO passed four resolutions in support of the UFW. AFL-CIO, *Proceedings of the Tenth Constitutional Convention of the AFL-CIO* (Washington, D.C.: AFL-CIO, 1973), 276–81, 454–65; Hahn, "The Influence of Organized Labor on U.S. Policy Toward Israel, 1945–1967," 154–77.

41. O. A. Johnson, "Explaining the Demise of the Black Panther Party," 407.

42. O. A. Johnson, "Explaining the Demise of the Black Panther Party," 405; Seale interview.

43. O. A. Johnson, "Explaining the Demise of the Black Panther Party," 391–94.

44. O. A. Johnson, "Explaining the Demise of the Black Panther Party," 407–8; Ferris and Sandoval, *The Fight in the Fields,* 191–92.

45. Ybarra interview; Jennings interview.

Conclusion

1. Michael Omi and Howard Winant argue that these "are not fixed and discrete categories, and that such 'regions' are by no means autonomous. They overlap, intersect, and fuse with each other in countless ways." Omi and Winant, *Racial Formation in the United States,* 68.

2. Cleaver, "An Open Letter to Stokely Carmichael," in Foner, ed., *The Black Panthers Speak,* 105.

3. Seale, *Seize the Time,* 210–11; Seale, *A Lonely Rage,* 210.

4. Seale, *Seize the Time,* 71–72.

5. Seale, *Seize the Time,* 270.

6. Varela, "Time to Get Ready," 570.

BIBLIOGRAPHY

Archival Collections

African American Museum and Library at Oakland, Oakland, California
    NAACP Collection
    Virna Canson Collection
Archives of Labor and Urban Affairs, Walter P. Reuther Library, Wayne State University, Detroit, Michigan
    Cesar Chavez Oral History
    Cesar Chavez Photo Collection
    David Cohen Collection
    Fred Ross, Sr. Collection
    Larry Itliong Collection
    Marc R. Grossman Collection
    National Farm Workers Association Collection
    United Farm Workers Administration Department Files
    United Farm Workers: Arizona State Office Files
    United Farm Workers: Audio-Visual Collection
    United Farm Workers Boycott: Idaho-Nampa Files
    United Farm Workers Boycott: Massachusetts-Boston Files
    United Farm Workers Boycott: Michigan Files
    United Farm Workers Boycott: New York Files
    United Farm Workers Boycott: Texas Files
    United Farm Workers Boycott: Washington, D.C. Files
    United Farm Workers Boycott: Washington State Files
    United Farm Workers Central Files
    United Farm Workers: Klamath Falls Collection
    United Farm Workers: Marshall Ganz Files
    United Farm Workers: Office of the President Collection
    United Farm Workers Organizing Committee Collection
    United Farm Workers Work Department Papers
Bancroft Library, University of California, Berkeley
    Eldridge Cleaver Papers
    Records of the National Association for the Advancement of Colored People, West Coast Region
    Social Protest Collection
Beinecke Rare Book & Manuscript Library, Yale University, New Haven, Connecticut

Jacques E. Levy Research Collection on Cesar Chavez
Leon F. Litwack Collection of Berkeley, California Protest Literature
Birmingham Public and Jefferson County Free Library, Birmingham, Alabama
Birmingham Police Department Surveillance Files, 1947–1980
Center for Southwest Research, University of New Mexico, Albuquerque
Alianza Federal de Pueblos Libres Collection
Francisco E. Martinez Papers
Peter Nabokov Papers
Tijerina, Reies Lopez—and Poor People's March—Washington, D.C., 1968 Vertical File
Department of Special Collections, Stanford University Libraries, Stanford, California
Dr. Huey P. Newton Foundation, Inc. Collection
Fred Ross Papers
Howard Gotlieb Archival Research Center, Boston University
Martin Luther King, Jr. Collection
Manuscripts & Archives, Sterling Memorial Library, Yale University, New Haven, Connecticut
Movement (Protest) Collection
Martin Luther King, Jr., Center for Nonviolent Social Change, Inc., Atlanta, Georgia
Martin Luther King, Jr. Papers
State Historical Society of Wisconsin, Madison, Wisconsin
Charles M. Sherrod Papers
Social Action Vertical File
María Varela Papers, Private Collection, Albuquerque, New Mexico

Archival Collections on Microfilm

FBI File on Cesar Chavez and United Farm Workers. Wilmington, Del.: Scholarly Resources, 1995.
FBI File on the Student Nonviolent Coordinating Committee, 1964–1973. Wilmington, Del.: Scholarly Resources, 1991.
Papers of the NAACP. Bethesda, Md.: University Publications of America, 2001.
Records of the Southern Christian Leadership Conference, 1954–1970. Bethesda, Md.: University Publications of America, 1995.
The Student Nonviolent Coordinating Committee Papers, 1959–1972. Sanford, N.C.: Microfilming Corp. of America, 1982.

Government Documents

Federal Bureau of Investigation. Freedom of Information Act File on Stanley Levison.
Gibson, Campbell and Kay Jung. *Historical Census Statistics on Population Totals by Race, 1790 to 1990, and by Hispanic Origin, 1970 to 1990, for the United States, Regions, Divisions, and States.* U.S. Bureau of the Census, Population Division Working Paper 56, September 2002.
———. *Historical Census Statistics on Population Totals by Race, 1790 to 1990, and by Hispanic Origin, 1970 to 1990, for Large Cities and Other Urban Places in the United States.* U.S. Bureau of the Census, Population Division Working Paper 76, February 2005.
U.S. Bureau of the Census. *1970 Census of Population*, vol. 1, *Characteristics of the Population, Part 6: California—section 2.* Washington, D.C.: U.S. GPO, 1973.
———. *U.S. Census of Population: 1960. Subject Report: Nativity and Parentage.* Washington, D.C.: U.S. GPO, 1965.
———. *U.S. Census of Population: 1960. Subject Report: Persons of Spanish Surname.* Washington, D.C.: U.S. GPO, 1965.
———. *U.S. Census of Population: 1970. Subject Report: Persons of Spanish Surname.* Washington, D.C.: U.S. GPO, 1973.

Internet Sources

Bracero History Archive. http://braceroarchive.org/.
Civil Rights Movement Veterans. http://www.crmvet.org.
Farmworker Movement Documentation Project. http://www.farmworkermovement.org.
Federal Bureau of Investigation, Freedom of Information Act File. http://foia.fbi.gov/.
It's About Time: Black Panther Legacy & Alumni. http://www.itsabouttimebpp.com.
National Center for Farmworker Health, Inc. http://www.ncfh.org/.
San Francisco Bay Area Television Archives. https://diva.sfsu.edu/collections/sfbatv.
SLATE Archives Digital Collection. http://archive.slatearchives.org.
TeachingAmericanHistory.org. http://teachingamericanhistory.org.
U.S. Bureau of the Census. http://www.census.gov.
U.S. Department of Justice, Civil Rights Division. http://www.justice.gov/crt/.
U.S. Department of Labor, Wage and Hour Division. http://www.dol.gov/whd/.

Documentary Film

I Am Somebody. Prod. Madeline Anderson. 30 minutes. Icarus Films, 1970. Videocassette.

Interviews

George Ballis, November 19, 2003, Oakland, California.
Wendy Goepel Brooks, September 13, 2004, by telephone.
Terry Cannon, December 11, 2003, by telephone.
Hardy Frye, November 18, 2003, Berkeley, California.
Marshall Ganz, November 25, 2003, by telephone.
———. May 4, 2004, by telephone.
Gene Guererro, October 1, 2000, by telephone.
Elbert "Big Man" Howard, November 19, 2005, Berkeley, California.
Bill Jennings, August 5, 2005, Sacramento, California.
Elizabeth Sutherland Martínez, October 30, 2000, San Francisco, California.
Vilma Martinez, October 9, 2000, by telephone.
Eliseo Medina, August 12, 2004, by telephone.
Mike Miller, December 20, 2003, by telephone.
———. February 19, 2004, San Francisco, California.
Gilbert Padilla, May 18, 2004, Berkeley, California.
Bobby Seale, May 24, 2004, Oakland, California.
María Varela, November 11, 2000, by telephone.
Baldemar Velásquez, September 22, 2000, San Francisco, California.
Richard Ybarra, October 12, 2004, by telephone.

Newspapers and Periodicals

Albuquerque Tribune
Arizona Republic
Atlanta Constitution
Bakersfield Californian
Black Panther
Black Politics
Black Scholar
Chicago Defender

Christian Century
The Crisis
Denver Blade
Dinuba Sentinel
Hardboiled
Inferno
Jet
Los Angeles Times
El Malcriado
The Movement
New Mexican
New York Times
Newsweek
Philadelphia Tribune
Playboy
Portland Scanner
Sacramento Observer
Salinas Californian
San Francisco Chronicle
Seattle Times
Student Voice
Sun-Reporter
Time
Turlock Daily Journal

Dissertations and Unpublished Papers

Behnken, Brian D. "Fighting Each Other's Battles: Mexican American/African American Coopera-
    tion During the Civil Rights Era in Texas." Paper presented at annual conference of the Western
    History Association, Incline Village, Nevada, October 13–16, 2010.
Ferreira, Jason. "All Power to the People: A Comparative History of Third World Radicalism in San
    Francisco, 1968–1974." Ph.D. dissertation, University of California, Berkeley, 2003.
Ganz, Marshall. "Five Smooth Stones: Strategic Capacity in the Unionization of California Agricul-
    ture." Ph.D. dissertation, Harvard University, 2000.
Krochmal, Max. "Labor, Civil Rights, and the Struggle for Democracy in Texas, 1935–1975." Ph.D.
    dissertation, Duke University, 2011.
Mantler, Gordon. "Black, Brown and Poor: Martin Luther King, Jr., the Poor People's Campaign
    and Its Legacies." Ph.D. dissertation, Duke University, 2008.
Michel, Gregg Laurence. "We'll Take Our Stand: The Southern Students Organizing Committee
    and the Radicalization of White Southern Students, 1964–1969." Ph.D. dissertation, University
    of Virginia, 1999.

Books and Journal Articles

Abernathy, Ralph David. *And the Walls Came Tumbling Down: An Autobiography*. New York:
    Harper and Row, 1989.
Abron, JoNina M. "'Serving the People': The Survival Programs of the Black Panther Party." In *The
    Black Panther Party: Reconsidered*, ed. Charles E. Jones, 177–92. Baltimore: Black Classic Press,
    1998.
Acuña, Rodolfo. *Occupied America: A History of Chicanos*. 4th ed. New York: Longman, 2000.

AFL-CIO. *Proceedings of the Tenth Constitutional Convention of the AFL-CIO.* Washington, D.C.: AFL-CIO, 1973.

Alkebulan, Paul. *Survival Pending Revolution: The History of the Black Panther Party.* Tuscaloosa: University of Alabama Press, 2007.

Alvarez, Luis. *The Power of the Zoot: Youth Culture and Resistance During World War II.* Berkeley: University of California Press, 2008.

Alvarez, Luis and Daniel Widener. "Brown-Eyed Soul: Popular Music and Cultural Politics in Los Angeles." In *The Struggle in Black and Brown: African American and Mexican American Relations During the Civil Rights Era,* ed. Brian D. Behnken, 211–36. Lincoln: University of Nebraska Press, 2011.

Anderson, Jervis. *Bayard Rustin: Troubles I've Seen.* New York: HarperCollins, 1997.

Aptheker, Bettina. *The Morning Breaks: The Trial of Angela Davis.* New York: International Publishers, 1975.

Arnesen, Eric, ed. *The Black Worker: Race, Labor, and Civil Rights since Emancipation.* Urbana: University of Illinois Press, 2007.

———. "The Quicksands of Economic Insecurity: African Americans, Strikebreaking, and Labor Activism in the Industrial Era." In *The Black Worker: Race, Labor, and Civil Rights Since Emancipation,* ed. Eric Arnesen, 41–71. Urbana: University of Illinois Press, 2007.

Babson, Steve with Ron Alpern, Dave Elsila, and John Revitte. *Working Detroit: The Making of a Union Town.* New York: Adama Books, 1984.

Behnken, Brian D. *Fighting Their Own Battles: Mexican Americans, African Americans, and the Struggle for Civil Rights in Texas.* Chapel Hill: University of North Carolina Press, 2011.

———, ed. *The Struggle in Black and Brown: African American and Mexican American Relations During the Civil Rights Era.* Lincoln: University of Nebraska Press, 2011.

———. "The Movement in the Mirror: Civil Rights and the Causes of Black-Brown Disunity in Texas." In *The Struggle in Black and Brown: African American and Mexican American Relations During the Civil Rights Era,* ed. Brian D. Behnken, 49–77. Lincoln: University of Nebraska Press, 2011.

Berg, Manfred. *"The Ticket to Freedom": The NAACP and the Struggle for Black Political Integration.* Gainesville: University Press of Florida, 1995.

Bernstein, Shana. *Bridges of Reform: Interracial Civil Rights Activism in Twentieth-Century Los Angeles.* New York: Oxford University Press, 2011.

Bloom, Joshua and Waldo E. Martin, Jr. *Black Against Empire: The History and Politics of the Black Panther Party.* Berkeley: University of California Press, 2013.

Boskin, Joseph. "The Revolt of the Urban Ghettos, 1964–1967," *Annals of the American Academy of Political and Social Science* 382 (March 1969): 1–14.

Branch, Taylor. *At Canaan's Edge: America in the King Years, 1965–1968.* New York: Simon & Schuster, 2006.

———. *Parting the Waters: America in the King Years, 1954–1963.* New York: Simon & Schuster, 1988.

———. *Pillar of Fire: America in the King Years, 1963–1965.* New York: Simon & Schuster, 1998.

Brilliant, Mark. *The Color of America Has Changed: How Racial Diversity Shaped Civil Rights Reform in California, 1941–1978.* New York: Oxford University Press, 2010.

Brown, Elaine. *A Taste of Power: A Black Woman's Story.* New York: Pantheon, 1992.

Burns, Stewart. *To the Mountaintop: Martin Luther King, Jr.'s Mission to Save America, 1955–1980.* New York: HarperSanFrancisco, 2004.

Camfield, David. "Re-Orienting Class Analysis: Working Classes as Historical Formations." *Science & Society* 68, 4 (Winter 2004/2005): 421–46.

Carmichael, Stokely (Kwame Ture). *Stokely Speaks: From Black Power to Pan-Africanism.* 1971. Chicago: Lawrence Hill, 2007.

Carmichael, Stokely (Kwame Ture), with Ekwueme Michael Thelwell. *Ready for Revolution: The Life and Struggles of Stokely Carmichael (Kwame Ture)*. New York: Scribner, 2003.

Carrigan, William D. and Clive Webb, "The Lynching of Persons of Mexican Origin or Descent in the United States, 1848 to 1928." *Journal of Social History* 37, 2 (Winter 2003): 411–38.

Carson, Clayborne. *In Struggle: SNCC and the Black Awakening of the 1960s*. 1981. Cambridge, Mass.: Harvard University Press, 1995.

———. Introduction to *Becoming King: Martin Luther King, Jr., and the Making of a National Leader*, by Troy Jackson, xi–xx. Lexington: University Press of Kentucky, 2008.

Charron, Katherine. *Freedom's Teacher: The Life of Septima Clark*. Chapel Hill: University of North Carolina Press, 2009.

Chepesiuk, Ron. *Sixties Radicals, Then and Now: Candid Conversations with Those Who Shaped the Era*. Jefferson, N.C.: McFarland, 1995.

Cherny, Robert W., William Issel, and Kieran Walsh Taylor, eds. *American Labor and the Cold War: Grassroots Politics and Postwar Political Culture*. New Brunswick, N.J.: Rutgers University Press, 2004.

Cleaver, Eldridge. *Target Zero: A Life in Writing*. Ed. Kathleen Cleaver. New York: Palgrave Macmillan, 2009.

Cleaver, Kathleen. "Back to Africa: The Evolution of the International Section of the Black Panther Party (1969-1972)." In *The Black Panther Party: Reconsidered*, ed. Charles E. Jones, 211–54. Baltimore: Black Classic Press, 1998.

Cleaver, Kathleen and George Katsiaficas, eds. *Liberation, Imagination, and the Black Panther Party: A New Look at the Panthers and Their Legacy*. New York: Routledge, 2001.

Cohen, Lizabeth. *A Consumer's Republic: The Politics of Mass Consumption in Postwar America*. New York: Vintage, 1994.

Cole, Stephanie and Alison M. Parker, eds. *Beyond Black & White: Race, Ethnicity, and Gender in the U.S. South and Southwest*. College Station: Texas A&M University Press, 2004.

Countryman, Matthew J. *Up South: Civil Rights and Black Power in Philadelphia*. Philadelphia: University of Pennsylvania Press, 2006.

Crawford, Vicki. "Coretta Scott King and the Struggle for Civil and Human Rights: An Enduring Legacy." *Journal of African American History* 92, 1 (Winter 2007): 106–17.

Cruse, Harold. *Rebellion or Revolution?* 1968. Minneapolis: University of Minnesota Press, 2009.

Daniel, Cletus E. "Cesar Chavez and the Unionization of California Farm Workers." In *Labor Leaders in America*, ed. Melvyn Dubofsky and Warren Van Tine. Urbana: University of Illinois Press, 1987.

DeGraaf, Lawrence B., Kevin Mulroy, and Quintard Taylor, eds. *Seeking El Dorado: African Americans in California*. Los Angeles: Autry Museum of Western Heritage, 2001.

D'Emilio, John. *Lost Prophet: The Life and Times of Bayard Rustin*. New York: Free Press, 2003.

Dickerson, Dennis. *Militant Mediator: Whitney Young, Jr.* Lexington: University Press of Kentucky, 1998.

Dittmer, John. *Local People: The Struggle for Civil Rights in Mississippi*. Urbana: University of Illinois Press, 1994.

Dobbie, David. "Evolving Strategies of Labor-Community Coalition Building." *Journal of Community Practice* 17, 1/2 (January–June 2009): 107–19.

Dr. Huey P. Newton Foundation. *The Black Panther Party: Service to the People Programs*. Albuquerque: University of New Mexico Press, 2008.

Dubofsky, Melvyn and Warren Van Tine, eds. *Labor Leaders in America*. Urbana: University of Illinois Press, 1987.

Dunne, John Gregory. *Delano: The Story of the California Grape Strike*. 1967. Berkeley: University of California Press, 2008.

Durant, Thomas J., Jr. and Joyce S. Louden. "The Black Middle Class in America: Historical and Contemporary Perspectives." *Phylon* 47, 4 (4th Quarter 1986): 253–63.

Etulain, Richard W., ed. *César Chávez: A Brief Biography with Documents*. Boston: Bedford/St. Martin's, 2002.

Fairclough, Adam. *To Redeem the Soul of America: The Southern Christian Leadership Conference & Martin Luther King, Jr.* Athens: University of Georgia Press, 1987.

———. Foreword to *Long Is the Way and Hard: One Hundred Years of the NAACP*, ed. Kevern Verney and Lee Sartain, vii–xiv. Fayetteville: University of Arkansas Press, 2009.

Fallows, Marjorie. "The Mexican-American Laborers: A Different Drummer?" *Massachusetts Review* 8, 1 (Winter 1967): 166–76.

Ferriss, Susan and Ricardo Sandoval. *The Fight in the Fields: Cesar Chavez and the Farmworkers Movement*. Ed. Diana Hembree. New York: Harcourt Brace, 1997.

Fink, Leon and Brian Greenberg. *Upheaval in the Quiet Zone: 1199SEIU and the Politics of Health Care Unionism*. 2nd ed. Urbana: University of Illinois Press, 2009.

Finks, David P. *The Radical Vision of Saul Alinsky*. New York: Paulist Press, 1984.

Fleming, Cynthia Griggs. *Soon We Will Not Cry: The Liberation of Ruby Doris Smith Robinson*. Lanham, Md.: Rowman & Littlefield, 1998.

Flug, Michael. "Organized Labor and the Civil Rights Movement of the 1960s: The Case of the Maryland Freedom Union." *Labor History* 31, 3 (Summer 1990): 322–46.

Foley, Neil. "Partly Colored or Other White: Mexican Americans and Their Problem with the Color Line." In *Beyond Black & White: Race, Ethnicity, and Gender in the U.S. South and Southwest*, ed. Stephanie Cole and Alison M. Parker, 123–44. College Station: Texas A&M University Press, 2004.

———. *Quest for Equality: The Failed Promise of Black-Brown Solidarity*. Cambridge, Mass.: Harvard University Press, 2010.

Foner, Philip S. *The Black Panthers Speak*. 1970. Cambridge, Mass.: Da Capo Press, 2002.

———. *Organized Labor and the Black Worker, 1619–1981*, 2nd ed. New York: International Publishers, 1982.

Forman, James. *The Making of Black Revolutionaries*. 1972. Seattle: University of Washington Press, 1997.

Freeman, Jo and Victoria Johnson, eds. *Waves of Protest: Social Movements Since the Sixties*. Lanham, Md.: Rowman & Littlefield, 1999.

Ganz, Marshall. *Why David Sometimes Wins: Leadership, Organization, and Strategy in the California Farm Worker Movement*. New York: Oxford University Press, 2009.

García, Ignacio M. *Chicanismo: The Forging of a Militant Ethos Among Mexican Americans*. Tucson: University of Arizona Press, 1997.

García, Mario T. *Memories of Chicano History: The Life and Narrative of Bert Corona*. Berkeley: University of California Press, 1994.

Garrow, David J. *Bearing the Cross: Martin Luther King, Jr., and the Southern Christian Leadership Conference*. 1986. New York: Perennial, 2004.

Gellman, Erik S. "'The Stone Wall Behind': The Chicago Coalition for United Community Action and Labor's Overseers, 1968–1973." In *Black Power at Work: Community Control, Affirmative Action, and the Construction Industry*, ed. David Goldberg and Trevor Griffey, 112–33. Ithaca, N.Y.: Cornell University Press, 2010.

Geschwender, James A. and Judson L. Jeffries. "League of Revolutionary Black Workers." In *Black Power in the Belly of the Beast*, ed. Judson L. Jeffries, 135–62. Urbana: University of Illinois Press, 2006.

Goings, Kenneth W. and Raymond A. Mohl, eds. *The New African American Urban History*. Thousand Oaks, Calif.: Sage, 1996.

Goldberg, David and Trevor Griffey, eds. *Black Power at Work: Community Control, Affirmative Action, and the Construction Industry*. Ithaca, N.Y.: Cornell University Press, 2010.

Gordon, Robert. "Poison in the Fields: The United Farm Workers, Pesticides, and Environmental Politics." *Pacific Historical Review* 68, 1 (February 1999): 51–77.

Grant, Joanne, ed. *Black Protest: History, Documents, and Analyses, 1619 to the Present.* New York: Fawcett, 1968.

Greenberg, Cheryl Lynn, ed. *A Circle of Trust: Remembering SNCC.* New Brunswick, N.J.: Rutgers University Press, 1998.

———.*"Or Does It Explode?": Black Harlem in the Great Depression.* New York: Oxford University Press, 1991.

Gregory, James N. *American Exodus: The Dust Bowl Migration and Okie Culture in California.* New York: Oxford University Press, 1989.

Griswold del Castillo, Richard and Richard A. Garcia. *César Chávez: A Triumph of Spirit.* Norman: University of Oklahoma Press, 1995.

Gutierrez, David G. *Walls and Mirrors: Mexican Americans, Mexican Immigrants, and the Politics of Ethnicity.* Berkeley: University of California Press, 1995.

Hahn, Peter L. "The Influence of Organized Labor on U.S. Policy Toward Israel, 1945–1967." In *Empire and Revolution: The United States and the Third World Since 1945*, ed. Peter L. Hahn and Mary Ann Heiss, 154–77. Columbus: Ohio State University Press, 2001.

Hahn, Peter L. and Mary Ann Heiss, eds. *Empire and Revolution: The United States and the Third World Since 1945.* Columbus: Ohio State University Press, 2001.

Hall, Jacquelyn Dowd and Eugene P. Walker. "I Train the People to Do Their Own Talking." *Southern Cultures* 16, 2 (Summer 2010): 31–52.

Hall, John R., ed. *Reworking Class.* Ithaca, N.Y.: Cornell University Press, 1997.

Hampton, Henry and Steve Fayer. *Voices of Freedom: An Oral History of the Civil Rights Movement from the 1950s Through the 1980s.* New York: Bantam, 1990.

Hayes, Edward C. *Power Structure and Urban Policy: Who Rules in Oakland?* New York: McGraw-Hill, 1972.

Hayes, Floyd W., III, and Francis A. Kiene, III. "'All Power to the People': The Political Thought of Huey P. Newton and the Black Panther Party." In *The Black Panther Party: Reconsidered*, ed. Charles E. Jones, 157–76. Baltimore: Black Classic Press, 1998.

Hogan, Wesley. *Many Minds, One Heart: SNCC's Dream for a New America.* Chapel Hill: University of North Carolina Press, 2007.

Holsaert, Faith, et al., eds. *Hands on the Freedom Plow: Personal Accounts by Women in SNCC.* Urbana: University of Illinois Press, 2010.

Honey, Michael. *Going Down Jericho Road: The Memphis Strike, Martin Luther King's Last Campaign.* New York: Norton, 2007.

———. "Martin Luther King, Jr., the Crisis of the Black Working Class, and the Memphis Sanitation Strike." In *Southern Labor in Transition, 1940–1995*, ed. Robert H. Zieger, 146–75. Knoxville: University of Tennessee Press, 1997.

hooks, bell and Amalia Mesa-Bains. *Homegrown: Engaged Cultural Criticism.* Cambridge, Mass.: South End Press, 2006.

Hooper, Hartwell and Susan Hooper. "The Scripto Strike: Martin Luther King's 'Valley of Problems': Atlanta, 1964–1965," *Atlanta History* 43, 3 (Fall 1999): 5–34.

Hsu, Hua. "Dave Hilliard: Former Black Panther Runs for Office." *Hardboiled* 2, 4 (Spring 2001).

Jackson, Thomas F. *From Civil Rights to Human Rights: Martin Luther King, Jr., and the Struggle for Economic Justice.* Philadelphia: University of Pennsylvania Press, 2006.

Jackson, Troy. *Becoming King: Martin Luther King, Jr., and the Making of a National Leader.* Lexington: University Press of Kentucky, 2008.

Jeffries, Hasan Kwame. *Bloody Lowndes: Civil Rights and Black Power in Alabama's Black Belt.* New York: New York University Press, 2009.

Jeffries, Judson L., ed. *Black Power in the Belly of the Beast.* Urbana: University of Illinois Press, 2006.

Jenkins, J. Craig. *The Politics of Insurgency: The Farm Workers Movement in the 1960s.* New York: Columbia University Press, 1985.

———. "The Transformation of a Constituency into a Social Movement Revisited: Farmworker Organizing in California." In *Waves of Protest: Social Movements Since the Sixties*, ed. Jo Freeman and Victoria Johnson, 277–99. Lanham, Md.: Rowman & Littlefield, 1999.

Jenkins, J. Craig and Kevin Leicht. "Class Analysis and Social Movements: A Critique and Reformulation." In *Reworking Class*, ed. John R. Hall, 369–97. Ithaca, N.Y.: Cornell University Press, 1997.

Jenkinson, Michael. *Tijerina: Land Grant Conflict in New Mexico*. Albuquerque: Paisano Press, 1968.

Jensen, Richard J. and John C. Hammerback, eds. *The Words of Cesar Chavez*. College Station: Texas A&M University Press, 2002.

Johnson, Cedric. *Revolutionaries to Race Leaders: Black Power and the Making of African American Politics*. Minneapolis: University of Minnesota Press, 2007.

Johnson, Ollie A., III. "Explaining the Demise of the Black Panther Party: The Role of Internal Factors." In *The Black Panther Party: Reconsidered*, ed. Charles E. Jones, 391–414. Baltimore: Black Classic Press, 1998.

Jonas, Gilbert. *Freedom's Sword: The NAACP and the Struggle Against Racism in America, 1909–1969*. New York: Routledge, 2007.

Jones, Charles E., ed. *The Black Panther Party: Reconsidered*. Baltimore: Black Classic Press, 1998.

Jones, William Powell. "'Simple Truths of Democracy': African Americans and Organized Labor in the Post-World War II South." In *The Black Worker: Race, Labor, and Civil Rights since Emancipation*, ed. Eric Arnesen, 250–70. Urbana: University of Illinois Press, 2007.

———. "The Unknown Origins of the March on Washington: Civil Rights Politics and the Black Working Class." *Labor: Studies in Working-Class History of the Americas* 7, 3 (Fall 2010): 33–52.

Joseph, Peniel E., ed. *The Black Power Movement: Rethinking the Civil Rights-Black Power Era*. New York: Routledge, 2006.

———. *Waiting 'Til the Midnight Hour: A Narrative History of Black Power in America*. New York: Owl Books, 2007.

Kelley, Robin D. G. *Race Rebels: Culture, Politics, and the Black Working Class*. New York: Free Press, 1994.

King, Coretta Scott. *My Life with Martin Luther King, Jr.* New York: Holt, Rinehart, 1969.

King, Martin Luther, Jr. *"All Labor Has Dignity."* Ed. Michael K. Honey. Boston: Beacon Press, 2011.

———. *Stride Toward Freedom: The Montgomery Story*. 1958. Boston: Beacon Press, 2010.

———. *Where Do We Go from Here: Chaos or Community?* 1968. Boston: Beacon Press, 2010.

Korstad, Robert and Nelson Lichtenstein. "Opportunities Lost and Found: Labor, Radicals, and the Early Civil Rights Movement." In *The Black Worker: Race, Labor, and Civil Rights Since Emancipation*, ed. Eric Arnesen, 222–49. Urbana: University of Illinois Press, 2007.

Kurashige, Scott. *The Shifting Grounds of Race: Black and Japanese Americans in the Making of Multiethnic Los Angeles*. Princeton, N.J.: Princeton University Press, 2007.

Kushner, Sam. *Long Road to Delano: A Century of Farmworkers' Struggle*. New York: International, 1975.

Lawson, Steven and Charles Payne. *Debating the Civil Rights Movement: 1945–1968*. Lanham, Md.: Rowman & Littlefield, 1998.

Lazerow, Jama and Yohuru Williams, eds. *In Search of the Black Panther Party: New Perspectives on a Revolutionary Movement*. Durham, N.C.: Duke University Press, 2006.

Lee, Taeku. *Mobilizing Public Opinion: Black Insurgency and Racial Attitudes in the Civil Rights Era*. Chicago: University of Chicago Press, 2002.

Leonard, Kevin Allen. "'In the Interest of All Races': African Americans and Interracial Cooperation in Los Angeles During and after World War II." In *Seeking El Dorado: African Americans in California*, ed. Lawrence B. DeGraaf, Kevin Mulroy, and Quintard Taylor, 309–40. Los Angeles: Autry Museum of Western Heritage, 2001.

Levy, Jacques E. *Cesar Chavez: Autobiography of La Causa*. 1975. Minneapolis: University of Minnesota Press, 2007.

Levy, Peter B. *The New Left and Labor in the 1960s.* Urbana: University of Illinois Press, 1994.

———. "The New Left and Labor: The Early Years (1960–1963)." *Labor History* 31, 3 (Summer 1990): 294–321.

Lewis, Earl. "Connecting Memory, Self, and the Power of Place in African American Urban History." In *The New African American Urban History,* ed. Kenneth W. Goings and Raymond A. Mohl, 116–41. Thousand Oaks, Calif.: Sage, 1996.

Ling, Peter J. "Gender and Generation: Manhood at the Southern Christian Leadership Conference." In *Gender and the Civil Rights Movement,* ed. Peter J. Ling and Sharon Monteith, 101–29. New York: Garland, 1999.

Ling, Peter J. and Sharon Monteith, eds. *Gender and the Civil Rights Movement.* New York: Garland, 1999.

Lipsitz, George. *A Life in the Struggle: Ivory Perry and the Culture of Opposition.* Philadelphia: Temple University Press, 1988.

Lopez, Esperanza Fierro. *The Chavista Daze: Volunteers, Rebel Rousers, Bleeding Hearts.* Bloomington, Ind.: AuthorHouse, 2007.

Mann, Geoff. "Class Consciousness and Common Property: The International Fishermen and Allied Workers of America." *International Labor and Working Class History* 61 (Spring 2002): 141–60.

Mantler, Gordon K. "Black, Brown, and Poor: Civil Rights and the Making of the Chicano Movement." In *The Struggle in Black and Brown: African American and Mexican American Relations during the Civil Rights Era,* ed. Brian D. Behnken, 179–210. Lincoln: University of Nebraska Press, 2011.

———. *Power to the Poor: Black-Brown Coalition and the Fight for Economic Justice, 1960–1974.* Chapel Hill: University of North Carolina Press, 2013.

Marable, Manning. *Race, Reform and Rebellion: The Second Reconstruction in Black America, 1945–1990.* Jackson: University Press of Mississippi, 1991.

Marger, Martin N. "Social Movement Organizations and Response to Environmental Change: The NAACP, 1960–1973." *Social Problems* 32, 1 (October 1984): 16–30.

Mariscal, George (Jorge). *Brown-Eyed Children of the Sun: Lessons from the Chicano Movement, 1965–1975.* Albuquerque: University of New Mexico Press, 2005.

———. "Cesar and Martin, March '68." In *The Struggle in Black and Brown: African American and Mexican American Relations During the Civil Rights Era,* ed. Brian D. Behnken, 148–78. Lincoln: University of Nebraska Press, 2011.

Martínez, Elizabeth Sutherland. "Neither Black nor White in a Black-White World." In *Hands on the Freedom Plow: Personal Accounts by Women in SNCC,* ed. Faith Holsaert, et al., 531–40. Urbana: University of Illinois Press, 2010.

Massey, Douglas S. "Residential Segregation of Spanish Americans in United States Urbanized Areas." *Demography* 16, 4 (November 1979): 553–63.

Matthiessen, Peter. *Sal si Puedes (Escape if You Can): Cesar Chavez and the New American Revolution.* 1969. Berkeley: University of California Press, 2000.

Mayer, Brian. "Cross-Movement Coalition Formation: Bridging the Labor-Environment Divide." *Sociological Inquiry* 79, 2 (May 2009): 219–39.

McCarty, Laura T. *Coretta Scott King: A Biography.* Westport, Conn.: Greenwood Press, 2009.

McWilliams, Carey. *Factories in the Field: The Story of Migratory Farm Labor in California.* Boston: Little, Brown, 1939.

Meier, August and Elliot Rudwick. *CORE: A Study in the Civil Rights Movement, 1942–1968.* New York: Oxford University Press, 1973.

Meister, Dick and Anne Loftis. *A Long Time Coming: The Struggle to Unionize America's Farm Workers.* New York: Macmillan, 1977.

Meyer, David S. and Nancy Whittier. "Social Movement Spillover." *Social Problems* 41, 2 (May 1994): 277–98.

Miller, Mike. *A Community Organizer's Tale: People and Power in San Francisco*. Berkeley, Calif.: Heyday Books, 2009.

Montejano, David. *Quixote's Soldiers: A Local History of the Chicano Movement, 1966–1981*. Austin: University of Texas Press, 2010.

Moore, Jesse Thomas, Jr. *A Search for Equality: The National Urban League, 1910–1961*. University Park: Pennsylvania State University Press, 1981.

Moore, Shirley Ann Wilson. *To Place Our Deeds: The African American Community in Richmond, California, 1910–1963*. Berkeley: University of California Press, 2000.

Motomura, Hiroshi. *Americans in Waiting: The Lost Story of Immigration and Citizenship in the United States*. New York: Oxford University Press, 2006.

Muñoz, Carlos. *Youth, Identity, Power: The Chicano Movement*. New York: Verso, 1989.

Murch, Donna Jean. *Living for the City: Migration, Education, and the Rise of the Black Panther Party in Oakland, California*. Chapel Hill: University of North Carolina Press, 2010.

Nabokov, Peter. *Tijerina and the Courthouse Raid*. Berkeley, Calif.: Ramparts Press, 1970.

National Association for the Advancement of Colored People. *Annual Report for 1968*. New York: NAACP, 1969.

———. *Annual Report 1969*. New York: NAACP, 1970.

Nelson, Eugene. *Huelga! The First Hundred Days of the Great Delano Grape Strike*. Delano, Calif.: Farmworker Press, 1966.

Newton, Huey P. *Revolutionary Suicide*. 1973. New York: Penguin, 2009.

———. *To Die for the People*. 1972. New York: Writers and Readers Publishers, 1995.

Ogbar, Jeffrey O. G. "Brown Power to Brown People: Radical Ethnic Nationalism, the Black Panthers, and Latino Radicalism, 1967–1973." In *In Search of the Black Panther Party: New Perspectives on a Revolutionary Movement*, ed. Jama Lazerow and Yohuru Williams, 252–86. Durham, N.C.: Duke University Press, 2006.

Omi, Michael and Howard Winant. *Racial Formation in the United States: From the 1960s to the 1990s*. 2nd ed. New York: Routledge, 1994.

Oropeza, Lorena. "Antiwar Aztlán: The Chicano Movement Opposes U.S. Intervention in Vietnam." In *Window on Freedom: Race, Civil Rights, and Foreign Affairs, 1945–1988*, ed. Brenda Gayle Plummer, 201–20. Chapel Hill: University of North Carolina Press, 2003.

Pagán, Eduardo Obregón. *Murder at the Sleepy Lagoon: Zoot Suits, Race, and Riots in Wartime L.A.* Chapel Hill: University of North Carolina Press, 2003.

Parris, Guichard and Lester Brooks. *Blacks in the City: A History of the National Urban League*. Boston: Little, Brown, 1971.

Pawel, Miriam. *The Union of Their Dreams: Power, Hope, and Struggle in Cesar Chavez's Farm Worker Movement*. New York: Bloomsbury Press, 2009.

Payne, Charles. *I've Got the Light of Freedom: The Organizing Tradition and the Mississippi Freedom Struggle*. Berkeley: University of California Press, 1995.

Peake, Thomas R. *Keeping the Dream Alive: A History of the Southern Christian Leadership Conference from King to the Nineteen-Eighties*. New York: Peter Lang, 1987.

Plummer, Brenda Gayle, ed. *Window on Freedom: Race, Civil Rights, and Foreign Affairs, 1945–1988*. Chapel Hill: University of North Carolina Press, 2003.

Polletta, Francesca. *Freedom Is an Endless Meeting: Democracy in American Social Movements*. Chicago: University of Chicago Press, 2002.

Pulido, Laura. *Black, Brown, Yellow, and Left: Radical Activism in Los Angeles*. Berkeley: University of California, 2006.

Raines, Howell. *My Soul Is Rested: The Story of the Civil Rights Movement in the Deep South*. New York: Penguin, 1983.

Ransby, Barbara. *Ella Baker and the Black Freedom Movement: A Radical Democratic Vision*. Chapel Hill: University of North Carolina Press, 2003.

Reed, Christopher Robert. "The Chicago NAACP: A Century of Challenge, Triumph, and Inertia."

In *Long Is the Way and Hard: One Hundred Years of the NAACP*, ed. Kevern Verney and Lee Sartain, 169–83. Fayetteville: University of Arkansas Press, 2009.

Reed, Touré F. *No Alms but Opportunity: The Urban League and the Politics of Racial Uplift, 1910–1950*. Chapel Hill: University of North Carolina Press, 2008.

Reisler, Mark. "Always the Laborer, Never the Citizen: Anglo Perceptions of the Mexican Immigrant During the 1920s." *Pacific Historical Review* 45, 2 (May 1976): 231–54.

Rhomberg, Chris. *No There There: Race, Class, and Political Community in Oakland*. Berkeley: University of California Press, 2004.

Robnett, Belinda. "African-American Women in the Civil Rights Movement, 1954–1965: Gender, Leadership, and Micromobilization." *American Journal of Sociology* 101, 6 (May 1996): 1661–93.

Rosales, F. Arturo, ed. *Testimonio: A Documentary History of the Mexican American Struggle for Civil Rights*. Houston: Arte Público Press, 2000.

Ryan, Yvonne. "Leading from the Back: Roy Wilkins's Leadership of the NAACP." In *Long Is the Way and Hard: One Hundred Years of the NAACP*, ed. Kevern Verney and Lee Sartain, 43–58. Fayetteville: University of Arkansas Press, 2009.

Salmond, John A. *Southern Struggles: The Southern Labor Movement and the Civil Rights Struggle*. Gainesville: University of Florida Press, 2004.

Sanchez, George. *Becoming Mexican American: Ethnicity, Culture and Identity in Chicano Los Angeles, 1900–1945*. New York: Oxford University Press, 1993.

Schrecker, Ellen. "Labor and the Cold War: The Legacy of McCarthyism." In *American Labor and the Cold War: Grassroots Politics and Postwar Political Culture*, ed. Robert W. Cherny, William Issel, and Kieran Walsh Taylor, 7–24. New Brunswick, N.J.: Rutgers University Press, 2004.

Seale, Bobby. *A Lonely Rage: The Autobiography of Bobby Seale*. New York: Times Books, 1978.

———. *Seize the Time: The Story of the Black Panther Party and Huey P. Newton*. 1970. Baltimore: Black Classic Press, 1991.

Self, Robert O. *American Babylon: Race and the Struggle for Postwar Oakland*. Princeton, N.J.: Princeton University Press, 2003.

Sellers, Cleveland with Robert Terrell. *River of No Return: The Autobiography of a Black Militant and the Life and Death of SNCC*. 1973. Jackson: University Press of Mississippi, 1990.

Sewell, Stacy Kinlock. "The 'Not-Buying Power' of the Black Community: Urban Boycotts and Equal Employment Opportunity, 1960–1964." *Journal of African American History* 89, 2 (Spring 2004): 135–51.

Spencer, Robyn Ceanne. "Inside the Panther Revolution: The Black Freedom Movement and the Black Panther Party in Oakland, California." In *Groundwork: Local Black Freedom Movements in America*, ed. Jeanne Theoharis and Komozi Woodard, 300–317. New York: New York University Press, 2005.

Stoper, Emily. *The Student Nonviolent Coordinating Committee: The Growth of Radicalism in a Civil Rights Organization*. Brooklyn, N.Y.: Carson, 1989.

———. "The Student Nonviolent Coordinating Committee: Rise and Fall of a Redemptive Organization." In *Waves of Protest: Social Movements Since the Sixties*, ed. Jo Freeman and Victoria Johnson, 349–364. Lanham, Md.: Rowman & Littlefield, 1999.

Storch, Randi. "The United Packinghouse Workers of America, Civil Rights, and the Communist Party of America." In *American Labor and the Cold War: Grassroots Politics and Postwar Political Culture*, ed. Robert W. Cherny, William Issel, and Kieran Walsh Taylor, 72–84. New Brunswick, N.J.: Rutgers University Press, 2004.

Strain, Christopher B. *Pure Fire: Self-Defense as Activism in the Civil Rights Era*. Athens: University of Georgia Press, 2005.

Sugrue, Thomas J. *Sweet Land of Liberty: The Forgotten Struggle for Civil Rights in the North*. New York: Random House, 2008.

Sullivan, Patricia. *Lift Every Voice: The NAACP and the Making of the Civil Rights Movement*. New York: New Press, 2009.

Taylor, Quintard. *In Search of the Racial Frontier: African Americans in the American West, 1528–1990.* New York: Norton, 1998.

Taylor, Ronald B. *Chavez and the Farm Workers: A Study in the Acquisition and Use of Power.* Boston: Beacon Press, 1975.

Terkel, Studs. *Working: People Talk About What They Do All Day and How They Feel About What They Do.* New York: Pantheon, 1974.

Theoharis, Jeanne and Komozi Woodard, eds. *Freedom North: Black Freedom Struggles Outside the South, 1940–1980.* New York: Palgrave Macmillan, 2003.

———. *Groundwork: Local Black Freedom Movements in America.* New York: New York University Press, 2005.

Ture, Kwame (Stokely Carmichael) and Charles V. Hamilton. *Black Power: The Politics of Liberation.* 1967. New York: Vintage, 1992.

Tyson, Timothy B. *Radio Free Dixie: Robert F. Williams and the Roots of Black Power.* Chapel Hill: University of North Carolina Press, 1999.

United States National Advisory Commission on Civil Disorders. *Report of the National Advisory Commission on Civil Disorders.* New York: Bantam, 1968.

Vaca, Nicolás C. *The Presumed Alliance: The Unspoken Conflict Between Latinos and Blacks and What It Means for America.* New York: HarperCollins, 2004.

Van Deburg, William L. *New Day in Babylon: The Black Power Movement and American Culture, 1965–1975.* Chicago: University of Chicago Press, 1992.

Van Peebles, Mario, Ula Y. Taylor, and J. Tarika Lewis. *Panther: A Pictorial History of the Black Panthers and the Story Behind the Film.* New York: New Market Press, 1995.

Varela, María. "Time to Get Ready." In *Hands on the Freedom Plow: Personal Accounts by Women in SNCC,* ed. Faith Holsaert et al., 552–72. Urbana: University of Illinois Press, 2010.

Vargas, Zaragosa. *Labor Rights Are Civil Rights: Mexican American Workers in Twentieth-Century America.* Princeton, N.J.: Princeton University Press, 2007.

Verney, Kevern and Lee Sartain, eds. *Long Is the Way and Hard: One Hundred Years of the NAACP.* Fayetteville: University of Arkansas Press, 2009.

Vivian, C. T. *Black Power and the American Myth.* Philadelphia: Fortress Press, 1970.

Vivian, Octavia. *Coretta: The Story of Coretta Scott King.* 1970. Minneapolis: Fortress Press, 2006.

Wallace, David M. "From the Fullness of the Earth: The Story of Chicago's Operation Breadbasket." *Chicago Theological Seminary Register* 57 (November 1966): 16–20.

Wallach, Jennifer Jensen. "Replicating History in a Bad Way? White Activists and Black Power in SNCC's Arkansas Project." *Arkansas Historical Quarterly* 67, 3 (Autumn 2008): 268–87.

Watson, Jonathan. "The NAACP in California, 1914–1950." In *Long Is the Way and Hard: One Hundred Years of the NAACP,* ed. Kevern Verney and Lee Sartain, 185–99. Fayetteville: University of Arkansas Press, 2009.

Weems, Robert E., Jr. "African-American Consumer Boycotts During the Civil Rights Era." *Western Journal of Black Studies* 19, 1 (Spring 1995): 72–79.

Weiss, Nancy J. *Whitney M. Young, Jr., and the Struggle for Civil Rights.* Princeton, N.J.: Princeton University Press, 1989.

———. *The National Urban League, 1910–1940.* New York: Oxford University Press, 1974.

Wendt, Simon. *The Spirit and the Shotgun: Armed Resistance and the Struggle for Civil Rights.* Gainesville: University Press of Florida, 2007.

Whitaker, Matthew C. "A New Day in Babylon: African American and Mexican American Relations at the Dawn of the New Millennium." In *The Struggle in Black and Brown: African American and Mexican American Relations During the Civil Rights Era,* ed. Brian D. Behnken, 257–85. Lincoln: University of Nebraska Press, 2011.

Williams, Yohuru. "A Red, Black and Green Liberation Jumpsuit: Roy Wilkins, the Black Panthers, and the Conundrum of Black Power." In *The Black Power Movement: Rethinking the Civil Rights-Black Power Era,* ed. Peniel E. Joseph, 167–91. New York: Routledge, 2006.

Wilson, Joel. "Invisible Cages: Racialized Politics and the Alliance between the Panthers and the Peace and Freedom Party." In *In Search of the Black Panther Party: New Perspectives on a Revolutionary Movement*, ed. Jama Lazerow and Yohuru Williams, 191–222. Durham, N.C.: Duke University Press, 2006.

Wilson, Sondra Kathryn, ed. *In Search of Democracy: The NAACP Writings of James Weldon Johnson, Walter White, and Roy Wilkins (1920–1977)*. New York: Oxford University Press, 1999.

Witwer, David. *Corruption and Reform in the Teamsters Union*. Urbana: University of Illinois Press, 2003.

Woodruff, Nan Elizabeth. "The Organizing Tradition Among African American Plantation Workers in the Arkansas Delta in the Age of Jim Crow." In *The Black Worker: Race, Labor, and Civil Rights Since Emancipation*, ed. Eric Arnesen, 178–94. Urbana: University of Illinois Press, 2007.

Young, Andrew. *An Easy Burden: The Civil Rights Movement and the Transformation of America*. New York: HarperCollins, 1996.

Zeiger, Robert H., ed. *Southern Labor in Transition: 1940–1995*. Knoxville: University of Tennessee Press, 1997.

Zinn, Howard. *SNCC: The New Abolitionists*. 1965. Westport, Conn.: Greenwood Press, 1985.

INDEX

ACKNOWLEDGMENTS

This book celebrates the spirit of cooperation and solidarity between the Black Freedom Struggle and the United Farm Workers. Just as the UFW would not have succeeded without the assistance of its allies, I could not have written this book without the help of a truly diverse coalition of supporters. To all of them, I owe my deepest appreciation.

The initial research for this project was funded by the University of California at Berkeley. At Berkeley I benefited from the guidance and support of an array of talented scholars. Waldo Martin has been an enthusiastic advocate of my work and has encouraged me every step of the way. Leon Litwack has demonstrated that one can be both an engaging writer and an excellent teacher. David Montejano in the Ethnic Studies Department asked me challenging questions that have improved the quality of this project. I would also like to thank Carlos Muñoz, Ula Taylor, and the late James Kettner. My colleague Kevin Adams has served as my academic guru, patiently and cheerfully advising me on all things scholarly.

At Denison University, the completion of the research and writing of this project was funded by the Professional Development Fund and the Bartlett Family Fellowship. I would like to thank Trey Proctor and Megan Threlkeld in the History Department for taking time away from their own important scholarship to critique some of my early drafts. I also appreciate the support of the Black Studies Program. Toni King has been an especially cherished colleague, always ready with sound advice, words of encouragement, and effusive praise.

This work has benefited from the input of talented scholars in a variety of fields. Ernesto Chavez, Diane Hotten-Somers, and Hasan Kwame Jeffries provided helpful feedback and asked thought-provoking questions of earlier drafts. Portions of Chapters 3 and 5 were previously published as "'In Common Struggle Against a Common Oppression': The United Farm Workers and the Black Panther Party, 1968–1973," *Journal of African American History* 94, 2 (Spring 2009). The material in these chapters was greatly improved by the critiques of V. P. Franklin and the anonymous reviewers of the *JAAH*, as well as the participants in the Workshop in Comparative and Transnational History at the University of California, San Diego in June 2008: Luis Alvarez, Jason Ferreira, Chrissonna Grant, Gaye Theresa Johnson, George Lipsitz, Pancho McFarland, Catherine Ramirez, Abigail Rosas, George Sanchez, and Daniel Widener. Parts of Chapters 1 and 2 were previously published in "Complicating the Beloved Community: The Student Nonviolent Coordinating Committee and the National Farm Workers Association," in *The Struggle in Black and Brown: African American and Mexican American Relations During the Civil Rights Era*, ed. Brian Behnken (Lincoln: University of Nebraska Press, 2011). The feedback of the editors and readers helped to improve this material. Political scientists Eric Boehme and Matt Jarvis provided valuable insight on municipal and mayoral politics. Tenisha Armstrong, associate director of the Martin Luther King, Jr., Research and Education Institute at Stanford University, provided helpful information on King's unpublished speeches. Finally, I owe a special debt of gratitude to my *compañeros* Brian Behnken and Gordon Mantler for reading multiple drafts, sharing insights and materials, and engaging in lengthy discussions and debates.

This book would not have been possible without the tireless work of dedicated activists. I would like to thank all the activists who allowed me to interview them: George Ballis, Wendy Goepel Brooks, Terry Cannon, Hardy Frye, Marshall Ganz, Gene Guererro, Elbert "Big Man" Howard, Bill Jennings, Elizabeth Sutherland Martínez, Vilma Martinez, Eliseo Medina, Mike Miller, Gilbert Padilla, Bobby Seale, María Varela, Baldemar Velásquez, and Richard Ybarra. They not only were generous with their time, but also openly shared their experiences with me. Each one of them gave me important information I could not have found elsewhere. I am especially grateful to María Varela, who welcomed me into her home and allowed me to pore through her extensive personal collection from her tenure in SNCC. I am in debt to Marshall Ganz for his doctoral dissertation and book on the UFW; the day-by-day calendar of UFW activities he compiled for the dissertation was indispensable to my first two chapters.

The assistance of numerous archivists was essential to the success of this project. I am particularly grateful to the staff of the Archives of Labor and

Urban Affairs at the Walter P. Reuther Library at Wayne State University, where the UFW papers are housed. Archivist Kathy Schmeling, who organized the UFW collection, has always been available to answer my myriad questions. Mary Wallace helped me navigate the extensive audiovisual collection. I am indebted to retired secretary Alberta Asmar, who arranged lodging for me during my research trips. During my first trip, Alberta connected me with Yates and Gail Haefner, who housed and fed me in their beautiful home and refused to take any payment except for a bottle of California wine. I am also thankful for the tireless work of Bill Jennings and LeRoy Chatfield. At their own expense, Bill and LeRoy have spent considerable time and effort to preserve the legacies of the Black Panther Party and the UFW, respectively, on the websites It's About Time (http://www.itsabouttimebpp.com/) and the Farmworker Movement Documentation Project (http://www.farmworkermovement.org/). They have uncovered and made publicly available a treasure trove of historical materials that will benefit both scholars and the general public for generations to come.

I have thoroughly enjoyed working with the University of Pennsylvania Press. Editor Robert Lockhart has been an indispensable guide in the publication process. His experience and knowledge have been vital to the success of this project and his kindness and generosity have made the process of publishing less overwhelming. Thomas Sugrue has been an invaluable advocate. Finally, thank you to my reviewers. Thomas Jackson's thoughtful and detailed comments on the manuscript have greatly improved this book.

I deeply appreciate artist Juana Alicia for allowing me to use the mural, *Vivir Sin Fronteras/Living Without Borders*, on the jacket of this book. Under Juana Alicia's direction, the students of the True Colors Mural Project painted this amazing mural on an exterior wall of Mi Tierra Foods in Berkeley, California. The images in the mural, as well as the creativity and collaboration the Project employed in both the creation of the mural and the pursuit of social change, truly represent the spirit of this book. Special thanks to Mark Brilliant, who has the fortune of admiring this mural while on his regular jogs, for bringing it to my attention.

I am grateful to the entire Fernandez and McNamara families for their support. I would especially like to thank my mother, Christine Fernandez, for her unwavering belief in my abilities, and my grandparents, Frank and Alta Fernandez, for never failing to ask how my "paper" was coming along each time I called or visited. Thanks also to Cynthia Fernandez and Anne, Mike, Becca, Ted, Erin, Tristian, and Addison McNamara for understanding that while this book was in progress, every vacation has been a working vacation. Finally, I am deeply appreciative of my husband, Charlie McNamara, to whom this book is dedicated. Charlie has been unfailingly supportive, patient, understanding, and encouraging. He is truly my helpmate and his love has sustained me through what has been a long and challenging process. For this I am eternally grateful.